sure
ll

...at Khrushchev's " darkness at...
...acted by torture. The chief
...rotskyites, Zinhvievites and
...ilitated. Khrushchev explicitly
...t the same time, he expresses
...'shook' them.

...uro in 1939, and in these last
...It is impossible not to wonder
...ges helter-skelter in tones ever
...military crassness; Stalin build-
...the films and the books about
...g roughshod over the Politburo
...tive force; Stalin shooting out
...ger supporters in the Leningrad
...he brilliant Chairman of the
...simply vanished in 1949).

...achinations of " traitor " Beria;
...hal Zhukov; his mass deporta-
...e Caucasus and the Black Sea
...te only because there were too
...place to deport them "); then the
...f the Doctors' Plot.

...max with the revelation that
...hilation " of the old Politburo
...ent of the U.S.S.R., was already
...glish agent; Andreyev had been
...; " baseless charges " had been
...olotov. " It is not excluded that
...r another few months, Comrades
...robably not have delivered any

...and no doubt for Khrushchev
...convenient.

Terror

Kamenev heard about it from her.
I have no intention of forgetting so
easily that which is being done
against me, and I need not stress
here that I consider as directed
against me that which is being done
against my wife. I ask you, therefore, that you weigh carefully
whether you are agreeable to re-
tracting your words and apologising
or whether you prefer the sever-
ance of relations between us.
(*Commotion in the hall.*)
Sincerely : Lenin, March 5, 1923.

Comrades !, I will not comment
on these documents. They speak
eloquently for themselves. Since
Stalin could behave in this manner during Lenin's life, could thus
behave towards Nadezhda Kon-
stantinovna Krupskaya, whom the
party knows well and values highly
as a loyal friend of Lenin and as
an active fighter for the cause of

THE FILM EXHIBITION

JANE BOWN

New Cyprus Proposal

By Our Diplomatic Correspondent

SIR JOHN HARDING is
expected to return to Cyprus
toward the end of this week,
taking with him a new proposal or
declaration on the political future of
the island. Just what form it will
take has not yet been decided by the
Cabinet. It is unlikely that it will
include any suggestion for associating
Nato with a political solution rather
internationalisation of the British
base there.

Sir John, it is understood, has given
a fairly reassuring report about the
progress of security measures and the
campaign against Eoka terrorists. It is
felt that, provided the momentum of
the anti-terrorist campaign can be kept
up and the efficiency of the measures
against smuggling arms from Greece
maintained, it is only a matter of perhaps three or six months before Eoka
ceases to be a major factor.

*The Countess of Harewood
opened* THE OBSERVER *Film
Exhibition in a reconstructed
building on Trafalgar-
square last Thursday with
workmen still on the premises
—due to a series of difficulties in the final days from
official regulations, Customs
delays and an unofficial
" go-slow " by casual paint-
ing labour. She and Lord
Harewood are seen sil-
houetted against a huge
photograph of the Thames
covering one wall of a room.*

More, on Page 12.

Eisenhower 'Excellent'

From Patrick O'Donovan

WASHINGTON, June 9

PRESIDENT EISENHOWER is
progressing " most satisfac-
torily " after his operation early
this morning, in the Walter Reed
military hospital here, for relief
of a non-malignant intestinal
obstruction.

His condition is described as
" excellent." His doctors say that he
should be able to return to his
" full duties " within four to six
weeks and that there is no reason, so
far as this particular illness is concerned, why he should not be able to
run for re-election as President.

At a crowded Press conference the
doctors said that the President
should be able to leave hospital in
some 15 days. They expected a
rapid and complete recovery. They
insisted that his heart had in no way
been affected.

" During the coming weeks," it
was stated, " he should be able to
sign official papers and carry on
those functions of the Government
which are necessary."

Harriman Decides

With this cautiously optimistic
diagnosis the political effects of this
attack have been minimised. Political
leaders of all sorts of opinion have
expressed their personal concern, but
almost all have refrained from public speculation. A notable exception
is Governor Harriman of New York,
who to-day declared himself at last
an " active " candidate for the
Democratic nomination for President.

Although it cannot be certain that
President Eisenhower will again be a
candidate—he gave a pledge to stand
down if he thought himself in any
way physically unfitted—there is no
doubt that this attack has a little
improved the Democratic chances.
It gives weight to suggestions that
he is not physically fit enough for
office and injects an element of
perilous uncertainty into the Repub-
lican claim for re-election, which is
based to a major extent on the personality and prestige of the President.

Fine and Warmer

A belt of relatively high pressure
over the British Isles is forecast for
to-day. Over much of the country it
will be fine with temperatures
approaching seasonal normal, but
rather cool in some eastern districts
with the chance of rain in south-
eastern areas of England. There will
be some low cloud or fog with drizzle
in places in parts of northern Ireland
and north-west Scotland.

David Astor
and The Observer

Other books by Richard Cockett

Twilight of Truth:
Chamberlain, Appeasement and
the Manipulation of the Press

My Dear Max:
The Correspondence of Brendan Bracken and
Lord Beaverbrook, 1928 − 58

David Astor and The Observer

RICHARD COCKETT

ANDRE DEUTSCH

First published 1991 by
André Deutsch Limited
105–106 Great Russell Street, London WC1B 3LJ

Copyright © 1991 by Richard Cockett

British Library Cataloguing in Publication Data
Cockett, Richard
  David Astor and the *Observer*.
  1. Great Britain. English newspapers, history. Astor, David
  I. Title
  072.092

ISBN 0 233 98735 5

Typeset in Hong Kong by Setrite Typesetters Ltd
Printed in Great Britain by
St Edmundsbury Press. Bury St. Edmunds Suffolk

For
MARK HETHERINGTON
1959—1990

Contents

Author's Note and Acknowledgments

The *Observer* is Britain's oldest Sunday newspaper, celebrating its bicentenary in 1991. During the paper's long and distinguished history it probably never achieved greater fame or influence than under its editor from 1948 to 1975, David Astor. At the urging of his friends, as well as of many of the *Observer*'s admirers, several attempts have been made by Astor and others to write an account of the paper's journalistic achievement under his editorship, and particularly of the circumstances in which he managed to gather round him on the paper probably the greatest array of literary talent in the history of British journalism, including Cyril Connolly, George Orwell, Isaac Deutscher, Sebastian Haffner, Arthur Koestler, Anthony Sampson, Patrick O'Donovan and Michael Frayn. When, in late 1987, David Astor turned to me to write an account of the *Observer* under his editorship, it soon became obvious to me, as it had been to others, that David Astor's *Observer* was just that: almost uniquely, a paper created and moulded in the image of its own editor. It was obviously a prerequisite for understanding the paper and the quality of its success to understand David Astor himself.

With some reluctance he therefore submitted to the ordeal of a biographical study, which concentrates, none the less, on his lasting and much acclaimed achievement: the creation of the modern *Observer*. This book is thus, I hope, a seamless blend of biography and newspaper history. That it should be so is a tribute to both David Astor and the many journalists and writers who worked with him on the *Observer*.

My greatest debt is to David Astor himself who, having invited me to write this book, has been unfailing in his cooperátion and support. As well as putting all his private papers at my disposal and granting me a series of long interviews, David and his wife Bridget have both offered many helpful suggestions on the manuscript, while always respecting my final judgement as to the content of the book. David has always been very generous with his hospitality; as many of the old *Observer* staff would testify, working with him is extremely pleasurable.

I also owe a special debt of gratitude to John Silverlight who, having done some work on a history of the *Observer* under David Astor, generously put his material at my disposal. I also owe a great debt to the following who kindly consented to what often turned out to be long and repeated interviews: Sir John (Jakie) Astor, Christabel and Peter Bielenberg, Nora Beloff, Jane Bown, Andrea Bosco, Dinah Brooke, Samuel Beer, Benjamin Buchan, William Curling, Michael Davie, Tamara Deutscher, Lord Deedes, Michael Foot, Alastair Forbes, Lord Goodman, Monty Guttman, John Grigg, Sir Peter Gibbings, Penelope Gilliatt, Kenneth Harris, Godfrey Hodgson, Anthony Howard, Jon Kimche, Rudolf Klein, John Heilpern, Roger Harrison, Tristan Jones, Colin Legum, Lord Longford, Clifford Makins, Patsy Meehan, Giles MacDonogh, Terry Kilmartin, John Littlejohns, Rafael Nadal, Kenneth Obank, Hermione O'Donovan, Jim Rose, Anthony Sampson, George Seddon, Bill Smart, Robert Stephens, John Silverlight, Clarita von Trott, Donald Trelford, Sir Peregrine Worsthorne, Gretta Weil.

I also benefited from correspondence with Laurence Gandar, Ronald Fredenburgh, Alastair Hetherington and Michael Frayn. I owe a special debt to Anthony Sampson, Roger Harrison and Christabel and Peter Bielenberg, who all read parts of the manuscript and suggested several important improvements. Needless to say, the opinions expressed in this book and the conclusions reached are, none the less, mine alone.

I would also like to thank the staff of the Bodleian Library, Oxford, the Reading University Archive Centre and the *Observer* library for their cooperation. Karmani Ward and Caroline Robinson both had the unenviable task of reading my handwriting and typing up the final draft. Finally I owe a considerable debt to Araminta Whitley who smoothed the passage of this book at some awkward moments, and to Diana Athill, a knowledgeable and sympathetic editor.

Sources. Unless otherwise indicated in the references, all the letters and documents referred to in the book are in the private archives of Mr David Astor at Sutton Courtenay. All the interviews with David Astor and with *Observer* writers quoted from in the book were conducted in 1989 and 1990. My thanks to everyone who talked to me. I am also grateful to Mr Ken Obank and Mr John Silverlight who generously put at my disposal a substantial amount of their own archival material on the history of the *Observer*: and I must record my debt to the official historian of the *Observer*, Dr John Stubbs, whose work is referred to in Chapter Four.

RC

1

Early Influences

David Astor was born in 1912 into the most sumptuous and affluent family environment that Edwardian Britain, then at the height of her Imperial power, had to offer. David's parents, the 2nd Viscount Astor and his wife Nancy, presided over their own empire of wealth, property, servants – and newspapers – which allowed them to live, and entertain, on a scale that has all but vanished today. As well as the main family home at Cliveden in Buckinghamshire, the Astors owned a substantial London house at 4 St James's Square, a seaside house, Rest Harrow near Sandwich in Kent, a house in Plymouth and a fishing-and-shooting lodge on the Isle of Jura off the coast of Scotland. Cliveden had about twenty indoor staff, and between fifty and sixty people working out of doors in the stables and gardens. When the family moved to London during the week, many of the staff travelled up to St James's Square with them, much like the stately progress of a medieval court.

The family owned two newspapers, the *Pall Mall Gazette* and the *Observer*, bought in 1911, and Lord Astor ran one of Britain's most successful racing stables at Cliveden. The Astors were multimillionaires, their fortune founded on investment by their ancestors in New York real estate during the nineteenth century; and at the age of twenty-one the Astor children, including David, each inherited enough money to make them independent for the rest of their lives. It was from this background that David Astor was to emerge as the editor of a paper, the *Observer*, that for over three decades under his direction was to be the most radical liberal newspaper in modern British journalism, battling on behalf of the oppressed, of minorities and of the persecuted in Britain and around the world.

That this was so stemmed from the unique political and cultural milieu in which David Astor grew up at Cliveden — a milieu which was markedly different from that of the other great country houses of Edwardian England — as well as his own rebellion against his family. For the Astors were outsiders in English society, and David was to grow up outside the Astors. He became, in the sense that really matters, a "self-made" man.

The salient fact about the Astors, apart from their wealth, was that they were American. The founder of the family wealth was John Jacob Astor, the son of a farmer at Waldorf in the Upper Rhineland. He emigrated to England, where his brother had become a prosperous harpsichord maker, then moved on to America at the time of the colonies' revolt. In America he made his money as a fur-trader, founding the American and Pacific fur companies. His greatest coup was to invest the profits from his commercial activities in land on Manhattan Island, so that he and his descendants became the main beneficiaries of the steady growth of New York City uptown on the Island throughout the nineteenth century. By the middle of the nineteenth century, the family was firmly established as probably the first of the fabulously rich American dynasties that were to dominate American financial and commercial life before the First World War, together with the Rockefellers, Vanderbilts, Morgans, and a few others. As John Grigg, Nancy Astor's biographer, has written, John Jacob's ". . . descendants had only to sit tight and the money would continue, inexorably, to roll in . . .",[1] as it does to this day.

John Jacob's great-grandson, William Waldorf, was the first Astor to break the family commitment to the New World by emigrating to Britain, via Italy, in 1890. Being a member of the new financial aristocracy in America was, apparently, not enough for William Waldorf; asked why he was leaving America, he gave

---

1. John Grigg, *Nancy Astor* (Hamlyn Paperbacks), p. 38.

the legendary — possibly apocryphal — reply "America is not a fit place for a gentleman to live". A more pressing reason for his emigration to Britain seems to have been his political and personal humiliation at the hands of the voters and journalists of New York City when he tried to run for office in his home-town in 1887. Once in England, William Waldorf busily set about buying the trappings of aristocracy and "civilization" which he felt America had so sadly lacked. He bought two historic country houses, Hever Castle in Kent and Cliveden in Buckinghamshire in 1893. He filled these two houses with some of the art treasures on which he had expended millions of dollars as he travelled round Europe, particularly Italy. In London he bought a house in Carlton House Terrace and built an office on the Embankment at Victoria. Feeling that newspaper ownership would give him a voice in — and access to — social and political life, he bought the prestigious *Pall Mall Gazette* in 1892, appointing Harry Cust to the editorial chair, and the Sunday *Observer* newspaper in 1911. (Cust refused to publish William Waldorf's own writings in the *Pall Mall Gazette*, complaining of their poor quality, and was peremptorily sacked for his pains.)

Astor's hopes for an aristocratic English life inevitably became focused on his children, Waldorf (David's father), John Jacob V, Pauline and Gwendolyn (who died in childhood). Both Waldorf, the eldest, and John Jacob were sent to Eton, and Waldorf then went up to New College, Oxford. At Eton he was Captain of Boats and treasurer of Pop, whilst at Oxford he belonged to the Bullingdon Club, a social élite similar to Eton's Pop, and represented the University at polo and fencing. So much sport left little time for work, and he graduated with only a fourth-class degree in Modern History.

After Oxford Waldorf's health declined and the rest of his life was to be dogged by frail health. It was in a state of some despondency and listlessness that he returned to England from New York after a visit to America in December 1905. On the same vessel was Nancy Witcher Langhorne, with whom he fell almost instantly in love.

Nancy Langhorne had been born in 1879, the eighth of the eleven children of Chiswell Dabney Langhorne of Danville, Virginia. "Chillie" Langhorne was a man of great resource and charm, who, like many in the South, enjoyed undulating fortunes due to the Civil War and the resulting economic dislocation. He made his first dollars as a tobacco auctioneer and Nancy spent the first six years of her life in a modest single-storey house, of no more than four rooms and a kitchen, in an unfashionable district of Danville. However, Chillie went on to make serious money in the railroad industry and in 1892 bought the country estate of Mirador in Albemarle County, which became the centre of the young Nancy's life. There was no great emphasis on education, but at Mirador she became a highly skilled and spirited horsewoman. In 1895, the eldest and most beautiful Langhorne daughter, Irene, married the painter Dana Gibson – thus becoming the original "Gibson Girl" – and this focused attention on Nancy as the eldest unmarried daughter. She was sent to a ladies' finishing school in New York, which she hated, and in 1896 met a rich Bostonian, Robert Gould Shaw II, whom she married, at the age of eighteen, in 1897, at Mirador. The marriage was an instant disaster, and within two days of the start of their honeymoon Nancy was back at Mirador.

Although she was prevailed upon to return to her husband, they were, in fact, fatally incompatible, a problem exacerbated by his alcoholism. They were divorced in 1903, after Bob's parents revealed to her that he had secretly married another woman. Nancy and Bob Shaw had one child, Robert Gould Shaw III, "Bobbie" as he was always known in the Astor family. He was born in 1898, and was to remain closest to Nancy of all her children throughout her life: not necessarily a good thing for either of them. Partly as a consolation for this failed marriage and partly out of a sense of adventure Nancy travelled to England, then a magnet for East Coast Americans. There, for the hunting, she spent the winters of 1903, 1904 and 1905; and it was on the last of these crossings that she met Waldorf Astor. They were married at All Souls Church, Langham Place, on May 3, 1906.

The match must have been founded on an attraction of opposites, for apart from the fact that they were both Americans abroad, they had little in common. Waldorf Astor was a serious young man with a highly developed sense of moral obligation (his son Michael wrote of the Astors that they were possessed of "a conscientious form of Lutheran orthodoxy..."[2]). His father, William,

---

2. Michael Astor, *Tribal Feeling* (John Murray 1963), p. 43.

was a notoriously shy person, but this quality he seems to have passed on more to John Jacob than to Waldorf. Waldorf was self-restrained, discreet and perhaps stern, but not shy. He was methodical; he weighed factors up before coming to a conclusion; and he was intelligent, although not an intellectual. Above all, as Christopher Sykes has written of him, "from his youth he had felt a deep sense of obligation and the duty of public service of an enlightened kind, such as was not to be traced, or not to any marked degree, in his father".[3]

Michael Astor, author of the best book on the Astors, *Tribal Feeling*, has written of his father that he

> ...recognised the fact that William Waldorf's attitude to affairs had been aristocratic, as well as autocratic. William Waldorf had paid scant regard to what people felt or thought of his behaviour. He had remained imperiously a law unto himself. My father did not applaud this attitude. Being American by birth he did not fit into the English aristocratic pattern. Being puritan by inclination he did not wish to. He wanted to succeed in a life of public service and make amends, as he saw it, for his father's negligence in this respect.... His handicap was that he had little instinctive feeling for people. His approach to life was that of reason, and he allowed his intuition very little play: consequently his methods, though admirably tenacious, were stern and not relieved by those flights of fancy and spontaneous outbursts which so enlivened my mother's life. Lord Brand, who knew Father all his life, described him as a saint, meaning, I fancy, that he was incorruptible, unselfish and ascetic.

He was, indeed, a remarkably kind and sympathetic man, who earned the respect and admiration of all who worked for him or knew him. David Astor's first generation of *Observer* journalists, recruited during the Second World War, or just after, were all to remark on Waldorf's often unwarranted and unsolicited acts of kindness and generosity towards them. Lord Brand was not the only person who described him as "a saint".

It would be harder to imagine a greater contrast with the Astors than the Langhornes of Virginia, and Nancy was every inch a

---

3. Christopher Sykes, *Nancy Astor* (Collins 1972), p. 80.

Langhorne just as much as Waldorf was every inch an Astor. Nancy was a highly intelligent, uneducated and intuitive woman of strong feelings. She was absolutely natural and uninhibited, with a flashing wit and a flair for conversation which became legendary. Whereas Waldorf was thoughtful and careful, Nancy was spontaneous and seemed to possess no capacity for reflective thought. Whereas Waldorf was possessed of self-doubt, Nancy had little capacity for self-criticism. Just as Waldorf, and to an even greater extent his English contemporaries, could be circumspect and evasive, so Nancy was very direct and always spoke her mind in any company, be it in the Cliveden drawing room or the House of Commons. Extraordinarily self-confident, she was also combative, aggressive and liked nothing better than spirited banter, whether with her own children or the voters of Plymouth. Above all she was natural — a rare quality in Edwardian England. Nancy could talk freely and meaningfully with anyone, poor or rich, high or low, without any inhibitions. She reflected on this characteristic in her unpublished autobiography:

> The trouble with so many English people is that they cannot, however hard they try, be quite natural with other people. It is difficult for them not to be just a little patronising. I don't know why that is. Maybe it has something to do with climate over here. In Virginia it is something we simply do not understand. I suppose it is because there never were the same class distinctions to make artificial barriers between people.[4]

Her ability to communicate rested on her simple love of individual human beings and her sheer cheek. She extended her sympathy and help to anyone whom she liked, whatever their station in life; she had a compulsion to help individuals in distress. During the First World War there was a Canadian army hospital at Cliveden, and she befriended several of the patients for life. There was one man in the ward for the most serious cases whom Nancy particularly respected and on one occasion, when he did not answer, she tried to reach him by a deliberate civic insult. Putting a hand on his shoulder she said: "It's no wonder you're dying. You come from Manchester." With a faint smile he answered: "Manchester's the

4. Sykes, p. 112.

finest city in the world." She often used to repeat the soldier's boast admiringly. She rallied another soldier, Frank Guy, by giving him a watch, inscribed with his name, shortly before he underwent his sixteenth operation on his legs, to show she expected him to live. He did and stayed on as the estate clerk at Cliveden for over twenty years. Another ex-soldier, a delightful but moody man named Dance, for whom she also found an estate job, disappeared one day and was found wandering depressed in Maidenhead. She went herself to fetch him back and he also lived out his life on the estate. By the same token, it was Nancy to whom the young Harold Macmillan turned in 1930 when his wife Dorothy fell in love with his parliamentary colleague Bob Boothby. Nancy also persuaded a woman tramp to leave the road and settle in a flat she provided, and in her extreme dotage she had to have her cheque book removed by her eldest son Bill to stop her sending near-strangers off on unsolicited holidays.

However, her kindness and sympathy towards individuals was matched by intolerance and a tendency to bully that lost her as many friends as she made. She was incapable of translating her capacity for individual love and kindness on to a wider emotional or political level. This characteristic was increased by her conversion to Christian Science in 1914, which made her more dogmatic and intolerant of her political and religious enemies — particularly Roman Catholics. She suffered all the faults of her virtues; she was spontaneous, intuitive, emotional and wilful, and could appear, by the same token, as unthinking, irrational and stubborn. As she grew older, the defects of her character tended to outweigh her virtues, particularly as revealed in some of her public comments.

However, in 1906 Waldorf and Nancy seemed to complement each other perfectly. John Grigg has written that Waldorf loved Nancy more than she loved him, but Nancy herself

> ...could see that their qualities were in many ways complementary — that he was almost ideally suited to act as the "straight man" to her inspired comedy, while on the serious side his patient, methodical mind could provide indispensable backing for her missionary flair. She also felt, and this was most important to her, that he would be a good stepfather to Bobbie.[5]

—————————

5. Grigg, p. 43.

As a wedding present, William Waldorf gave the couple Cliveden, while Waldorf's younger brother, John Jacob, inherited Hever Castle on William Waldorf's death in 1919. Waldorf also bought a substantial town house at 4 St James's Square.

Between her second marriage and the First World War Nancy gave birth to three children, William Waldorf (Bill) in 1907, Phyllis (Wissie) in 1909 and Francis David Langhorne in 1912. During the war she gave birth to two more sons, Michael in 1916 and John Jacob (Jakie) in 1918. At the time of David's birth in 1912 Waldorf and Nancy were cultivating the parliamentary seat of Plymouth for Waldorf's political career, so David was known as the "Plymouth baby". He was also christened Francis in honour of Sir Francis Drake, to help endear Waldorf and Nancy to the electors of Plymouth. The childhood regime at Cliveden, the principal home of the family, was in many ways typical of that enjoyed — or suffered — in other Edwardian upper-class families. The children's lives were run by Nannie Gibbons, described by Nancy as the "backbone" of the family. They saw less of Nancy, especially after she became a Member of Parliament in 1919, and Waldorf was regarded with distant admiration: his formal, reserved nature made him awkward with young children and he came into his own when they were somewhat older. As a result, the children's lives were centred around the staff, in particular Nannie Gibbons and Mr Lee, the butler.

David has described Mr Lee "...as God ought to be...omnipotent and seemed to know everything...also a thoughtful man". Strongly built, coming from Herefordshire farming stock, he served throughout the Great War, ending as a still young sergeant-major. It was to Mr Lee that David, like the rest of the children, looked in times of trouble; he remembers Mr Lee accompanying him all the way back to prep school on one occasion when he could not face going back alone, and being reassured by Mr Lee that this was how soldiers had reacted to the prospect of going back into the trenches after being on leave — an unintentionally poignant insight into the English prep and public school system. Mr Lee was not only a fount of wisdom and common sense, but was also remarkably sensitive and caring. After David had moved out of Cliveden, he discovered that Mr Lee, on his annual seaside holiday, took with him a member of the Cliveden household known as Sailor Walker. Sailor's job was the humble one of "odd man", the carrier of luggage and heavy trays. Mr Lee took him along because he knew Sailor's secret: that he was illiterate and could not organise a holiday for himself.

Most country houses of Cliveden's size and grandeur stand at the centre of large agricultural estates and represent the authority of land ownership. Cliveden's 450 acres of garden and woodland, its stud farm and its model dairy farm at White Place, over the Thames at Cookham, enabled the house to be pretty well self-sufficient but were large-scale pleasure-grounds rather than working acres. The Sutherlands and Westminsters, who rebuilt the house in the nineteenth century, had their family estates elsewhere and wanted this house to be a place for occasional retreat from London. When Sir Charles Barry redesigned it in 1850–51, he therefore created an Italianate villa, grand but not too large for comfortable family habitation.

The romance of Cliveden lies in its situation, on a man-made plateau astride the chalk cliffs overlooking the Thames, a few minutes' drive from Taplow, Buckinghamshire. The house commands sweeping views over the serene and fertile Thames valley, Maidenhead and beyond being easily visible in the distance. Below the thickly wooded cliffs, the river flows through one of its most beautiful passages at Cliveden Reach. To this day, although many fields have given way to suburbia, it remains one of the most striking panoramic views in England. Perhaps the most remarkable fact about the house is that although so much can be seen from it, it is all but invisible from the countryside spread out beneath it, remaining haughtily discreet and very private on its eminence. David's room was at the top of the house, on the left, facing the garden, with views east and south.

To David living in Cliveden was like "...living in a hotel which was also partly a museum". With the constant round of entertainment that the Astors indulged in between 1893 and the Second World War, the house did have something of the character of a luxury hotel. There could be up to ten or twelve guests at weekends, some of whom might stay on, and one was never quite sure who would be there at breakfast. Together with all the servants, gardeners and other outside workers they formed a constant stream of people which, though fascinating, could be a strain. In its "museum" aspect, the house was stuffed with the artistic trophies of William Waldorf's peregrinations in Europe, which made it a very precious environment to grow up in. And because of the size of its grounds on the one hand and the moat-like protection of the river on the other, it felt cut off from the outside world. It was something of a gilded cage.

What set it most apart from other English country houses, and what profoundly influenced David, was the fact that his parents were American. This meant that their social and political ideals were quite unlike those of their English contemporaries. Waldorf Astor's father had hoped that he would marry into the English aristocracy and was none too pleased when he chose an American wife. For all Waldorf's Eton education, he was notably unlike the Edwardian youth with whom he grew up, his seriousness and earnest demeanour contrasting with their languid and carefree ways. Nancy was, of course, vigorously American — she never lost her slight Virginian accent. And unlike many Americans, including Waldorf's father, they were not ashamed of their country: to them America was "the great experiment" in human and social organisation, a young country with a potential yet to be fulfilled. (Interestingly, at the time of greatest danger to the Anglo-American alliance, the Suez crisis in 1956, all the Astor children spoke publicly against Eden's attack on Egypt, singling out the strain it put on the "Western" Anglo-American axis. Jakie Astor, a Conservative MP at that time, was often taunted by fellow Tories for being American or "half-American".) Indeed, Waldorf and Nancy consciously took on the role of self-appointed ambassadors for the land of their birth, making Cliveden a centre of hospitality for visiting Americans.

Almost every American of any consequence during the inter-war years stayed at Cliveden at least once, and often more frequently. Nancy's family were often invited, particularly her sisters — her favourite sister, Phyllis, married the English banker Bob Brand, who became an integral part of the extended Astor family. Then there were successive American ambassadors who, according to David Astor, "were part of the furniture...and some were very dull", and celebrities ranging from senators and journalists to Fred Astaire, Helen Wills the tennis star and the honorary American Charlie Chaplin, who stayed several times.

A striking example of Waldorf and Nancy Astor acting usefully in their capacity as unofficial ambassadors came when Joe Kennedy was about to give up his ambassadorship in London just after the beginning of the Second World War. It was rumoured — correctly — that Kennedy was leaving Britain with a poor view of the country's determination to continue fighting the war and also feeling personally neglected. This could have had a bad effect on his close friend President Roosevelt and thus on America's vital support for Britain. So Nancy Astor first got herself invited to Kennedy's home at Sunningdale to probe his feelings. (David accompanied her and found Kennedy in a silk pyjama suit, mainly interested in showing his two guests a number of trivial and uninteresting films.) This visit seemed to confirm Nancy's misgivings. Finding that there was no government intention to give Kennedy a farewell meal, she decided to give him one at Cliveden — if she could get the King and Queen to come. She did, and the Kennedys and their children duly arrived for a very successful evening. The only slight problem arose with George VI, who did not seem fully to grasp the role he was supposed to play and sat chatting for much of the evening with the extremely pretty Argentinian girlfriend (later wife) of Jakie, "Chiquita" Carcano, leaving the Queen to do her conversational best with the Kennedys. It was Nancy who managed to interrupt and recall the King to his duty. Nancy and Waldorf were aware of the fact that many people resented them as Americans, but they were too proud of the land of their birth to mind. Nancy was a consummate mimic, and one of her favourite acts for the children was to mimic haughty English county ladies talking about "those vulgar Americans".

The Americanism which set the Astors apart from the English "aristocracy" also set them apart politically from their contemporaries. Waldorf was essentially a democrat, both in the literal sense and in the American party sense of the word. Far from viewing America, as many Englishmen did, as an uncivilized, degenerate country he always remained loyal to the vision of America as a classless, mobile and vigorous democracy from which England had a lot to learn. With his sense of responsibility and the duty of public service it was inevitable that Waldorf should go into politics, and in 1910 he was elected to Parliament for Plymouth. Although he was elected as a Conservative, he was only nominally a Tory and from the beginning he took up a position on the left of the party. He immediately made his views known and his presence felt by voting with the Liberal Government against his party for Lloyd George's Health and Unemployment Insurance Bill in 1911.

His main political interest remained social reform, and he quickly joined the Unionist Social Reform Committee, under the patronage of F. E. Smith, in 1912. Amongst other youthful members of that committee were those who were to direct the policy of "appeasement" during the 1930s, Stanley Baldwin, Samuel Hoare and Edward Wood (later Lord Halifax). In 1917, by which time he was working as a member of Lloyd George's "Garden Suburb" in Downing Street, he produced a penny pamphlet entitled *The Health of the People*, which brought the idea of a Ministry of Health into more popular discussion. He was appointed by Lloyd George as Chairman of the State Medical Research Committee and in 1918 became Parliamentary Secretary to the new Ministry of Health under Christopher Addison.

Waldorf's political career was effectively ended in 1919 by the death of his father, for William Waldorf had accepted a peerage in 1916, becoming the 1st Viscount Astor, without consulting or even telling Waldorf and Nancy. This angered Waldorf, who was thus denied the satisfaction of a longer political career, and the family rift this caused was such that the 1st Viscount Astor partially disinherited Waldorf, authorizing his money to be passed on to Waldorf's sons when they reached the age of twenty-one.

Having put down his marker as a "radical", or "progressive" in politics, Waldorf was to support and sponsor a number of causes during the inter-war period, including experiments in modern housing in Plymouth and agricultural methods on his own model farm. At the end of the Second World War, Waldorf gave Cliveden over to the National Trust and in a speech to the House of Lords recommended the nationalization of the land, mainly to facilitate the rebuilding of Plymouth after the German bombing. It is small wonder that George Bernard Shaw used teasingly to refer to Waldorf as "that Commie" in his letters to Nancy; Waldorf's liberalism and progressivism were to be a great influence on David and the *Observer*, especially during the Second World War when David found a natural ally in his father for his plans for changing the *Observer* from a conservative paper into a very much more liberal one.

Indeed, the strongest expression of political abuse in the Astor household was to refer to someone as a "die-hard". The die-hards of the Conservative right were regarded as the enemy, rather than the Labour politicians. Nancy Astor's own political inclinations were also radical and to the left, although she never kept still long enough to evolve what could be characterized as a coherent political philosophy. George Bernard Shaw wrote to her giving advice on how to woo the voters of Plymouth in 1929, and summed up her politics thus:

> ...You are in a difficult situation; a violently Radical Conservative, a recklessly unladylike lady, a Prohibitionist member of the Trade Party, and all sorts of contradictory things, including (on the authority of the late Speaker) the most turbulent member of the Party of Order.[6]

Intellectual coherence was certainly never Nancy's forte, she was a politician of instinct. Like Waldorf, she had little time for the stuffiness and pretensions of the English class system, and, of course, her feminism put her at odds with the bulk of the Conservative Party. When Waldorf had to go to the House of Lords as 2nd Viscount Astor in 1919, it was natural that Nancy should fill his shoes in Plymouth and she took her seat in the House of Commons as the first woman MP on December 1, 1919. Her mere presence in the House of Commons was enough to give many Conservative members apoplexy, particularly the despicable Horatio Bottomley and the ultra-Conservative Sir Frederick Banbury. Winston Churchill also objected to women MPs, which exacerbated a long-running feud between Nancy and Churchill. She had to demonstrate enormous reserves of moral courage and sheer guts to survive the first few years in Parliament, which she later admitted was "a time of almost continual and unbearable strain".[7] In her eighties, she admitted to David that if she had known how hostile the House of Commons would be, she would probably never have tried to become an MP. As it was, once she sensed that the men were trying to break her nerve in the hope that if she was seen to fail so other women would not be chosen by constituency parties as parliamentary candidates, she drew on all her considerable fighting qualities and stuck it out. Probably no other woman could have

6. G.B.S. – Nancy Astor: May 18, 1929, *Collected Correspondence of G. B. Shaw*, Vol. IV, p. 142.

7. Sykes, p. 216.

done it, or survived all the petty — and often obscene — provocations and humiliations to which she was subjected during her first years in the House of Commons. Even her own relations would not speak to her in the House.

In Parliament, like Waldorf, she was only nominally a Conservative and all her campaigns and speeches on behalf of women and such issues as child care marked her out as an equally independent figure. Most of her Parliamentary friends were thus to be found on the Labour benches, particularly amongst the women MPs such as Eleanor Rathbone. Mrs Wintringham, the second woman to sit in Parliament, a Liberal, was also a firm ally, as was Nancy's rival for the affections of the Plymouth electorate, the great Liberal West Country lawyer, Isaac Foot, father of Michael Foot, whom David was later to recruit as a contributor for the *Observer*, and Dingle Foot, chairman of the trustees of the *Observer* during the 1950s. Emotionally, Nancy Astor was always for the underdog in society, just as she was in her element coming to the rescue of distressed individuals. In this sense, she was, again, much more like an American missionary than a Conservative peeress. David inherited her concern for the "underdog", though he also inherited Waldorf's more reflective, thoughtful qualities that enabled him to build this basic emotional sympathy into a more coherent and embracing political philosophy.

Nancy Astor was also very catholic in her taste for people. Unlike many other country houses, Cliveden's house parties were not a country extension of political club-life. The tradition of Cliveden entertaining was to do with bringing together people of a wide variety of backgrounds so that they could exchange ideas. It was the same ideal that persuaded Waldorf Astor to help found the Royal Institute of International Affairs at Chatham House. Nancy and Waldorf were always independent of the Conservative Party machine, had no ambitions for high office, and thus devoted little time to cultivating the grandees of their Party. Nancy's criterion for judging people was simple — they had to be interesting. This accounted for her close friendship with people as diverse as Hilaire Belloc, Sean O'Casey, Brendan Bracken and, most famously, George Bernard Shaw. There was no "Cliveden Set"; such a thing was impossible at Cliveden. The Astors were thus not only outsiders in England in the sense that they were American, but they were also outsiders in the sense that they were politically and socially radical. It was David, more than any of the other children, who identified strongly with this grain of independent radicalism that manifested itself in different ways in both Nancy and Waldorf.

The other feature of Cliveden that was to leave its indelible mark on David Astor was its vibrant intellectual atmosphere, for under the Astors the house, especially at weekends, became a continuous talking shop. Waldorf and Nancy were not an intellectual couple in the ordinary sense of the word, for they did not surround themselves with books or pore over learned journals in search of enlightenment. Indeed, there were very few books at Cliveden, Nancy having largely given up anything more than occasional literature since her conversion to Christian Science in 1914. However, Nancy, especially, was an inveterate talker and she and Waldorf absorbed most of their information through talking and listening. Cliveden echoed to the sounds of endless conversation and banter, sometimes serious, often not. For a boy to grow up in this atmosphere was tremendously stimulating, as most of the great talkers of the era, such as J. L. Garvin, G. B. Shaw, Lloyd George or Belloc, might be found of an afternoon exchanging views, or shouting to be heard, on the terrace or in the garden. For the children, this was the most exciting element of Cliveden; the best intellectual upbringing they could have. *Observer* journalists could not help noticing in later years that David Astor's *Observer* was run largely as a mini-Cliveden talking shop, the paper's weekly intellectual content taking shape at a series of perpetual conferences where the editor would listen and debate with the most interesting minds of the day that he could gather around the table. In this sense the *Observer* was David's own little Cliveden. And at the centre of this constantly shifting intellectual firmament at Cliveden were the men of "Milner's Kindergarten", who were to have the biggest influence on David's intellectual development.

"Milner's Kindergarten" was the unlikely nickname for the group of young Oxford graduates which gathered around the High Commissioner in South Africa, Alfred (later Lord) Milner, who was largely credited with having started the Boer War. In the wake of the Boer War, however, he worked on an attempt to reconcile British and Boer interests in South Africa by adopting an elaborate scheme for a federal Union of the South African colonies.

It became known as the Selborne Memorandum, after the High Commissioner who succeeded Milner. To help him in this task, Milner gathered around himself in South Africa a group of the ablest young Oxford graduates, predominantly products of New College and All Souls, who took up positions of territorial or administrative responsibility in South Africa. This group of men included Philip Kerr, whose father was the younger son of the seventh Marquess of Lothian, Robert Brand, Geoffrey Robinson (later Dawson) and Lionel Curtis. On their return to England, these men founded the Round Table group in 1909, an endeavour in which they were joined by Edward Grigg and F. S. Oliver, a businessman who was also an enthusiast for imperial federalism. These men were to become the closest political and personal friends of Lord and Lady Astor. Waldorf was at New College with Kerr and Brand, and he was to become an enthusiastic supporter of their cause over the years. It was the Round Table group together with Waldorf Astor who founded the Royal Institute of International Affairs, an enterprise with which Waldorf Astor and Lionel Curtis became closely connected. All of the Round Table group became intimately connected with the Astors in one way or another; Geoffrey Dawson became editor of *The Times*, which was owned by Waldorf's brother John Jacob, Bob Brand married Nancy's sister Phyllis, Edward Grigg was closely connected with the *Observer* and sat on the various tribunals to settle Garvin's contract as editor, while Curtis was Waldorf Astor's principal collaborator at Chatham House. None of the Round Table group — except Grigg — ever sought, or held, political office. They preferred to make their contribution to public affairs by writing and acting as advisers to Government.

The most important member of the Round Table as far as the Astors, and particularly David, were concerned was Philip Kerr, later Lord Lothian. Kerr was a political colleague of Waldorf's, but, more significantly, was Nancy's closest friend; indeed, there is little doubt that he loved her platonically. They came together in the years just before the First World War when Kerr had a nervous breakdown at much the same time as Nancy herself suffered a prolonged bout of ill-health. Together they found solace in Christian Science, an American interpretation of Christianity pioneered by Mary Baker Eddy, whose works became central to the life of the Astor family. The parents took it in turn to conduct an hour's Christian Science reading with David and the other children every morning. Christian Science held that the root of all physical malady lay in the mind, and that prayer was the only answer for such mental affliction. Kerr himself was to be a martyr to Christian Science. When he was Ambassador to Washington in 1940 he refused to see a doctor for a relatively minor condition which quickly killed him. With their dual conversion to Christian Science in 1914, Lothian and Nancy shared a bond that lasted for the whole of their lives — Waldorf was only converted ten years later.

As well as being Nancy's spiritual confidant, and later go-between with her and her children, Kerr was probably the most original political thinker of the Round Table group and his ideas on world government and international problems had a profound effect on Waldorf Astor, and even more so on the young David. As a thinker on foreign affairs, Kerr spent his intellectual life grappling with the problem of the decline of British world power, and the vacuum that this would create at the heart of world affairs. Even before the First World War Kerr and the Round Table group were concerned with this scenario and, drawing on their work with the concept of federalism in South Africa, they evolved the idea that the British Empire should set out to federate. Naturally, this would mean that those dependent territories, such as India, that were not yet self-governing under a representative government should be helped to become so. They went on to suggest that such a new federation should seek a political union with the United States, and they accepted that the United States would become the centre of such combined federations. They considered that, in time, the democracies of Europe should be welcomed into this world-wide federal union. Such a development was, they believed, the rational way to create a political system strong enough to keep the peace in the world and to provide the nucleus of an eventual system of world government. This grand concept was largely the creation of Kerr and Curtis, and today Kerr is regarded by many Europeans as one of the spiritual fathers of European federalism and the EEC.

In 1917, Kerr was taken on as Lloyd George's Private Secretary for foreign affairs on the recommendation of Lord Milner, who had a seat in Lloyd George's War Cabinet; he was thus in close proximity to Waldorf Astor, who in December 1916 had been appointed Lloyd George's Parliamentary Private Secretary, a post he shared with David Davies. Kerr's most important job for Lloyd George was to advise the Prime Minister during the negotiations leading up to the Treaty of Versailles in 1919. It was Kerr who, on request, personally drafted the notorious "War Guilt" clause of the treaty which he later came to believe was directly responsible for the rise to power of Hitler; it was to atone for this piece of punitive diplomacy that Kerr became one of the most ardent supporters of the policy of "appeasement" during the late 1930s, visiting Hitler twice in 1935 and 1937. Although the League of Nations which emerged out of the Treaty of Versailles should have been welcomed by federalists, Kerr was always deeply sceptical of the ability of the League to fulfil its functions, because of the absence of the USA.

Kerr and David were close, and David took naturally to the atmosphere of liberalism and the sense of the importance of international relationships which surrounded the older man and his friends. He did not necessarily agree with Kerr on every subject — particularly not on the value of talking to Hitler's Germany in the nineteen-thirties — but he did inherit Kerr's central interest: the problem of developing a system of world order, possibly federalism, that would prevent international anarchy and therefore war. This interest would be clearly reflected in the *Observer*. Kerr's pamphlet *Pacifism is not Enough* was the most important text of David's early life.

It was inspiring for a young man to sit at the feet of such people, as well as of the great statesmen of the day such as A. J. Balfour, whom David visited with his mother on his death-bed. It also allowed him to see politicians as human beings, an opportunity denied to most aspiring journalists. This was very important for David's later career as it meant that the *Observer* never stooped to the level of gratuitous belittling of politicians that characterized some other papers, and it also made David Astor "guidance-proof" as an editor, because it made him more sure and self-confident in the presence of politicians who might have sought to exert undue influence on him.

The other man, closely associated with the Round Table group, who was to have a great influence on the Astors, and particularly David, was Dr Thomas Jones, known to the family as "TJ". TJ was a Welsh-speaking child of the South Wales coal valleys who gained renown in his own country as a wise and commonsensical professor of economics and man of character. After an academic career, he returned to Wales as adviser to David Davies, the philanthropic Welsh coal-owner, who introduced TJ to Lloyd George. Lloyd George brought TJ into Whitehall in 1916 as assistant and then as Deputy Secretary of the Cabinet. Although a lifelong Socialist of a moderate hue, he worked best with his Conservative masters Bonar Law and Stanley Baldwin, to whom he became a valued confidant. TJ lived and died like a Socialist. He never owned shares or employed a housekeeper and always washed up — on principle. TJ met Waldorf Astor in Whitehall during the First World War, and he became a life-long friend of both Waldorf and Nancy Astor. Although by no means an original thinker or intellectual in the class of Kerr, TJ was a steady and consistent adviser to the Astors, who supported him in the various philanthropic activities that he indulged in after his retirement from Whitehall in 1930. As a Socialist, he reinforced Waldorf Astor's sense of social duty and liberalism, and, as we shall see, became a valuable guide and mentor to David Astor when he was transforming the *Observer* along more liberal lines during the Second World War. The Astor and Jones families virtually grew up together: Tristan Jones was a contemporary of David's at Balliol, and later became general manager of the *Observer*.

Growing up among some of the most intelligent and influential people of the era, none of whom could be easily classified according to normal party political lines, was probably more important to David Astor's intellectual development than his formal education. The latter began at West Downs preparatory school in Winchester, where he endured the rigours of a very Victorian establishment, including cold baths every day. At the age of twelve, after a short spell at a Christian Science school at Uckfield, David, like his brothers, was sent to Eton, his father's old school. He was in Conybeare's House, named after the housemaster of the day. After a slow start he took a "double remove" (jumping up two classes) and won a school English Literature prize and later managed to get "credits" in all six subjects for school certificate. For much of his career at Eton he seemed to fulfil the expectations of his family, particularly his mother. He followed the cause of Christian Science and, like his father, seemed to accept the responsibilities towards the wider community that such a privileged education and background conferred on him. He wrote often to his mother about his devotion to the practice of Christian Science. In 1926 he reported that

> ...I went to the lecture at Maidenhead on Friday, and I thought it was very good. My Tutor, Mr Conybeare, did not seem to like my going and my classical tutor, Mr Rowlatt, made a dutiful fuss because I had to miss some work for him. I think they are both very prejudiced against C.S.[8]

He also wrote long letters commenting on the rest of the family, as at that time he was probably closest to Nancy Astor of all the children. He was also developing the interest in the world outside Eton that was so important to his father, and one of his first visits was to a mission in the East End of London. Such missions, in his youthful opinion, were

> not going to solve the country's problems, in a bang like some people [think] but it is undoubtedly a good thing and from my point of view very useful as it gives me an opportunity of becoming acquainted with members of the middle and lower classes (I hate the word!) in an unofficial and convenient way even if at first it is all a trifle forced.

He was also developing the Astor sense of duty and responsibility to others — what the English might have called "noblesse oblige" — which characterized his own approach to life. In 1929, aged seventeen, he sent his mother the following definition of "nobility", which sums up what both he and his father worked for in a personal way throughout their careers:

NOBILITY

Undoubtedly exists but has no connection with economic position [it is] a quality of thought...an appreciation of the common good and the unselfishness and ability to minister it....He is essentially a man of balanced character. Not an aesthete or a fanatic about anything. An enrolled man of the world.

---

8. D.A. — N.A.: undated, Nancy Astor Papers, 14/6/1/3, 28.

These were the qualities that David Astor was to aspire to, and which he was to find in a succession of mentors: Robert Birley at Eton and later Adam von Trott and George Orwell. Conscious as he was of his obligations, he was equally conscious of his advantages in life and the special benefits that these conferred on him. Just before he left Eton, he compared his situation to that of a less privileged boy of his age, such as a bank clerk:

> The difference is really this I suppose. My possibilities are almost boundless. I have apparently every external advantage imaginable. Here's this fellow starting from scratch. He *may* go far if he's very able but the odds are a hundred to one that he will be a dull mediocrity. Everything is against him. But then there are similar odds that in my particular sphere I will also be a dull mediocrity. My sphere is bigger and more exciting but our mediocrities are equally as dull...the only difference that I can think of is that given favourable conditions in your individuals my position gives me a bigger scope for good....You can sneer at material possessions and circumstances but their presence seems to save years of donkey-work even if it necessitates the same amount of spade work to get character.

This, again, was part of the Astor creed that he shared with his father. David and Waldorf derived no particular enjoyment from material possessions and money for their own consumption, it merely gave them a "bigger scope for good". Waldorf was an austere man, who lived a relatively frugal life for a person of his wealth; he preferred channelling his money into supporting causes, hosting conferences and founding institutes or model farms. This was David Astor's inheritance, as he too lived a comparatively austere life, and used his property largely for the benefit of other people. *Observer* journalists used to note that there was rarely a time when David Astor's London house did not shelter at least one or two refugees or political exiles; and just as Cliveden was often put at the disposal of organizations for their conferences, so David Astor's country house at Sutton Courtenay, near Oxford, rarely passes a year without a dozen or more similar events. Material wealth was understood to be principally a means to help others; in that sense both Waldorf and David were of the "high thinking, plain living" school.

Smooth as David Astor's progress through the educational system of his day might have seemed, from Eton onwards he was plagued by a deteriorating family relationship. In any other family he might have been free to exploit his intellectual background and education, and carve his own path in life, but not with a mother as dominating as Nancy Astor. His childhood memories of her are primarily of an entertainer, ceaselessly mimicking, miming, provoking, laughing. There was much gaiety, mainly created by her, but aided and abetted by Bobbie Shaw, the only one of her children who could tease and scold her as mercilessly as she teased and scolded everyone else, and by Jakie, who also possessed her razor-sharp wit. Bill, David and Michael shared the laughter but were quieter by temperament and did not compete. But delightful though she could be, Nancy suffered from the most dangerous vice of motherhood — parental possessiveness. She loved her children, but was incapable of the kind of love which benefits no one but the recipient: as David has remarked, "She loved me...she just did not know how to go about it the right way." As a result the nursery quickly developed into a battlefield. John Grigg has written perceptively that:

> As a blood relation Nancy gave a lot of blood and drew a lot of blood. Whether she gave more than she drew is open to question. Her children were in the front line and none of them escaped unscathed...She went through life firing from the hip...though temperamentally more flexible than Waldorf, she was more assertive and therefore seemed more masterful. She was also intensely possessive — of children, other relations or friends. She could never let people who were attached to her go. They were *hers*, and her rights of ownership had to be maintained. So far as her children were concerned, the harmful effects of this possessiveness were aggravated by a good deal of neglect. Nancy was too busy to see very much of them, but when she did see them she tended to be over-powering.[9]

Curiously, Nancy herself seems to have been aware of this trait in her family. In her unpublished autobiography, she referred to

9. Grigg, p. 121.

what she analysed as the ill-effects of the possessiveness of her own father Chillie — but she might just as well have been describing herself:

He was not so good with his sons. He never let them go. From time to time he would say: "You ought to get out and earn your living". Delighted at the prospect, off they would go, but before they got very far, Father would call them back.[10]

She could not bear to let any of her children succeed or shine on any but her own terms, and was constantly directing them to this end. They were not allowed an independent life, or to search for their own particular spiritual or political path to follow — freedom to do so could only be gained by revolt against Nancy. Michael Astor has written of the peculiar consequences of this on the family situation:

Despite enchanting moments when the family felt happily united, moments that were infinitely reassuring, it was usually a relief when there were outsiders present. When we were just the family all sense of personal privacy evaporated. Visitors, especially if they were what I thought of as "worldly" rather than "religious" people, formed a silent court of appeal, their presence imposing a modicum of restraint.

Allied to her destructive possessiveness was her inability to give praise: "She could not give the immediate word of encouragement or reassurance that a child, in particular, so badly needs."[11] She did not support her sons in the way that they needed, and to the end of her days would apparently take delight in criticizing them quite freely to other people. This could be the most bruising experience of all, and David had to endure such treatment on several occasions when Nancy took exception to the politics of the *Observer* under his editorship. All the children suffered from Nancy's bewildering parental behaviour, and the oldest three, Bobbie, Bill and Wissie probably suffered the most. The most

---

10. Sykes, quoted p. 41.

11. Grigg, p. 135.

tragic was Bobbie, the only child who could repay her in her own coin in conversation. He suffered imprisonment as a homosexual as early as 1931, and committed suicide after the death of his mother. If Bobbie suffered from an excess of misdirected love, Bill suffered from a lack of it, and never succeeded in breaking out of his mother's suffocating emotional grip. Wissie was seen by Nancy largely as a threat to her own position as the woman of the family, and endured the inevitable battles as a consequence. As David Astor has remarked of the first three children, they were "shockingly treated", and bore the scars for life. David, on the other hand, suffered the most as a child and as a consequence was the only son who broke totally with his mother in order to survive. His position at home was particularly difficult because for a time he was Nancy's favourite, and so was the son of whom she was most possessive. Moreover, Nancy pinned her hopes on him as the son who would become a Christian Science "practitioner". At Cliveden Nancy used to say to David as a joke: "I wish you'd been born an ugly girl, then you couldn't leave here." It was said in jest, but she was absolutely serious in her intent. For David Astor to develop his own personality, and become an independent man, involved a struggle with Nancy which began at Eton.

He faced his first crisis at the age of about sixteen when he tried to confront Nancy with the argument that he could no longer be treated as a possession, or as a Christian Scientist. The initial struggle between his love for Nancy and his conflicting and natural interest to break away from her led to an emotional break-down, which was to recur with greater severity at Oxford. He was unable to make Nancy understand the problems that she posed her children, as she was quite unselfcritical. Instead, as on other occasions, Nancy insisted on seeing David's problems in Christian Science terms and Philip Kerr was dispatched to act as a spiritual adviser. Kerr visited Eton frequently and exchanged a series of letters with David, in which he tried to explain David's problems in Christian Science terms; a task to which he was, perhaps, particularly well suited as he himself had suffered a similar emotional and spiritual breakdown in 1911, prior to renouncing Roman Catholicism in favour of Christian Science. David was helped by Kerr, and to a certain extent surmounted his difficulties. He wrote to Nancy from Eton in 1929:

Mr Kerr came over and helped me more than I can say. He

was so practical about everything, especially Science. It was so good of him to come over and you can't think how it's helped me to understand what I can do here and how to do it. I hope he will come over soon again....I find Mr Kerr so helpful.[12]

Nancy Astor, for her part, never fully understood the unfortunate pressures that she put on David and the rest of her children, although she was dimly aware of her shortcomings, writing rather later, in 1940, to Kerr when he had moved to Washington as Ambassador:

I wish to goodness you were here, and not in Washington, for I do seem to need advice with the men folk in the family. It is most wearing, I can assure you.[13]

David's difficulties with Nancy accentuated a natural shyness and diffidence and damaged his self-confidence. Shyness was a family trait, especially evident in William Waldorf, which David seemed to have inherited. In a burst of self-analysis he admitted as much in a letter to his mother, written just before he left school:

On paper, of course, my Eton career has been dim in the extreme...I'm an oddish mixture. To the ordinary Etonian I'm very obscure and retiring. Beaks [tutors] consider me most precocious and even provocative and I certainly cut ice in the house but I don't get across outside it. I haven't got the faculty for ready friendship on first acquaintance like you have.

It thus took an enterprising master to pick David Astor out from the crowd of Etonians, but such a man was the legendary Robert Birley. Like many people disorientated or overawed at public school, David's school career was salvaged by an inspiring teacher. Birley later told an *Observer* writer, Dinah Brooke, that David Astor sat in silence throughout his "divisions" (classes), but once singled out and allowed to speak in a more intimate atmosphere was one of the most interesting schoolboys he had ever met.

---

12. D.A. – N.A.: undated, N.A. Papers 14/6/1/3/28.

13. N.A. – Lothian: Feb 20, 1940: N.A. Papers 14/6/1/4/59.

Birley, born in 1903, arrived at Eton as a history master in 1926 straight from Balliol, Oxford, and went on to become probably the most distinguished public school headmaster of the century, headmaster of Charterhouse at the age of thirty-two and later of Eton. He was a free thinker, and, to a certain extent, a Socialist, supporting the general strike in 1926. To any boy with intellectual inquisitiveness and a yearning to learn he was, in David Astor's own words, "a breath of fresh air at Eton. He didn't behave like a master at all....but as though we were all on an equal footing." He introduced Astor, and others, to a range of literature which otherwise would have been closed to the young Etonians, including left-wing books such as Harold Laski on Marxism — indeed to the whole world of music and art, which was seldom mentioned at Cliveden. Birley also held an evening conversation party once a week to which certain boys were invited, including David Astor and his contemporary Guy Burgess. His influence on David was great, and the latter remained devoted to his history teacher for the rest of his life. Birley shared in many of David Astor's later campaigns, on behalf of Africans in South Africa and the German anti-Nazi resistance. His lodgings at Eton were an "open house", a little corner of intellectual excitement for David and others; and unlike Nancy Astor, he treated David as if he had considerable intellectual promise and inclined him towards Balliol. Birley also got on very well with Waldorf and Nancy Astor, and was an occasional visitor to Cliveden. At one point Nancy took particular exception to one of David's housemasters and decided that the boy should therefore leave the school. Birley was convinced that such a move so late in his Etonian career would sabotage his education and travelled several times to London to talk Nancy out of it, which he succeeded in doing. David Astor had good reason to describe Birley as his "saviour" at school.

As a result of Birley's interest, David's final year at Eton was relatively successful and fulfilling. It was Birley and TJ together who persuaded Waldorf Astor that David should go to Balliol rather than, like the rest of the Astors, to New College — evidence that at this stage David was already regarded as rather more intellectual, and perhaps more "leftist", than the rest of the family. He arrived at Balliol in October 1931. Between Eton and Balliol David stayed for three months with the family of the Professor of Music in Heidelberg to learn German. This, again, was TJ's idea.

The impact of this visit on David will be discussed in the next chapter.

Before returning to England, David was a party to one of the most celebrated tourist trips in history, the visit of Nancy Astor, the "arch-capitalist" and G. B. Shaw, the "arch-socialist", to Soviet Russia. The genesis of the Shaw/Astor visit to Moscow is uncertain. By 1931, Shaw had become one of Nancy Astor's closest friends, sharing a talent for radicalism, directness and humour. Shaw wrote to Horace Plunkett of the trip:

> My going is a bit of an accident; the Astors suddenly took it into their heads to see for themselves whether Russia is really the earthly paradise I had declared it to be; and they challenged me to go with them. I felt, at my age, that if I did not seize the opportunity, I should never see Russia at all; so I agreed.[14]

David Astor remembers the Astor version, that Shaw invited the Astors to accompany him to Moscow on the occasion of his seventy-fifth birthday. David saw Shaw essentially as a "prankster", and there could be no greater "prank" than the doyen of British socialists travelling to the heart of the workers' paradise with a couple of millionaire capitalists! This would have amused Shaw, just as Nancy Astor always teased Shaw that behind his bold, "Shavian", bohemian manner lay a very prudish, meticulous, careful man who had an almost spinsterish life and who cleaned his own shoes every day. Whatever the reason for the visit, the party set out from Victoria Station on July 19, 1931, at a time when the pilgrimage to the Soviet Union was almost *de rigueur* for the British far left and still strictly taboo for the British of the centre or right. The party consisted of Waldorf and Nancy Astor, Shaw, Philip Kerr, Charles Tennant, a Christian Scientist, and Maurice Hindus, a writer who was Russian by origin so could translate and give expert comment. Two Americans also joined them, Anna Louise Strong and Gertrude Ely. David Astor met the party in Berlin, and then travelled with them via Warsaw to Moscow.

The visit of the Astors and Shaw made irresistible copy and excited world-wide publicity. The Russians took Shaw extremely

---

14. Shaw – Plunkett, July 16, 1931: *Collected Letters* Vol. IV, 1926–1950. (Max Reinhardt, ed. Dan H Lawrence.)

seriously as a sympathetic writer to be cultivated, which accounted for the presence of Maxim Litvinov, the Commissar of Foreign Affairs (1930—39) at the Russian border to greet them and accompany them on the train to Moscow. Litvinov had an English wife, so could talk adequate English and David got to know him quite well. Indeed, Litvinov was later to stay at Cliveden on one of his trips to England. In Moscow a band and hordes of journalists and photographers met them at the station. They stayed in the Metropole Hotel, and were guided round the sights of Moscow with considerable reverence. Naturally, they saw nothing of the famine which was gripping parts of Russia or the collectivization of the farms which was leading to the elimination of the *kulaks*, so Shaw was able to return to London with his ideals pretty well intact. David and his father were taken to see an officers' training barracks and also a model collective farm just south of Moscow. David was not affected politically by the visit, like so many others, but noted the large hoardings of Stalin all over the place, which gave Moscow something of "the atmosphere of a school", and signs of the extreme defensiveness and paranoia about the outside world which gripped the population — impressions that were to chime with the work of the two *Observer* writers, George Orwell and Arthur Koestler. Shaw seemed to treat the whole visit with a high degree of amusement, especially as the Russians tried to lay on increasingly inappropriate festivities for his delectation. On Shaw's birthday itself the Russians arranged for the party to go to a race-track, presumably thinking that, being Irish, Shaw was a devotee of the turf. However, as Shaw arrived to take his seat he declared to his hosts that he was "the only Irishman who had never been on a racecourse". He took his place in the "royal box" and slept through the races, whilst Lord Astor, an authority on bloodstock, was very unimpressed by the quality of the horses. The same sense of mischief informed Shaw's reaction to the climax of the visit, the audience with Stalin himself. David was excluded from the party, and thus missed Nancy Astor's famous question to Stalin — "How long will you have to rule by Czarist methods?" At first the interpreter refused to pass this question on, but when Shaw insisted Stalin replied that he did not use "Czarist methods" and argued that any oppression was used because the revolution was in a transitional stage and then riposted to Nancy "What about Cromwell?" The Astors were impressed by his solid, undemonstrative grasp of affairs, as were all Westerners who saw him at work during the wartime "Big Three" Conferences. David Astor, however, was waiting, together with a number of American journalists, at the Hotel Metropole, for Shaw's reaction to the interview. Shaw entered the hotel to tremendous excitement and walked in silence to the stairs to go to the lift. He studiously ascended one step, and then turned round, very theatrically, and in answer to all the questions of "What was Stalin like?" merely replied, very slowly and deliberately. "He has big black moustaches", thus annoying all the journalists who were expecting some gem of Shavian wit. David recalls Shaw on the journey as not "listening to anybody but treating everybody well". Shaw's only printed remark about David was wholly in character; writing to his wife he remarked that "David is the beauty success of the party. He really looks like an Italian picture of the late XV century. All the Communists notice it."[15] The party returned to England with all their political expectations intact. Shaw remained devoted to the Soviet Union, while Waldorf Astor wrote a piece for a Plymouth paper outlining the deficiencies of the Soviet system as he had observed them. David returned an agnostic, but went back again in the summer of 1932 with a school friend to see the country without the razzmatazz. Unlike many of his generation, he was never passionately attracted by the USSR, but also never felt the fear of it that he had felt of the Third Reich during his stay in Heidelberg.

Back in London, David furthered his political education by meeting Gandhi, who was attending the Round Table Conference on Indian constitutional reform in London. Nancy invited Gandhi to 4 St James's Square, which like many similar invitations to anti-imperialists, communists, pacifists and the like outraged many of her fellow Tories at a time when Gandhi was treated with either extreme deference or extreme hostility. Nancy, typically, did neither. Her opening gambit was: "I know what everyone's saying about you, they think you're a saint, but I know you're just an old politician like me!" Gandhi was delighted by this, and proceeded to have a very friendly, general talk. A few days later David breakfasted with Gandhi alone in the Knightsbridge flat where he

---

15. Shaw — Charlotte Shaw: July 23, 1931.

was staying for the Conference, and was enormously impressed by the man whom Churchill had just denounced as a "naked fakir". (He had also, incidentally, denounced the Astors for visiting Stalin.) Such political contact widened David's horizons in a way afforded to few people, while also demonstrating how far the Astors were outside the Conservative political mainstream. It was a very catholic political upbringing.

In October 1931 David Astor duly arrived at Balliol College, Oxford, which enjoyed a reputation, inspired by its great Victorian Master Benjamin Jowett, as the intellectual powerhouse of the university. His basic character was already shaped, he had absorbed the lessons of his mentors and the emotional responses of his parents. He combined the concern for the disadvantaged which his mother showed with the more reflective, intellectual methodology and curiosity of his father. His main interest, like that of the Round Table group, was in foreign affairs and the management of international relations. He was liberal in politics and, more importantly, had acquired a set of values from his father that were to last him for the rest of his life. Balliol was the ideal environment for such a student; which made it all the more unfortunate that he was not able to profit from the opportunities that the college offered.

The first person whom David Astor met in the porter's lodge on his first day at Balliol was the German Rhodes Scholar Adam von Trott zu Solz, to whom he was immediately drawn and who was to become the most influential single person in his life. Their friendship is discussed in more detail in the next chapter. Due to his interest in Germany as a consequence of his recent stay in Heidelberg, David Astor naturally gravitated towards the Germans at Oxford; another Rhodes Scholar whom he befriended within the first year was 'Fritz' Schumacher, then at New College (who was to write *Small is Beautiful*). Schumacher and Trott were both anti-Nazis at a time when the Nazis were making their bid for power, and with their concern for the alarming political situation in their home country they both added a note of seriousness to the essentially carefree lives of the young English undergraduates. Schumacher was later to play a considerable role in David Astor's *Observer*. Tristan Jones, the younger son of TJ, who had won the Brackenbury Scholarship to Balliol from Stowe school, was also in David's year, and would also play an important part in the life of the paper. David's group of friends at Balliol was completed by the American Rhodes Scholar Samuel Beer, who arrived at Oxford in 1932. Beer later became Professor of Politics at Harvard and an expert on British politics, and remained a lifelong friend of David's. Charles Collins, who later joined the Foreign Office, also became a friend at Oxford. Other direct contemporaries included Jo Grimond, who had come up from Eton and who was later to lead the Liberal Party, and Christopher Hill, the Marxist historian and subsequent Master of Balliol. The friends who were most important to David (in addition to Adam Trott) were Tristan Jones, Sam Beer and Charles Collins. Sam found David Astor markedly different from any of his English contemporaries, because he was "...unreserved and approachable...", free of many of the more disagreeable English characteristics.

The 1931 generation of Oxford students was the hinge generation between the "bright young things" of the 1920s and the committed ideologues of the later 1930s. In 1931 the spirit of Oxford was still essentially that of Waugh rather than of Auden and Spender, although the years that the 1931 generation spent at Oxford did witness those world events — the rise of Fascism and the Great Depression — which were to form the political context of the following generation. In 1931, however, the tone was still essentially frivolous and sceptical — there was a light-hearted and innocent atmosphere, and the political gestures of the next generation of Communist poets were yet to come. None the less, the under-graduates of David Astor's generation were already aware on which side of the barricades they might have to line up. For the Balliol generation, this impending struggle was exemplified by "the battle for Hawser's Trousers". In the Hilary or Trinity Term 1934, after a customarily high-spirited and alcoholic dinner, some of the college hearties decided to try to debag a student called Hawser for their post-prandial evening's sport. Hawser was a Jew from Cardiff High School, quiet, hard-working and withdrawn, who went on to become a QC and the Recorder for Portsmouth. The drunken cries of "debag Hawser" echoed round the back quad, only to alert the left-wingers, who rallied to Hawser's defence, barricading his rooms and preventing the assault. Hill and Beer were both there; it was Hill who coined the battle-cry "Save Hawser's Trousers!" David Astor attended the Communist

October Club and Labour Club as well as a number of other political clubs. Tristan Jones did join the Communist Party at Oxford, whilst Christopher Hill joined some time later. Collins was a Socialist, but, unlike Beer, not a Party member. It was very difficult *not* to be of the left in that generation at Oxford, but David's Oxford exploration of its more extreme reaches never seduced him from the basically liberal principles of his father and his American ancestors.

But while Oxford offered David so much, and his contemporaries competed to outshine each other and collect their glittering prizes, he began to fall behind, much as he had done at Eton. This time, the emotional and spiritual breakdown arising from the continuing struggle with Nancy Astor was more dramatic. He had drifted into rebellion against Christian Science, which his brother Bill had already discarded. Because Nancy had hoped that David might actually become a "practitioner", his rejection of the faith was particularly painful to her, and for the rest of her life Christian Science was to be one of many battlegrounds between them. She refused to see that it could be irrelevant to someone's needs. She wrote to Kerr in 1940 of David: "...he thinks C. S. has failed him. Needless to say, it never occurs to him to think that he has failed C. S."[16]

The long-standing personal strain which David's unsatisfactory relationship with his mother put on him brought on bouts of intense depression and ill-health that led him to abandon serious work after only a year at Balliol. Nancy was impervious to reasoning as to how she might help by curbing her possessiveness or by supporting David in what *he* wanted to do rather than in what *she* wanted him to do, and he still felt that Waldorf was too aloof to talk to. Having been brought up without any contacts with the medical profession and absolutely ignorant of psychoanalytical methods, he was courageous in deciding to see Dr Gillespie, a senior consultant in psychiatry at Guy's Hospital in London, with whom he had some relieving talks; but these did not have a lasting effect.

David's psychological and, to a certain extent, physical exhaustion was to reduce him to a state of semi-activity for some six years. At

---

16. N.A. Papers 14/6/1/4/59.

Oxford he was encouraged to take time off, and TJ recommended getting clean away and working in Glasgow at an engineering works which made coal-cutting machines, owned by an acquaintance of TJ's. David took the spring term off in his second year at Balliol to follow this advice, and had his twenty-first birthday in Scotland, spending the day with Philip Kerr on one of his estates outside Edinburgh. On that birthday he came into the money left to Waldorf's children by William Waldorf, the token of his displeasure at Waldorf's objection to his accepting a peerage — "Grandfather's revenge", as the money was known in the family. It was fortunate timing, as he could now be independent of his family.

David returned to Balliol, but he had not yet recovered. One of his tutors, Roger Mynors, summoned him to his study to give him a dressing-down about his lack of work. A little while after this embarrassing episode, David arrived one day for a tutorial with his celebrated history tutor, Humphry Sumner, a "terribly nice man", and a friend of Trott and Beer. His essay was only half-done, and when he was half-way through reading this wretched piece of work Sumner gently stopped him and said that he was not going to manage Finals, and it would be better to stop there and then. To David this came as "...some relief...". He left the university at the beginning of his third year, in 1933. This decision was made much against the wishes of his mother, who even enlisted Sam Beer to try to change his mind. Once again, Nancy Astor failed to understand her son's needs and motives, and the tension between them became worse.

The unfortunate termination of his Oxford career, leaving him without a degree, left its permanent mark on David Astor. Of all the Astors he was the most intellectual, in the sense of being interested in ideas, but he had failed to acquire the academic discipline needed for the management and orderly expression of his intellectual preoccupations. This meant that he came to substitute talking and listening for reading and writing.

Added to a natural diffidence, this lack of intellectual self-confidence, which might at first appear to be a handicap, turned out to be a most valuable quality in a newspaper editor. An over-eagerness to be a participator is a vice in an editor, and of this David was free. Instead, he became a great listener. This made him attentive to a series of "mentors" ("David's gurus", *Observer* journalists sometimes called them) such as Trott, Orwell, Haffner and Koestler, who at one time or another helped to guide him and his newspaper. Rather than wishing himself to dictate to people, he became an organizer of ideas, working to put important minds at the disposal of a wide public through discussion and publication in the *Observer* and other papers.

Soon after his departure from Balliol, having failed to make his mother understand his point of view, David went to see his father alone at 4 St James's Square, to tell him that he could no longer endure his mother's attitude towards him and would have to leave the family. Waldorf listened and was perturbed, but did not rebuke his son; he probably understood the problem very well. He asked David to keep in touch and let him go; and from then on they shared both a political empathy and a secret emotional under-standing that was to be of critical importance when the family battle for the soul of the *Observer* commenced during the Second World War.

For the rest of the thirties David lived on his own in London, and later in Yorkshire, visiting Cliveden very rarely. The only member of the family of whom he saw much was his half-brother Bobbie, to whom he was close because both of them were "out-siders", in family terms. The difference between them — that Bobbie, though he could put up a fine show of resistance to Nancy, was ultimately the most dependent on her of all of them, while David had made a real break — cannot at that time have been apparent to them.

David's break with his mother, painful though it was, was the making of him, allowing him to develop a greater degree of inde-pendence than any other member of the family. As Sam Beer observed, David became "a self-made man in the moral sense", in that he had to make his own emotional way in the world, out of reach of a dominating parent. The self-examination to which David was driven, and the effort he had to put into rebuilding his life, gave him an important feeling of sympathy for anyone in trouble: a feeling which, of course, stemmed partly from Nancy's remarkable "instinctive human sympathy", as well as from his reaction against her. The experience of failure and humiliation at Oxford, and in the eyes of his mother, was not, therefore, profitless, but gave him the essential understanding of human and political failure that did so much to shape the policy of the *Observer*. It was the newspaper's identification with the victims of political and social disorder that was to become famous.

After leaving Balliol David Astor rented a flat in London and, at the suggestion of his uncle, Bob Brand, worked in his merchant bank, Lazards for two years as a clerk. In 1936 he moved to Yorkshire to work on the *Yorkshire Post* for a year. Journalism had already been mentioned as a possible career for him by his father, and he was attracted by the idea but less so if it meant working on the *Observer* under the tutelage of J. L. Garvin, the paper's celebrated editor. Garvin was revered by Waldorf, but not by David, who found him overbearing and arrogant. The *Yorkshire Post*, on the other hand, was edited by Arthur Mann, a shy yet authoritative figure who earned a lasting reputation for journalistic integrity by his fearless attack on Chamberlain and appeasement in the late 1930s.

David saw little of Mann during his year on the *Yorkshire Post*, but Mann was later instrumental in the affairs of the *Observer*. David Astor's journalistic input to the *Yorkshire Post* was slight, but he did write several pieces on riding and hunting in Yorkshire, signed "F.D.L.A". The importance of his connection with the paper lay in the friends he made. During this year in Leeds he came to know several journalists who were to form the core of the *Observer* under his editorship, including Charles Davy and Fred Tomlinson. Ken Obank, the key man on his *Observer*, was also on the *Yorkshire Post*, slightly after David left the paper; which he did with something less than a glowing reference from Arthur Mann.

David then lived in Whitby for two years, until September 1938. He tried to write, but was more concerned with putting on pantomime shows for the summer seasons, rekindling an early interest in the theatre and film-making, which he was also attracted to. He shared a love of the music-hall with Bobbie Shaw. It was while doing a concert party at Whitby that he heard on the radio that Neville Chamberlain had ceded the Sudetenland to Nazi Germany in the Munich agreement of September 30, 1938.

By 1938, therefore, David was both recognizably an Astor, and yet in rebellion against the Astor family. His politics were largely adopted from his father and the Cliveden milieu; he was never to lose the Anglo-American liberal internationalist outlook of his father, Philip Kerr and the rest of the Round Table group. He also shared with his mother an instinctive human sympathy for the underdog and with his father a desire to use his wealth and position to help others. During the late 1930s he founded the York Trust, which under the direction of the omnipresent TJ was to be the main arm of his charitable activities. His early charitable donations reflect concerns that he was to retain all his life: under the auspices of Dr Gillespie he founded the York Clinic, which housed the psychiatric department of Guy's Hospital, and he gave money to Dame Lillian Barker, the first woman Prison Commissioner, to help in the rehabilitation of ex-prisoners. All his donations remained anonymous.

David was a synthesis of his parents' qualities. He was impetuous and reflective; talkative and receptive; intuitive and intellectual; stubborn and tolerant. He was thus on the one hand — as many *Observer* colleagues noted — a paradoxical character, and on the other hand very well-balanced. The most important of the paradoxes in his nature was that he carried the mantle of Cliveden on his shoulders, and yet was in rebellion against it. It was largely this unresolved tension that gave him the extraordinary drive and energy needed to re-fashion the *Observer* during the war; but for most of the 1930s that energy remained dormant. It was the return of Adam von Trott into David's life, in 1938, that ensured its creative release into useful channels.

2

Adam von Trott

David Astor heard about the Munich agreement on September 30, 1938, at Whitby. He was "horrified" by the results of the Munich conference which handed Czechoslovakia to Nazi Germany on a plate, and was unimpressed by Chamberlain's assurance that he had secured "peace for our time", let alone "peace with honour". However, David was in no position to do anything about it and travelled back to London in the autumn of 1938 to take up a trainee management position on *The Times* in order to learn the newspaper business outside the orbit of J. L. Garvin. But this smooth progression into journalism was to be interrupted by the sudden intervention of his old Oxford friend, Adam von Trott zu Solz, who came to Britain in a desperate attempt to avert war between Britain and Germany. It was David's involvement in Trott's efforts to avert war which gave the hitherto well-meaning but aimless young Englishman a sense of political purpose which was to change his life profoundly.

David had always been interested in what was usually called the "German problem" in inter-war Europe, but what marked him out from many of his generation, particularly his family and their immediate entourage, was the fact that he had seen Nazism at first hand and had few illusions about what it meant. During his stay in Heidelberg in 1931, two years before Hitler came to power,

David had already seen the frighteningly mesmeric effect that the Nazis could exert on a German people bewildered and disillusioned by their experiences in the inter-war years. As well as being kept awake by the singing — or chanting — of rival parties of Communists and Fascists walking home at night in the ancient university town, he had also witnessed a Reichsparteitag, a sort of electioneering rally held by the Nazi Party in different towns up and down the country.

It began in a large rugby football field on the edge of town, where a row of dark figures was lined up on the far side.

They turned out to be the widows of private soldiers from the first world war. A parade of Brownshirts was drawn up opposite them. Medals were presented to the widows. You were made to feel that everyone else had forgotten these women. It was rather moving.

They then marched through the town, passing the trade union house which flew red flags and was crowded with jeering, determined-looking men. At the back of this house were van loads of silent police, waiting to quell a possible riot. The Nazi parade was not particularly well-drilled, their uniforms were homemade; but they marched as though they had a right to be there.

Who were these people? I looked at their faces. Were they a type? Would they show the sort of peculiarities one thought one saw in Goering, Goebbels or Hitler himself? It hit me quite strongly that these were ordinary people. It seemed more alarming that they were ordinary, rather than eccentric. It seemed that Hitler's idea could capture the man in the street.

That night the Nazis paid for a Schlossbeleuchtung (illumination of the castle). Half of the town watched a blazing swastika appear below the castle walls and heard individual Nazis call out "Deutschland Erwache" (Germany awake) into the night. Nobody chanced contradicting these calls. As the spectators walked home in the dark it was noticeable that they spoke quietly. Were they already anxious?

Whereas David, like many others in England, had been brought up on a horror of war after the blood-letting of the First World War, here were the Nazis marching to recover national pride, and winning a following. David found the scene "almost pathetic, but frightening too".

His stay in Heidelberg gave David an interest in Germany which was strengthened at Oxford by his friendship with Germans there such as Trott and Fritz Schumacher. It was no coincidence that all David's German friends were anti-Nazi, as they belonged to a social and intellectual tradition that was very remote from the roots of the Nazi Party. David paid several visits to Germany during the 1930s, none of which persuaded him to change his mind about the Nazis. David's attitude towards the Nazis also created a further cleavage in his relationship with his family and their friends, as although none of them ever sympathized with Nazism as an ideology, neither could they ever fully appreciate the dangers of Nazism and Fascism. On a tour of Italy with his mother in the mid-1930s, David noted how Nancy would ridicule the pompous pretensions of the Italian Fascists, but she also refused to "take them seriously". A certain *frisson* entered into his relationship with Philip Kerr (Lord Lothian) as well, who had travelled to Berlin to meet Hitler in 1937 and had been persuaded by his conversations with the Führer into energetically promoting a rapprochement between Britain and Nazi Germany based on a formula of mutual concessions, a policy that was later characterized as "appeasement". David had some earnest discussions with Lothian on the subject, but he was not to be swayed on his chosen course, which probably had as much to do with Lothian's own sense of guilt about his participation in the unwisely punitive Versailles Treaty as with any realistic assessment of Germany and Hitler in the late 1930s. The one man in the family circle with a sound understanding of Nazism was Waldorf Astor, who had been afforded a glimpse of the darker side of the Führer which had been successfully concealed from men as able as Lothian, Lloyd George and many others. Lord Astor met Hitler as a representative of the Christian Science Movement, to plead for toleration of Christian Science in Germany. Hitler asked his guest why relations between Britain and Germany were so bad — to which Lord Astor replied that as long as Hitler persevered with his Jewish policy there could be no friendship. At this Hitler burst into one of his seldom-witnessed manic tirades and Lord Astor left the Führer in a spluttering frenzy.

All these different emotions and political complexes were on display at 4 St James's Square at a lunch that Lord and Lady Astor gave for Ribbentrop, the German Ambassador to London, in 1937. This lunch was held largely at the instigation of Lothian; for the Astors it represented a chance to question Ribbentrop and to build bridges of friendship and understanding over a widening Anglo-German divide. It was the same impulse that had made them invite Maxim Litvinov, Shaw and Ramsay MacDonald to 4 St James's Square and Cliveden, and that had taken them to see Stalin in Moscow. David learnt that Ribbentrop was to be the lunch guest only when he reached the house. By 1937 many of his German friends were already in exile, or, like Trott, were planning active opposition to Hitler, so his first instinct was to go away again, but it seemed that it was not meant to be a very meaningful or serious occasion, so on second thoughts he stayed; but the decision to lunch with Ribbentrop that day still makes him feel "uneasy". It was a large party of about twenty guests and as usual Nancy Astor immediately got into her stride, trying to bring about general conversation by calling for silence and then asking a pro-vocative question. Nancy misjudged Ribbentrop, the totally humourless former champagne salesman, from the start:

> She said to him, "Now you tell us all about Germany but you must realize before you begin that this country is never going to take Hitler seriously as long as he wears that little Charlie Chaplin moustache."
>
> It was a very silly thing to say because it wasn't a profound or meaningful remark but she said it and you could see Ribbentrop wonder should he leave the room, should he refuse to answer, what should he do? He was completely flummoxed. . . and it was very difficult to have any conversation after this insulting start. It was a very stilted conversation and Ribbentrop left rather early and that was that.

It was probably this impertinence of Nancy Astor's that earned her a place on the Nazis' famous "black list" for immediate arrest as soon as they had invaded England.

If David was, by 1938, fully alive to the dangers of Nazism and the threat that it posed to the peace of Europe, Adam von Trott had for long been impressed by the same danger — to Germany as well as Europe. Trott had made a tremendous impact on Oxford when he was there as a Rhodes Scholar from 1931 to 1933. He was two or three years older than his "year", and the relatively youthful and inexperienced public schoolboys who mainly populated Oxford were much attracted to this wiser, more mature and experienced creature in their midst.

As Trott's widow, Clarita, has pointed out, Adam was both "natural and intellectual", a very rare combination at Oxford, which made him a man of real human interest. Amongst his Balliol contemporaries he was admired for his humour, his breadth of knowledge and his intelligence — to say nothing of his easy naturalness with women, something that must have been beyond many of his English friends. He, more than anyone else at Balliol, seemed to convey that "effortless superiority" which was supposed to mark out the Balliol man. His and David Astor's friend Charles Collins has written of Adam at Balliol:

> The impression which he made on meeting one was immediate; it was produced by his very tall figure, striking features, and a sense of power in his manner. But one came to like him for more important things than these; for his quick sympathy and understanding, his good humour, his great kindness, his intelligence, and his complete integrity of purpose. He was always good company. No one to my knowledge ever found any serious flaws in his sense of humour; he would equally readily joke at other people's expense and take a joke at his own. We used to tell him, in fun, that no one had a right to *look* so imposing as he did; and it would have been easy for anyone with so much natural dignity of appearance as well as his other claims to distinction, to be conceited or pompous, but he never was. I was always impressed by the ease with which he got on with all classes of people, both in Germany and in England; and he had the same sense of ease of manner with children, who at once took to him.

There was no one more attracted to Trott than David Astor. The two quickly struck up a firm friendship that was to be the most important of David's life. At the end of the war he wrote a letter to Adam's widow, Clarita, about their friendship:

> To me he was a teacher, and elder brother as well as a well-loved friend. He was the greatest member of my generation

in any country that I have ever met....He was a striking figure and his conversation and manner of carrying out his studies were so out-of-the-ordinary — there was both distinction and power in all he did — that his presence was soon felt by everyone. I was very attracted by the side of his nature that was both boyish and warm-hearted, by his extraordinary historical perception and by his obvious goodness.

Trott and Astor had very similar backgrounds and attitudes to life. They were both well-born, and beneath their humour and charm they were both of a basically serious disposition and were possessed of an elevated sense of responsibility for their respective countries. Trott was born in 1909, into the old nobility of Hesse, and his family had been, in varying degrees, loyal servants of Hesse and later of Germany for nearly four hundred years. Adam was very conscious of the weight of family tradition and studied law and public administration at the University of Göttingen before going to Oxford, in preparation for a life of public service. Hitler came to power during his time at Oxford (1931—33), and his increasing anxiety about Germany's fate was hard to conceal. It was his strongly personal concern with the future of his country, and the role that *he himself* should play in that future, that inevitably placed him apart from his more carefree undergraduate contemporaries. Charles Collins noted this:

Much as he enjoyed his time in England, he was never unmindful of the real business of his life, which was the future of Germany. He knew that even in the most favourable circumstances that future would be difficult; he feared that it would be tragic. He took it for granted that he would play an active part in his country's affairs; his family tradition, the advantages he would have in taking up a place in public life, and his personal abilities made it a duty which it did not occur to him to evade. Consequently life in Oxford, which was on the whole carefree, seemed somewhat unreal to him, and depressed him, though never so as to mar the pleasure which his acquaintances took in his company. This preoccupation with a future which he saw as a grim one added to his maturity...and indeed made him seem maturer than his company even among many members of the teaching staff of

Oxford, with whom, rather than with undergraduates, his intellectual attainments more naturally placed him.

David Astor and Trott spent many hours discussing politics and the German "problem" as events moved inexorably to Hitler's appointment as Chancellor of Germany in January 1933. Those who knew Trott best never had any doubt as to where he stood as regards the calamity that had befallen his country. David Astor always thought Adam the "exact opposite of what Hitler represented".

He was more deeply and thoroughly anti-Nazi than any English or American. His international spirit and outlook, his unselfish generosity, his kindness and gentleness, his breadth of understanding, his culture, learning and love of beauty and his complete disregard of himself and of what people thought of him — these qualities, which were those of a Christian, a gentleman and a citizen of the civilized world, made him the very embodiment of what Hitler always had tried to crush and what all who fought against Hitler ought to have been inspired by.

Some thought that Adam's opposition to Hitler was inspired by mere nationalism, that he was a German patriot trying to save Germany from Hitler. He was certainly that, but David and his other close friends cherished him mainly for his internationalism, for he was trying to save Germany, and the peace of Europe, by enlisting the aid of the international community in combating the *universal* evils of racialism, bigotry and intolerance that ruled in Germany from 1933. This was the grounds of a dispute between Adam von Trott's first English biographer, Christopher Sykes (*Troubled Loyalty*, Collins 1968) and Adam's friends, as Sykes preferred to lay stress on Adam's loyalty to Germany and his "nationalism". One of Adam's closest friends, Christabel Bielenberg took issue with Sykes over this matter and wrote to him that ". . . I had always felt him to be the first true internationalist that I had ever met in my life".[1]

---

1. Christabel Bielenberg to Christopher Sykes, May 1968: Papers of Clarita von Trott, Berlin.

It was this "international" outlook that David valued, and which was later to inform so much of his own life. David Astor and Adam von Trott were fighting for shared *values*, and against nationalism.

The rise of Hitler represented the negation of all those values. Charles Collins was with Adam in the Balliol Junior Common Room when Adam read in an evening paper that Hitler had become Chancellor.

He knew at once that a terrible disaster had befallen his country; that the prospects for his own future had undergone a fundamental change; that it was a future in which a bitter struggle would be needed to achieve even the smallest result; that many of his friends and acquaintances were at once in personal danger. A number of things he was sure of immediately; that overt opposition to the new regime would be useless for a long time to come; that nevertheless he must oppose it by all the means in his power; that a common ground must be found for as many opponents of the regime as possible, and that he himself would try to find that ground in a struggle for the "liberal" rights; that, although it would certainly be at the cost of handicap to his own career he would not join the Nazi Party unless it should ever become his clear duty to do so in furtherance of his anti-Nazi activity. All these things he expressed to me on the same night that he learned of Hitler's coming to power.

Adam was never to deviate from this course.

It was the future of Germany that was uppermost in his mind when he accompanied David to the Astor family home on the Scottish island of Jura in July 1933. They went there with Jo Grimond, and were joined on Jura by a German friend of David's from Heidelberg, Otto Schnetzler. He was a quarter Jewish, an engineer who had already decided to emigrate from Germany. Adam and David travelled to Jura via Glasgow, where they visited the McNairs who had put David up while he had been working at the factory of Mavor and Coulson the year before. Their stay in Jura consisted of little more than eating, drinking and walking but Adam and David talked about Adam's prospects in Germany. David was already convinced that he should not return to his native land, and he later recalled one walk which he took with

Adam "...and I said to him you're a fool to go to Germany, you won't be able to deal with these people. You can deal with people in a civilized way by arguing with them but these people don't argue, they will just use physical force on you and you won't be able to get out. And he just said, well maybe so but I've got to try, I've got to go. I really tried to say to him that this isn't your matter, you shouldn't get mixed up in this because he wasn't the sort of person you would think would make a good conspirator or a good man of violence and that was what he was heading towards and I felt he might underestimate the Nazis. I think I was wrong, I think he estimated them very clearly but I didn't think he did.... We were walking over a sort of moorland on the Atlantic ocean side and although Adam was very tall he wasn't very strong, physically — he was slender and I just, when talking to him, put my leg out and tripped him up and pushed him over and I said how easily your arguments can be flattened and that is what they will do to you. I sort of pulled him over backwards and he just continued arguing from lying down. He didn't take the slightest notice. He just thought it was very childish and I felt my attempt to make him aware of one's physical fragility had completely failed. He wasn't going to think in those terms. I always knew I wouldn't have dared to do what he did...."

David's arguments made no impression on his friend, and in August 1933 Trott returned to Germany to take up his own personal mission against Hitler's regime. He had made many other friends at Oxford; younger dons like A. L. Rowse, Richard Crossman and Maurice Bowra as well as important politicians such as Sir Stafford Cripps (John Cripps, Stafford's elder son, was a contemporary at Balliol) and Lord Lothian. As well as these men, he also formed a close attachment to two women, Sheila Grant-Duff and Diana Hopkinson. Sheila and Adam pledged themselves to form "the best friendship in Europe", a relationship that can be followed from Oxford to the eve of war in their correspondence published as *A Noble Combat*, edited by Klemens von Klemperer (Oxford 1988). David was certainly not among the most distinguished of Adam's friends at Oxford, but by the end of their holiday together in Jura in 1933 there was probably no one amongst his English friends who had a clearer understanding of the task that Adam had set himself. It was to David that Adam would return in 1939 when those youthful Balliol discussions on Adam's future role in Germany took on an altogether more serious and darker aspect.

In the intervening years there was little contact. While David worked out his own life in his self-imposed exile in Yorkshire, Adam devoted himself to his legal training in Germany, giving a great amount of his time to helping the victims of Nazism. By the end of 1936 he had come to accept that a "popular rising" against Hitler — the original hope of the German left — was an impossibility, and he therefore conceived the plan of making a journey to America and the Far East. His object was partly to look at Germany from the outside and partly to consider what role he himself should play in the fight against Nazism. The choice was whether to pursue his opposition from inside or from outside Germany. Should he join the opposition he knew was beginning to exist inside the Government service and the Army? Or should he try to influence events from outside Germany, using his contacts in England and America?

To fund his trip he turned to the Rhodes Trust, the sponsors of his years at Oxford, and it says much for the esteem in which he was still held at Oxford, mainly by Lord Lothian, that Trott was given sufficient money to complete his two years of study abroad. Sir Stafford Cripps also helped to finance Trott's Far Eastern journey out of his own pocket. Cripps became, undoubtedly, his closest political friend in Britain. Leaving Germany in January 1937, Adam travelled to London on his way to America and the Far East. Before staying in London, he spent a few nights in Oxford, where he not only took his BA on February 27 but also met, for the first time, Count Helmuth von Moltke at a dinner in All Souls. Moltke was the great-nephew of the famous Field Marshal, and was to become a friend and fellow conspirator. In London Adam stayed at 4 St James's Square, where he met Nancy Astor for the first time. Nancy seems to have taken an immediate shine to him, and demonstrated her customary attention to the personal needs of her friends by despatching the impecunious, rather shabbily dressed "student" to a Mayfair tailor where he bought a suit and an overcoat. Trott wrote to Sheila Grant-Duff:

> I really liked Lady Astor for all her wiry liveliness — she said the last day, "I am sorry the little Trott is leaving", and I am

about twice as big as she is, and I told her so — she gave me a letter to Charlie Chaplin....[2]

Nancy was also her customary indiscreet self. Adam told his mother that his hostess

believes us [the Germans] to be encircled by Roman Catholic powers who she hates....I get on very well with her, although she is a somewhat wild lady....[3]

During his two years in China Trott toyed with the idea of deserting Germany and getting an academic post in America or Britain, but in the end, and entirely alone, he made the fateful decision to return to Germany and work from within the Government, where he would be most effective, in active treason against the Hitler regime. In China and America he had been visiting German Embassies and keeping up his Nazi contacts to smooth his entry into the German Foreign Ministry; but this inevitably raised suspicions amongst the British and American intelligence officers who now began to observe his comings and goings. Trott could never reveal the active, treasonable side of his life after his return from China; it was only the loyal, German side that he could put on display — with disastrous consequences for himself and his reputation.

Adam chose to tell David Astor of his decision to return to Germany in a letter from China in the autumn of 1938. His letter was, necessarily, cryptic but it left David in no doubt as to what Adam subsequently intended to do. He said that he would become "active" in opposition in Germany, and also warned his friend that he might need his help in the future. (Unfortunately this letter does not survive.)

On his return to Germany in December 1938 Adam began to seek out the forces of opposition to Hitler and was amazed and encouraged to learn from a Foreign Ministry friend that it existed within the German Government and Army, was highly organized

2. Quoted by Giles MacDonogh in *A Good German* (Quartet 1990), p. 96.

3. Quoted by Christopher Sykes, *Troubled Loyalty* (Collins 1968), p. 183.

and to be found amongst a wide range of officers. Indeed, he soon learnt that the previous September, just before the Munich Conference, there had been a full-scale plot to topple Hitler the moment the Führer gave the order to cross the Czechoslovak border. This plot had been led by Ernst von Weizsäcker, the permanent head of the German Foreign Ministry, and General Ludwig Beck. Through Theodor Kordt, counsellor at the German Embassy in London, the plotters conveyed to Lord Halifax, the British Foreign Secretary, at a meeting in London on September 7, 1938, that if the British stood firm against Hitler over the annexation of the Sudetenland, this would force Hitler to commit a blatant act of war by invading Czechoslovakia — at which moment the military plotters would arrest Hitler, with, as they hoped, the blessing of the German people, who at that time dreaded another European war. The British Government, however, chose to ignore the message of the plotters as conveyed by Kordt, and Chamberlain, by ceding the Sudetenland over the heads of the Czechs, thereby gave Hitler another bloodless victory that further enhanced his reputation with the German public. Never was Hitler to be in so vulnerable a position again; in retrospect Halifax's neglect of Kordt's proposals has come to be seen by some as the greatest missed opportunity of the entire period leading up to the war itself.

However, the fact that such a plot had existed must have come as an enormous tonic to Trott, and he was astonished at the seniority of some of the officers involved. Equally important was the involvement of the Army, which Adam knew was the only institution capable of moving against Hitler. In order to further his plans, he managed to secure an informal connection with a department of the Auswärtiges Amt, the German Foreign Ministry, although he did not join it formally until June 1940 when he also had to become a member of the Nazi Party. This informal connection allowed him to travel on his peace mission in June 1939 supported by the pro-Nazi head of the department, Walter Hewel. Hewel, who liked Trott and never suspected his young subordinate's real reasons for visiting London, was skilfully exploited to give him access to funds and also to the higher echelons of the German government and Party bureaucracy.

It is likely that the plan to save the peace and remove Hitler from power which Trott took to London in June 1939 was of his own making, although he certainly had the support of Weizsacker and other members of the opposition. It is impossible that Weiszacker would not have known about it, or backed it. And with the support came the quandary that faced Weizsacker and other members of the opposition at the time. As D. C. Watt has written, in the wake of Munich the disappointed and desperate plotters were confronted by a conflict of choice which they never succeeded in resolving.

> Put very crudely, the choice lay between attempting to sharpen the points of international conflict so that a general realisation of the perils into which Hitler was leading Germany could cause the army leadership to remove him, and working to deter the oncoming conflict so that Germany should not be involved in a European war which could only end in disaster. Throughout Weizsäcker inclined towards the second of these choices. This was to lead him again into advocating a solution which, to British opponents of Hitler, seemed to differ hardly at all from surrender, from ignominious appeasement.[5] It was to just such a scheme that Adam von Trott lent himself in May and June of 1939.[5]

During his visits to England in 1939, Trott argued with his friends for negotiations to delay war — which sounded little different from more appeasement. What he could not tell them, but hoped to tell Halifax or Chamberlain, was that such a delay would be followed by an internal coup. The difficulties of conveying this message were evident on his first visit to England in February 1939, a visit on behalf of Weizsäcker with the modest aim of sounding out British opinion. It came as a surprise to him to note that among his British friends whom he visited at Oxford there was now a strong feeling against delaying the outbreak of war any longer and that there could be no more talks with Hitler. Trott later told David Astor that he was amazed how even his most idealistic Oxford friends seemed actually to want war. But Adam, because of his need for secrecy, could not argue with them that, if peace could only be prolonged, there might be a further chance of a military coup inside Germany. Already he noted a certain coolness

---

5. D. C. Watt, *How War Came* (Heinemann 1989), p. 392.

towards himself, and wrote to his mother that Oxford was "somewhat disappointing" and that he had noticed a "severe frostiness" amongst his friends, "which I have not met with before". Trott then returned to Germany in the company of Geoffrey Wilson, a confidant of Sir Stafford Cripps, to show Wilson, through private meetings with individuals, that the German opposition really existed and to discuss their plans.

David Astor, informed by Trott from China of what he was going to do, had observed Adam's activities with mounting interest, and in June 1939 was directly enlisted by Adam to help his peace-saving mission to London. The international atmosphere had changed drastically since February 1939, with the German invasion of Prague and the rump of Czechoslovakia on March 16, after Hitler had promised solemnly at Munich that the Sudetenland was his last territorial demand. This finally removed any shred of legitimacy that Hitler might have claimed for his actions, and war was now considered to be almost certain. Chamberlain quickly guaranteed the borders of Poland, Romania and Greece. It was in this last-minute atmosphere that Trott flew to London on June 1 to try to place before the British Government his plan to prevent war and topple Hitler. It was natural that Trott should look to David to assist him in this task, since the Astors could provide an entrée into Government circles. Trott confided some of the plot to David because he knew he could trust him and because David's parents were his swiftest route to the top.

Trott's plan was a fantastic one. The plotters proposed that Hitler should restore freedom to Czechoslovakia, except for the Sudetenland, and that in return he should be helped by Britain to get back the Danzig Corridor from the Poles. This would restore Europe to a sort of pre-Munich peace situation; but — and this was the essence of the German opposition's idea — Hitler would surely break this peace soon, as he had broken the Munich agreement; in which case the German Army would arrest him whilst Britain stood her ground and threatened war. This was an exceptionally convoluted and impractical scheme in the context of June 1939, although it is hard to think of another one that might have achieved their tremendous purpose. It shows that Trott made a grave error in seriously misjudging the mood in Britain, for by the summer of 1939 the hesitancy and confusion of the past had hardened into a feeling that, after the outrageous invasion of Prague in March, there must be no more deals with Hitler — let alone the kind of lengthy diplomatic haggling that Trott was proposing. The plan was unworkable and the British Government could not possibly have accepted it. David Astor was told little about it, but Trott gave him indications that the people for whom he was working were substantial figures in Germany and that they had shown themselves willing to take action. David needed this to convince his father that Trott was worth taking seriously. Once Trott was in London, David Astor worked energetically on his behalf and invited him to a dinner at Cliveden on June 3 at which the Foreign Secretary would be present.

It was a bright summer evening as the Astors and their twenty or so guests sat down to eat. The conversation during dinner was general, but after the ladies withdrew, while the men passed round the port, Lord Astor beckoned Trott to sit by his side, next to Halifax. Waldorf then led Trott into the conversation by asking him questions about Germany and Halifax listened very attentively. Adam started hesitantly but gained in confidence as he went on. All he could say at this semi-public occasion, without revealing the extent of the opposition, was that ordinary Germans did not want war, but who could they listen to? He said that these Germans were eager to listen to another voice — that the British should talk to these other Germans who had exactly the same fear of war as the British. He said that the British should talk *past* Hitler. One listener was William Douglas-Home, who later wrote that Trott "...spoke with a deep sincerity and a sense of urgency. Listening to him I understood how it was that so many Germans, loathing and despising Hitler as they did, yet felt that in his insistence on the rights of Germany he was voicing the wishes of his people...."

Halifax listened in silence, but was obviously impressed, as he took TJ, who was also present, by the arm on the terrace after the dinner party had dispersed and told him that Chamberlain should listen to Trott. Adam left his telephone number with TJ and it was the latter who then actually telephoned Trott to fix a meeting with the Prime Minister. Trott saw Chamberlain at Downing Street on June 7. Lord Dunglass (Alec Douglas-Home), Chamberlain's PPS, was the only other man present at this meeting. Unfortunately, no record of their conversation survives and Lord Home, as he now is, can remember nothing of it. However, what is certain is that Trott put his plan to Chamberlain, and that Chamberlain was unimpressed. David Astor saw Trott immediately afterwards and Trott said that talking to Chamberlain was like talking to "a very old and tired man who was at the end of a very long and uncongenial road", and that the Prime Minister was too tired to think of anything new — although in this case it would have taken a mind of extraordinary activity and fertility to make something of Trott's "plan". However he did not alienate Chamberlain and left a favourable impression on Halifax, Chamberlain and Dunglass. Indeed, there is some evidence that Halifax incorporated some of what Trott was saying into a speech that he gave in the House of Lords on June 8, and later in a speech at Chatham House on June 29. This speech certainly cheered Trott and the German opposition. Other than this, it is hard to see whether Trott achieved much more than Kordt had done — with a much better proposal — the previous September. It was just after his interview with Chamberlain that Trott came nearest to revealing to David Astor what he was doing. Asked what, in the simplest terms, he was trying to achieve, Adam put his answer in an allegory: "You could imagine Hitler as a heavily armed village drunkard, whose wild behaviour was endangering the lives of his own family and those of his neighbours. The best way to deal with him might be for two people to take him one by each arm. One arm would be taken by his strongest relative (the German plotters) and the other by his strongest neighbour (Britain). These two would then persuade him, with much pretence of friendly helpfulness (negotiations on Danzig, colonies, anything at all) to come for a long walk. Having got him into a quiet field, they should then hit him on the head with his own revolver (the German Army)." This is the closest that Trott got to explaining the exact nature of his mission to Astor, but the latter did not press him any further, recognizing the danger of his work and the need for secrecy. He took his friend on trust.

Others clearly did not. He flew back to Berlin on June 9, and then returned to London on Sunday June 11, going to Oxford a few days later. During his weekend in Berlin he composed a colourful and highly imaginative report on his visit to Britain, portraying his activities from the point of view of a dedicated Nazi. With the help of his comrade-in-arms, the lawyer Peter

Lord Astor, David's father, a few years before his death

photo Michael Peto

Lady Astor, David's mother, addressing the electors of Plymouth

Philip Kerr, Lord Lothian   J. L. Garvin

A portrait of Dr Thomas Jones—'TJ'—

David Astor (right) and Adam von Trott in the garden at Cliveden in the summer of 1939

Christabel and Peter Bielenberg in the garden of David Astor's London house in the summer of 1989.

photo Jane Bown

David Astor in the editorial chair, 1964

photo David N. Smith

Sebastian Haffner

photo Tony McGrath

Isaac Deutsch

photo Jane Bown

William Guttman

photo Tony McGrath

Jon Kimche

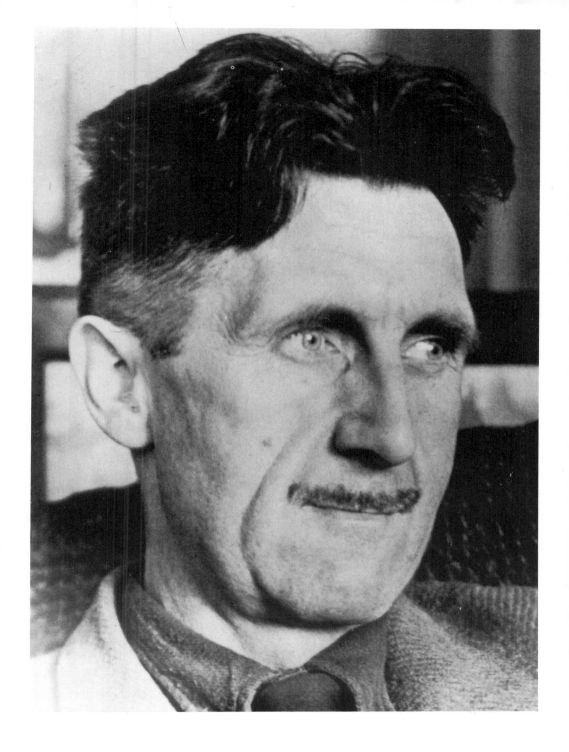

George Orwell

E. F. Schumacher

Arthur Koestler

photo Donald McCullin

Patrick O'Donovan

photo Tony McGrath

John Gale

photo Tony McGrath

Bielenberg, he succeeded all too well, but his attempts to place the document before Hitler and Goering were thwarted by the ever-zealous and ever-jealous Ribbentrop, his political chief as Foreign Minister. Once again, his efforts produced no short-term benefit, but this ferociously "Nazi" document was to muddy his reputation further when it came into the hands of the British Foreign Office after the war.

Trott returned to London on June 9 and stayed at 4 St James's Square before going to Oxford. It was during these few days at Oxford that, speaking to his "friends" such as Stuart Hampshire, Christopher Hill and Maurice Bowra, he was to create a fatal impression as an arch-appeaser, if not an actual Nazi agent. At this distance in time it is not difficult to see why, for everywhere he went he collided with the new defiant mood in Britain that he does not seem to have understood or taken into account in his dealings with his Oxford contemporaries. For what Trott was proposing was more talks with Hitler — without being able to say that the time thus gained would be used to attempt a military coup in Germany — which he had, of course, indicated to the British ministers he met. He thus appeared to be suggesting further concessions, possibly at the expense of the Poles and Czechs, for no other purpose than to humour Hitler. David Astor admits that Adam was "crazy to go back to Oxford to see all his Oxford friends without being able to give them a full explanation of his activities". He confided most in Maurice Bowra of Wadham College, but could still not be totally frank with him, merely conveying the impression that he wanted more appeasement of Hitler in a doubtful cause. Bowra, furious, showed him the door. However, Bowra did not stop there, and wrote a letter to Felix Frankfurter, President Roosevelt's close friend, warning him against Trott in very hostile terms. Bowra knew that Trott was contemplating a mission to America in the autumn, and this letter effectively scuppered any chances he might have had of making a favourable impression on the Americans. One of the reasons that Trott chose to be a good deal less than frank with these Oxford dons was because of the dangers of gossip in the small, hothouse world of Oxford academia. He was right to fear this gossip, as in a few days his name was mud. Just as Bowra sabotaged his American trip (although he was later to recognize his mistaken rejection of Trott as "one of my bitterest regrets"[6]) so another young don, Richard Crossman, was later to ruin his advances to the British Government in 1942 with another hostile letter to the Foreign Secretary. At the same time as leaving this trail of bitterness and confusion at Oxford, Trott also broke his friendship with Sheila Grant-Duff over the issue of Czechoslovakia. From now on, only David Astor of his Oxford friends would stand square behind him, supported by the equally loyal Stafford Cripps and Wilfred Israel.

Trott flew back to Berlin on June 22. David Astor's next service for his friend was to fly out to Berlin at the beginning of July to stay with him for a few days. One of the reasons why Adam wanted David to come to Berlin was so that he could show off his friend with the famous name at a cocktail party, chiefly to impress Hitler's personal representative in the Foreign Ministry, Walter Hewel, who would then look favourably on his taking more trips abroad. Astor was thus introduced as an important political contact in Britain, and he played up to the part. Hewel arrived with his son, with a rose in his button-hole; he was obviously convinced that he was indeed meeting someone grand. The party seems to have done the trick, as Trott continued to be allowed to travel anywhere at will during the coming years. It was also on this trip to Berlin that David Astor first met the Bielenbergs, the couple whom Adam "most depended on". Christabel, of Anglo-Irish stock, was later to write her own account of these anxious months in her celebrated autobiography, *The Past is Myself*. Peter was a young lawyer by training, who had met Adam in 1935 and a few years later had dedicated his life in Germany to working for him and the opposition. Adam told David that he could depend on Peter because he "could always be relied to risk his neck for him" (as indeed Peter did after the July 20, 1944 bomb plot in a thwarted attempt to free Adam), and he depended on Christabel because she "kept him sane" with her English pragmatism and good sense. It was indeed, a strong and reassuring combination, and they were to become lifelong friends of David's.

On his last day in Berlin, David and Adam went driving in Adam's extremely small car to the northern outskirts of the city,

---

6. Sir C. Maurice Bowra, *Memories 1918–1939* (Cambridge, Mass., 1967), p. 305.

principally so they could talk out of microphone-range of the Gestapo. After some time, Adam drove beyond the suburbs until they came to a long, dead straight road only one field's distance from the main road, "at the end of which was a concentration camp". Adam stopped the car at the beginning of the road leading to the gates, and the two just sat for a while, much to David's initial alarm, in front of the ugly, forced-labour-built prison gates surrounded by tidy turnip fields. Adam remarked on the complete silence of the place and said that "this is what Nazism amounts to".

On his return to London, David Astor wrote a memorandum for Lord Halifax on his visit to Berlin and his talks with "Adam von Trott and some of his friends". Dated July 9, the memo conveyed some of the current thinking of Adam and the opposition, in particular the idea that Goering might have been suitable as an intermediary between the British Government and the Germans as he was able to gather the more moderate forces behind him. This was a fashionable idea at the time, especially as Goering was sending his own emissaries over, unknown to Trott, to try to come to a last-minute settlement. Astor's document was described as "rather woolly" by one Foreign Office official, and was subsequently consigned to the files.[7]

In mid-July, Trott made his last visit to England, but on this occasion appears to have seen only the Astors and Cripps. While staying in David's Regent's Park mews house, Adam spoke of the evil of Hitler, but argued that allowing him to have his war would only spread his evil influence. During the course of one conversation, Adam suddenly asked, "Why don't you like Hitler?" and before David could answer, said:

> because he is a fanatic nationalist, because he's cruel and guilty of the murder of his fellow men, because he is blind with hate. I agree with you in all that — but can't you see that if we have war, then everyone will become a nationalist fanatic, everyone will become cruel, and you and I will kill our fellow men and perhaps each other. We will do all these things that we condemn in the Nazis, and the Nazi outlook

---

7. Document in Public Record Office, FO 800/316.

will not be suppressed but will spread. Is that what you want?

There was a lot of truth in this. Trott stayed only a few days, and then returned to Berlin. It was the last time that David was to see his friend.

It was through Trott that David Astor got involved that summer in a much more practical scheme to save the peace. It was brought to London by a professional Army officer, the audacious Colonel Count Gerhard von Schwerin. Schwerin, an English-speaking officer in the Atlantic Group of the German High Command, was like many other German officers profoundly sceptical of the consequences of fighting what he liked to call "Hitler's War". With the knowledge of his immediate superiors, he took it upon himself to travel to England in July 1939 to impress upon the British the fact that even after all the guarantees to Poland and related sabre-rattling in the summer of 1939, Hitler still did not believe that Britain would actually go to war over Poland — which, given Britain's past record, was not an unreasonable assumption. That he was operating on authority was made clear and was not later doubted. But what he needed in London was contacts. David Astor's name was given to Schwerin by a Bremen businessman, Wilhelm Roloff, whom David had met through Erwin Schueller, an émigré German who had worked with David at Lazards. David had stayed with Roloff outside Hamburg. On being approached by Schwerin, Astor checked with Trott who said that Schwerin was definitely not a Nazi and should be met. Schwerin thus arrived in London at the beginning of July and installed himself in a flat off Piccadilly, presenting himself on Astor's doorstep complete with printed visiting cards giving his Piccadilly address and full military status. At first sight, Schwerin appeared to be a caricature of a German officer, "with his almost clean-shaven head". He was also, however, very genial and extremely blunt in the message that he wanted to convey to the British Government. This message was much simpler and more direct that Trott's and Weizsäcker's complicated formulations and was therefore much better suited to the mood of the moment. The message he brought was as follows: the German High Command expected an attack by Hitler on Poland that summer and Hitler definitely did *not* believe that Britain and France would go to war over Poland. It was useless for the High Command to tell Hitler that this time they would, because when they had previously predicted that the West would fight they had always been wrong. If Britain this time really meant to fight, there was surely no advantage to Britain in keeping Hitler in any doubt. But the only thing that would convince Hitler was action. Schwerin thus proposed several concrete military actions, including a high-profile exercise by British warships in the Baltic, the swift dispatch of RAF units to France and the replacement of the weak compliant British Ambassador to Germany, Sir Nevile Henderson, by a military man. As Schwerin said:

> Hitler will scream but that does not matter. At least he will believe that you mean war. If you really do, you should also invite some friends of Goering, such as Air Marshal Milch, to see for himself that you really have a serious aircraft industry — they only believe their own cronies.

Schwerin's message had the virtue of simplicity, and unlike Trott's plan, it was also very practical in the circumstances. Astor promised to help him. He approached his only contact in the War Office who was a friend of Bill's, Robert Laycock, later the dashing wartime chief of Commandos. Laycock was interested enough in Schwerin to direct Astor to a brigadier at Military Intelligence who apparently specialized in German affairs. Astor outlined Schwerin's case and was then rather surprised to be told by this brigadier, "...sitting back behind his desk in the grandest of manners, that he regarded Schwerin's visit to London at a time when relations between his country and ours were as bad as they were in 1939 as 'bloody cheek'". The brigadier clearly had no intention of following up the matter and there was nothing more Astor could do for Schwerin.

In fact, Schwerin, through his other contacts, did get to see Admiral Godfrey, the Chief of Naval Intelligence, who arranged for him to meet James Stuart, the Conservative whip, Gladwyn Jebb of the Foreign Office and General Marshall Cornwall, the former British military attaché in Berlin. Schwerin outlined his plan at a dinner, ending his discourse forcefully with the words "Hitler is the only person in Germany worth convincing, and he can only be convinced by deeds, not words".[8] However, Schwerin's

---

8. The account of this dinner is in *Documents on British Foreign Policy, 1919–39*, Third Series, Volume IV, pp. 295–98.

appeal, like Kordt's and Trott's, fell on deaf ears. Astor's last contribution to this frantic summer of clandestine, amateur diplomacy was on August 19, when he received Peter Bielenberg who had flown from Berlin to London on behalf of Trott in a last-minute gamble to avert what now looked like certain war. He stayed with David Astor, who once again took upon himself the task of getting Bielenberg's message placed before the British Government. The message this time was mercifully simple: that to pre-empt Hitler's imminent invasion of Poland the British should send some uncompromising military figure such as General Gort direct to Hitler, bearing a letter from the King warning him that if he crossed the Polish border he would be plunging Europe into war. If this visit were to take place in a blaze of publicity, then it might not only persuade Hitler to think again but would also warn the German people of what they were letting themselves in for and might persuade the generals to act.

Unfortunately Bielenberg arrived at an awkward moment: the week following the "glorious twelfth", which left Whitehall and Westminster very depleted. None the less, Astor hand-delivered a letter at the Foreign Office for Halifax, informing the Foreign Secretary that Astor and Bielenberg would be available to be seen throughout the weekend. There was no response; according to Christopher Sykes, Lord Halifax was supposed to be away, but was, in fact, in the office over the weekend but elected not to see Bielenberg. This was not really so important, as just such an idea as Bielenberg was suggesting had been discussed in official circles, with the minor alteration that Whitehall's preferred soldier to talk man-to-man with Hitler was General Sir Edmund Ironside. As it was, Bielenberg returned to Germany on August 20, having apparently achieved nothing at great personal risk to himself, as he had already received his call-up papers.

With the signing of the Nazi-Soviet pact on August 24, war could only be a few days away, yet still Trott persisted in trying to make the British Government aware of the possibilities of the opposition in Germany. On that same day, August 24, Trott managed to communicate to Astor through a friend in the British Embassy a short memo on the aims of the German resistance, entitled "Inner Political Situation in Germany Today". In this memo he painted an optimistic picture of the opposition, warning that it would be ready to "use the same *methods* against Fascism as

Hitler uses now. In Germany itself there is an idea of *force* in all directions." He ended with this prediction:

> If there is a war it is hoped that the inner development of the opposition is strong enough to become really active. If the war is long the Generals are likely to gain much greater influence. *The English must then make a new European Order, without Hitler, but with a new opposition from outside.*

On September 1 Hitler's tanks rolled into Poland and on September 3 Britain declared war on Germany. The peace-keeping endeavours of Trott and his colleagues were at an end. Despite David Astor's valiant efforts on their behalf, the German opposition had achieved nothing. During the process Trott had also besmirched his reputation amongst his English friends to such a degree that — unknown to him — his use as an emissary for the opposition was now at an end. This was partly due to his own enforced lack of frankness, but it may also have had something to do with his intimate association with the Astors, who at the end of 1937 had appeared in the Communist Claud Cockburn's weekly newsletter *The Week* as hosts of the pro-Fascist "Cliveden Set", surreptitiously pulling the strings of an alternative British foreign policy at their famous weekend parties. In fact, this myth was not the fancy of Cockburn's admittedly fertile imagination, but more probably the invention of Sir Robert Vansittart, the Permanent Under-Secretary at the Foreign Office from 1931 to 1938, who was contemporaneously engaged in what he saw as a struggle to save his job against the "appeasers". Vansittart did indeed lose his job, but Eden, the Foreign Secretary, had a great deal more to do with it than the Astors.[9] Despite all the evidence to the contrary and frequent letters to the press pleading their case, the Astors found that the mud stuck, and some of this must have rubbed off on to Trott.

The effect of all his efforts on Trott's — and Schwerin's — behalf on David Astor himself was galvanizing. All thoughts of working on *The Times* disappeared as he threw himself energetically into

---

9. See Richard Cockett, *Twilight of Truth* (Weidenfeld & Nicolson, 1989) pp. 33–38.

promoting Trott's cause. With the beginning of war and the deser-
tion of most of Trott's friends, David became virtually his proxy
in Britain. The only other person in Britain to maintain a similar
interest in Trott was Sir Stafford Cripps, but by the end of 1939
Cripps had taken up his own idea of acting as "Ambassador" to
Moscow, which was to remove him from the domestic political
scene until 1942. David had always been aware of the menace of
Fascism, but it was Trott who gave him a positive plan for
combating it, not just in a German context but a European
context as well. The simple message that David carried away was
that the fight against Fascism should not be that of an out-dated
nationalist conflict, but had to be an international anti-Fascist
crusade, in which the anti-Fascist Germans were just as willing to
play their part as anyone else. But it was up to Britain to create
the idea of a new European order, to rival Hitler's "New Order";
as Trott had said in the last sentence of his August 24 memo,
"The English must make a new European Order, without Hitler,
but with a new opposition from outside." This was the goal that
David Astor would devote his war to with considerable single-
mindedness.

In England, David Astor quickly started to act on Trott's ideas
and to make contact with the nucleus of a group that could start
giving Trott's ideas a more concrete shape. Under the auspices
of the York Trust, Astor set up the Europe Study Group to
examine the problems of Europe, and more specifically the prospects
of creating a new non-nationalistic order in Germany and Europe
that would operate as an alternative vision to Hitler's Europe. At
the core of the Europe Study Group were a number of émigré
Germans who were later to play a considerable role in David
Astor's *Observer*. Through his contacts with the Socialist "Neue
Beginnen" group, Astor met "Rix" Lowenthal, later to become a
leader-writer on the paper, and it was also at this time that Willi
Guttman started working for David. Guttman was a Jew, born in
1903 in Upper Silesia, who trained as a lawyer but had to flee
Hitler's Germany in 1933 because as a Jew he lost the right to
practise law. He emigrated to Italy, but came to London in
February 1939 and was introduced to David Astor through his
brother, a neurologist at the Maudsley Hospital, in May of that
year. In October David Astor started to employ Guttman, who
was fluent in both German and Italian, as a one-man monitoring

service of Axis radio broadcasts. David paid for a wireless set and Guttman was paid £5 a week to provide Astor and the Europe Study Group with transcripts of the broadcasts. Guttman was later to become a highly popular and respected librarian at the *Observer*. Erwin Schueller, David's friend from Lazards, also joined the group. However, the central figure in this group was supposed to be Trott, who in September 1939 had sailed for America to take part in the Institute of Pacific Relations Conference at Virginia Beach. Ostensibly, Trott was attending the conference on behalf of the Foreign Ministry, but he was using as a pretext for more of his undercover work on behalf of the opposition.

However, it was soon clear to Trott, as perhaps it should have been before, that due to the confusions arising from his visit to England in July 1939, there was now considerable resistance to having any dealings with him at all, and his American trip was a hopeless failure. In his last letter to David Astor on December 26, 1939, he admitted as much, writing:

> ...my usefulness over here is very limited. I too have interested myself in "groups" who are discussing with varying degrees of seriousness and authenticity the conditions of a future peace...but frankly I do feel that not very much can be expected from these groups other than an influence to keep passions from getting hold of the problems completely....There is another point which makes my staying here definitely inadvisable. You never gave any importance to the fact that during this summer I seemed to develop the ill-deserved reputation of an "appeaser" in certain quarters in England. They have, apparently, proceeded to warn some Americans against me whose confidence under the circumstances was essential. So it wasn't in this case a matter, merely, of "touchiness" to which you very rightly objected, but quite an obstructive and harmful falsification of my intentions here, by way of establishing me in the minds of some of these worthies as undoubtedly "out for another Munich". Under the circumstances I am obviously defenceless against such and other accusations; they originate, I feel, in certain "clever" quarters in Oxford you and I know and hinge on to Felix [Frankfurter] and his friends here, who in spite of a genuine degree of personal high-mindedness, and, possibly,

even friendly feelings to what you and I try to stand for, are violently suspicious and antagonistic to anything that might result from the wider implications of cooperation such as yours and mine etc.

Even Lothian, the new British Ambassador to Washington, was unable to help Trott. With his American mission a failure, David Astor saw it as even more urgent that Trott should come and work for the Europe Study Group, and not return to Germany. A string of letters from David pursued Trott across America, arguing that "There are many people here who would wish you to be in this country. What you should do in this matter you can best judge for yourself. I must, however, emphasise that my own feeling is that your usefulness is ten times as great outside Germany as a planner for the future than inside Germany as a revolutionary." David warned, quite frankly, of the possible fate awaiting Adam in Germany on his return, particularly as his close contacts with the British and Americans were already known to be an object of interest to the Gestapo. But in his last letter on December 26, Trott indicated his firm resolve:

> Though I shall listen carefully to the advice you may still send me...not to return, I have definitely made up my mind that apart from *definite* indications of presumable liquidation my place during this coming time is at home. You and your friends may be right that my capacities to do a lot there may be limited, but the urgent need for every single individual with any scope and insight seems to be overwhelmingly on the side of inside work. If this is not recognised by people like ourselves we must resign to an almost helpless determination, because the drift of things, left to themselves, is definitely against what we hope for.

Trott returned to Germany in the second week of January 1940 a disappointed man. In his last weeks in Washington he sent David several long letters, outlining his hopes for Europe and Germany, as though he was passing the torch to David. In his letter of December 26, 1939, Trott delineated their common goal:

> We are not fighting within the framework of a constitution on sectional interests and principles, but for the formation of a constitution — which has become an elemental necessity, for

the life of Europe as a whole, if our individual countries and what we consider worth preserving in them is to survive. In this sense I think we stand on common ground, not only with responsible conservatives and socialists in our own, but with the analogous alliance in every other country.

Trott outlined a clear course which Britain should take to enlist the German people in the fight against Nazism:

If your country were to develop a clear vision of the new Europe in which the survival of her own liberties were coupled with a working prospect of restituted freedom all round, with no overshadowing suspicion of monopoly and sectional supremacies, that mood would probably change. The effectiveness of your propaganda on the continent would be incomparably more powerful and a basis for realistic cooperation in all countries would form itself automatically.

It was this propaganda that David Astor and the Europe Study Group threw themselves into producing throughout the winter of 1939—40. David recognized that educating the British public along the lines that he and Trott wanted was going to be an uphill task, as British propaganda seemed only to reflect, as he wrote to Lord Lothian on October 20, 1939, "...the negative, cautious and uninspiring approach of the rest of the Government". He went on:

Another depressing "sign of the times", is the marked tendency to depart from the PM's idea that we are fighting Nazis and not Germans and to revert to the clap-trap of 1914—18. I have sat through some pretty painful meals at the family table. My father is the only one in the family whose ideas are firmly against this atmosphere produced by Khaki.... My general view of the outlook is that;
a) If we just pit our armed forces against those of the Germans and fight it out it will be a long and destructive war, at the end of which the Europe which we are supposed to be fighting for will be replaced by breakdown and totalitarianism.
b) If we apply enlightened statesmanship and propaganda to the situation, the war can be shortened...I don't underrate the difficulty of dealing with the eighty million Germans now or hereafter, but there are certain obvious things — such as not condemning them en masse, promising not to destroy

"Germany", starting some non-committal but non-punitive war aims — which any half-wit should be able to see will help us win this war more quickly....

This was the message of several memos and papers produced by David Astor and his fellow students of Europe during the first winter and spring of war. These were sent to anyone who might have been expected to take some interest, particularly the Ministry of Information. However, David's appeals fell on deaf ears. It was because of this solid wall of official obstruction that they encountered that he turned to an institution somewhat nearer to hand on which he could exert some influence to publicize his propaganda aims, namely, the family newspaper, the *Observer*. From 1940 onward David's efforts were to be concentrated on promulgating his and Trott's joint ideal for Europe in the *Observer*, living up to his final pledge to Trott's widow in the first letter that he wrote to her after the war:

...we must try to remember his spirit and his ideals and attempt with our more limited talents and powers to continue living as he would have wanted his friends to live.

As a footnote to David Astor's involvement in the German opposition, he also attracted the attentions of the British Secret Intelligence Service, SIS (also known as MI6). David was interviewed by the SIS at the beginning of the war, but turned down. However the SIS permitted him to attempt to establish contact between SIS and the German opposition through Holland. In October, David was sent to Holland to help the officers running this operation, Major Stevens and Sigmund Payne Best. David did not warm to either of these rather "arrogant" officers, but he did become a firm friend of Lionel Loewe, an MI6 officer, later a prominent barrister, who set up his meeting with the other two.

After only a few days he returned to Britain as it was clear he could be of no assistance. However, the consequences of this MI6 operation were to be of importance to David, as Payne and Best were duped by the Gestapo into making contact with a fake "opposition" on November 9, 1939 at the border town of Venlo. As soon as the Englishmen arrived, they were bundled over the border by the waiting Gestapo. The "Venlo incident", as it became known, was not only deeply humiliating for SIS but it removed any faith that Whitehall might have had in the reality of a German opposition. Once bitten, permanently shy; having been duped by the Gestapo, this was to be the last time that Britain made any attempt to contact the German opposition.

Meanwhile Trott had returned to Germany and carried on his work for the opposition in the Foreign Ministry. In one of his letters to David, typed on chinese flower-paper, Adam had written "whatever happens to you and me we'll remain friends, anyway, I know".

David was true to this friendship and worked for the ideals that they shared throughout the war. Trott's last letter to David was his long one from America on December 26, 1939, for after his return to Germany there could be no further communication. David was thus wholly unaware of the fraught path of secret opposition that led up to the July 20, 1944 bomb plot, the most serious attempt to topple Hitler's Government. The story of Trott's wartime opposition to the Nazis belongs to the growing array of Trott biographies, but Richard Lamb, author of the *Ghosts of Peace, 1939—45*, (Michael Russell 1987) has chronicled his frequent attempts to persuade the British Government to cooperate with the German opposition. These attempts, which were unknown to David, all foundered on the twin rocks of British distrust of Trott personally, and, after the Russian entry into the war, the British Government's pledge to the unconditional surrender of Germany, which effectively ruled out any dealings with the German opposition. Churchill personally forbade any such negotiations. Trott's trips to Oxford in July 1939 came back to haunt him in May 1942, when his most promising approach to the Foreign Office was spiked by a personal testimony by Richard Crossman which was hostile and destructive in the extreme. Even by Crossman's standards, it was a document of astonishing deviousness and intellectual irresponsibility. Cripps, by this time occupying a prominent position in the Government, tried to come to Trott's aid but the damage had been done and Eden, the Foreign Secretary, rejected Trott's approach out of hand. It was this consistent refusal of the British Government even to recognize the existence of a German resistance, let alone help it, that eventually drove the plotters to act unilaterally and plan the bomb plot of 1944. Colonel von Stauffenberg planted the bomb at Hitler's headquarters, whilst Trott waited in Berlin, perhaps expecting to become the Foreign Minister in the new Government. On hearing the news that Hitler had survived, Trott again had the chance to flee Germany, but elected to stay. He was arrested, tried at the mock-court that sentenced many of the other 4,980 people to death as a result of the plot, and he was executed by slow strangulation on August 26. In the end, Trott probably recognized that the chances of success for the plotters, acting on their own, was minimal, but they did not wish future generations in Germany to live with the disgrace that no Germans had risked their lives to destroy Hitler.

Astor heard of Trott's death in a hospital in Naples in September 1944. In Christabel Bielenberg's last conversation with Adam von Trott he had told her, "the last friend I would have in England now was David Astor". Barring Cripps, this was probably correct. Just as David had devoted himself to fighting for Adam while he was alive, so David was to fight an almost equally important campaign after his death to clear Adam's name of the charges of duplicity and Nazism that his death did little to dispel.

David Astor's first act after the end of the war was to make contact with Trott's widow, Clarita, whom he had married in 1940. In January 1946 he applied to Ernest Bevin, the Foreign Secretary, for a visa for Clarita to travel to England. In making this request, David added that,

> I would also suggest that the mere fact that she was allowed to come here would represent to his [Trott's] surviving friends in Germany a mark of this country's recognition of their efforts in the fight against Hitler. I hope you may consider it desirable to give these few Germans who have definitely proved themselves to be our friends, this small and indirect sign of our appreciation...

His application was supported by Sir Stafford Cripps. Clarita thus became the first German to be allowed to enter Britain after the end of the war. David Astor became a close friend and benefactor of Clarita and her two daughters. He also helped Peter and Christabel Bielenberg to come to Britain and eventually to set up a farm in Ireland. Christabel was also briefly employed as a correspondent in post-war Germany for the *Observer*, and it was partly with David's encouragement of her literary talents that she produced *The Past is Myself*, a graphic record of her friendship with Adam von Trott and her life in wartime Germany. David was also instrumental, with the Bielenbergs and Diana Hopkinson, in setting up the "July 20 Memorial Fund" to provide for the families and children of those executed as a result of the bomb plot. A few years later he helped to found, together with his mentor of Eton days, Robert Birley, that most lasting institution to post-war Anglo-German friendship, the Königswinter Conference. Starting in 1950 and meeting annually ever since, this institution provided a forum whereby British and German Members of Parliament, businessmen and representatives of the press could meet and discuss subjects of mutual interest.

On a more personal level David waged an often lonely campaign in the post-war years to clear the name of Adam von Trott. He was prompted mostly by the anger he felt at the shabby treatment that his friend had received at the hands of the British Foreign Office immediately before and during the war. In 1956, with the publication of a large volume of German diplomatic documents relating to the period March-August 1939, the Foreign Office, presumably in an attempt to justify their neglect of Trott, drew the attention of the press to the report, written by Trott in a style deliberately aping the Nazi manner, of his visit to Cliveden in June 1939 referred to on page 51. This gave birth to a rash of "Nazi Spy at Cliveden" articles in the press by journalists taking Trott's report at face value, out of context. David Astor wrote a long reply to these press articles in the *Manchester Guardian* on June 4, 1956.

The confusion still surrounding Trott led the Bielenbergs and David Astor to appoint Christopher Sykes to write a biography of Trott, *Troubled Loyalty*. However, as has been seen, David and the Bielenbergs, as well as Clarita von Trott, disagreed sharply with Sykes in his portrayal of Trott, which, in their view, presented him too much as a nationalist, sentimental, unworldly German aristocrat obsessed by the finer points of Hegelian philosophy. David took the unusual step of publicly disclaiming the book in an article for *Encounter* in June 1969, which produced a lively debate in the letters page in which all the old wounds were opened again. Trott was fully rehabilitated only in 1983, with a course of Adam von Trott memorial lectures in Balliol Hall during Hilary term, organized by Professor Hedley Bull and David Astor. David's own lecture, "Adam von Trott: A Personal View", was published in *The New York Review of Books* in April 1983. In addition, David Astor has been unfailingly generous with his time and money in helping what has developed into a small army of scholars now working on Adam von Trott and the resistance. Giles MacDonogh's latest biography, *A Good German* (Quartet, 1990) demonstrates how far the rehabilitation has come: that students now write PhDs on Trott's "early political thought" testifies to his new status as a significant historical figure, one previously neglected compared to his fellow conspirators such as Moltke and Stauffenberg. To date (1990) he has had more biographical studies devoted to him than most British prime ministers — including Anthony Eden, the man who as Foreign Secretary so brusquely turned down Adam's approaches on behalf of the resistance in 1942.

If David Astor felt angry at being ignored by British official circles during the war when he might have testified on Adam's behalf, he has certainly made up for it since then. That the name of Trott is now not only familiar to, but respected by, every student of Anglo-German relations, as well as a wider public, owes much to David Astor. He has perhaps been a better friend to Adam in death than he could ever hope to have been during his life. For David Astor's part, Trott was the single most influential person in his life. David was alert to the same enemy, Fascism, before he was enlisted to help the German opposition in 1939, but it was Adam who showed David what could be done against the enemy and how racism, intolerance, bigotry and rabid nationalism should be defeated everywhere. It was Adam who galvanized David into action and gave him the confidence and political purpose to look to the *Observer* to fight this international anti-Fascist crusade. Asked to define the "ideal" of the *Observer* in 1959, David wrote:

> In the character of this paper, ethics matter more than politics. Its particular ethics could be defined as trying to do the opposite to what Hitler would have done. In fact, that may be the historic origin, as the paper's present personality was established in the last war by people drawn together more by being anti-Fascist than by anything else.

Adam von Trott could not be one of those people, but it was their dual policy that David carried with him to the *Observer*. It would not be too much of an exaggeration to say that David Astor's *Observer* was Adam von Trott's political monument.

Perhaps theirs was "the best friendship in Europe".

3

The Going of Garvin

The end of the "phoney war" and the beginning of the "real war" in May 1940 did nothing to diminish David Astor's belief in the efficacy of Adam von Trott's ideas. Indeed, the immediate failure of the Allied war machine in France in May and June of that year, and the desperate air battle for Britain's survival in the skies of southern England that summer, seemed to confirm their analysis that if Hitler was to be defeated something more was needed than mere militarism − a unifying, anti-Fascist idea which would set Europe (including the anti-Nazi Germans) alight. One person who was very sympathetic to this idea, whom David Astor met through Trott's introduction soon after the war began, was Sir Stafford Cripps, a politician of great independence and stern idealism. A little later in the war, David Astor wrote to Cripps to explain

> ...the need for developing a new political front of stronger appeal than a mosaic of old ideas in our world-wide struggle against the false Messiah and his false promised land. The sterility of the anti-Nazi world makes Hitler's job too easy. This is the line which still needs recognition....The line that Adam von Trott was representing to people in the early summer of '39.
>
> ...Not that what I am proposing is a simple task. The new political front must not only be a unifying one − and there

are very diverse elements to be united. It must also have a militant or even a militarist character. You can't beat Hitler unless you inspire a sterner fighting spirit and build up a better fighting organisation than he possesses. There is no primrose path of easy ideologies which like Joshua's trumpets will make the walls fall down by blowing alone. We must inspire such a fighting spirit that we become the best soldiers of the modern world and the conquered people resist Hitler with any improvised weapons. Cromwell combined high ideals and good soldiering; for freedom, the American colonists and the Boer farmers resisted better armed troops. But what spirit are Winston and his motley crew of old party hacks creating that is comparable. . . .

David thus pledged himself to collecting around him the "younger people who have a really avid interest in the anti-Hitler crusade". Motivated by Trott, he was convinced that Hitler could only be fought with the pen *and* the sword, with ideas *and* weapons. And with Britain isolated and virtually defenceless from June 1940 until the tide of war turned towards the end of 1942, ideas were about all that the British had to play with. Britain could hold out no hope of liberating Europe by military invasion, but she could foster a battle of ideas, an anti-Fascist crusade, which would make Europe ungovernable for the Nazis.

In May 1940 David enlisted in the Marines, spending most of the following months in the Royal Marine barracks at Portsmouth and on Hayling Island. This did not prevent him from energetically going about the task of organizing those "younger people who have a really avid interest in the anti-Hitler crusade". The vigour and energy which David was able to bring to bear on this task often surprised those who took his shy, diffident and hesitant manner at face value. Behind the mask lay great firmness of purpose, and his mother's quality of energetic directness. This could make him seem to an older generation impatient and impetuous; even his father, always an admirer, could warn TJ that David was "rather inclined to go too fast".[1] Just as Wilfrid Eady, a Treasury civil

---

1. Lord Astor to TJ, April 10, 1942; Thomas Jones Papers, University of Wales, Aberystwyth.

servant at one time tipped to be editor of the *Observer* after Garvin, was inclined to see David as "a bit impatient for results".[2] But if he was "too fast" for some of his elders, he was much more in tune with his own generation, many of whom held the easy-going "Baldwinism" of the inter-war establishment responsible for landing Britain in its gravest peril in the summer of 1940.

David was not alone in thinking that the Second World War had to be fought along radically different lines from the First if Britain was to triumph. As soon as hostilities started there was a swift proliferation of *ad hoc* institutes and bureaux dedicating them-selves to the problems of "war aims" and propaganda policy. In his search for like-minded souls, David joined some of these bodies, the most important of which was probably the Post-War Bureau. This was the brainchild of Edward Hulton, the young and wealthy proprietor of *Picture Post* magazine, founded in 1938 and already by 1940 doing impressively well with its blend of photo-journalism and progressive politics. Hulton set up the Bureau in his house in Hill Street, Mayfair. Its purpose was to "provide contacts and publicity for all those groups and individuals who were interested and working on the correlated subject of war aims, peace terms, general European Construction and World Order". Amongst those who gathered at Hill Street were Gerald Barry (editor of the *News Chronicle*), Tom Hopkinson (editor of *Picture Post*), Francis Williams (editor of the *Daily Herald* until January 1940) and E. H. Carr (assistant editor and leader-writer on *The Times*). As an organization in its own right, the Post-War Bureau was a singularly ineffective body which soon petered out; but it was important as a precursor of what was to come.

With the fall of France and the Battle of Britain, minds were temporarily focused on other things, but by the autumn of 1940 the dying embers of the Post-War Bureau were rekindled by the novelist, playwright and broadcaster J. B. Priestley. It was in his capacity as a broadcaster that Priestley left a lasting impression on the hard-pressed population of Britain during the summer of 1940, for his "Postscripts" on the BBC offered an arcadian vision of honest, earthy socialism that was so appealing that his broadcasts

---

2. Eady to TJ, December 16, 1941; Thomas Jones Papers.

were temporarily as popular as Churchill's (something which did *not* please the Prime Minister). Priestley instantly became the focus for all those interested in post-war aims and alternative methods of fighting the war: the radical alternative to old-fashioned militarism and nationalism. Edward Hulton joined forces with Priestley, and it was largely through their combined efforts that the 1941 Committee was born, out of which grew the radical 'Commonwealth Party' which contested (and won) a few Parliamentary seats during the war. Sir Richard Acland, the radical baronet who was to lead the Commonwealth Party and was later to become a Labour MP, summed up the convictions of this group and the ways in which they differed from Churchill's coalition Government in a letter he wrote to W. P. Crozier, editor of the *Manchester Guardian*, on December 9, 1940:

> It is all nonsense to think that the *only* thing this country has to do is to turn out war materials, build up terrific armed forces and so win a military victory...it just cannot work that way. Hitler is fighting with an idea. We must fight back with an idea...it is quite certain that we cannot hope to win without real support from the people on the continent and we will not get that support and in the way we need unless we stand for something which they can see is worthwhile. Today, it is assumed that those who speak of a New Order are stirring up trouble, disrupting unity...it is not true. In all these circumstances it is those who like to think that we can go right on with the war with nothing unchanged who are the traitors to our cause. They are snails leading us to failure.

As Britain stood alone from June 1940 to June 1941, this line of reasoning was appealing. Even after Russia entered the war in June 1941, neither Russia nor America was able to make any military impression on the Wehrmacht until the end of 1942. It was thus natural that the younger, progressive thinkers should cast around for an alternative strategy to ordinary military action. As David Astor described it, their aim was to broaden the war into "an international civil war conducted by the methods of total war, i.e., propaganda and fifth column activity as well as maximum output". Their criticism of Churchill was that he was "attempting to fight this war as though it were one of Marlborough's, i.e., by soldiers only".[3] The nascent 1941 Committee attracted not only those concerned with the Post-War Bureau, but also journalists such as Michael Foot (editor of the *Evening Standard* 1942—44 and a close family friend through his father Isaac Foot) and Philip Jordan (of the *News Chronicle*), and politicians such as Ellen Wilkinson and the famously charming and persuasive barrister Sir Walter Monckton (a close friend of Cripps and adviser to Edward VIII during the Abdication crisis).

This was an impressive array of people; but David Astor was soon questioning whether they could actually do anything. On December 19, 1940 he wrote to TJ expressing his dismay:

> The Priestley-Hulton committee has taken a turn for the worse — very distinctly the most active members of the Committee are, of course, the cranks and the doctrinaire, intellectual backwoodsmen. I mean Acland, Julian Huxley, Zilliacus, Balogh. Hulton himself has not shown practical commonsense, but quixotic enthusiasm and an immense ignorance of politics. Priestley is limited by his temperament (he is beginning to get peevish with those who don't accept his views in toto), by his prejudices (he believes a few, very few evil privileged capitalist aristocrats are at the back of all evil).

To create at least something out of the Priestley-Hulton committee, David proposed forming a "core of *sensible* 1941-ites which would operate separately from the Priestley-Hulton group". This core of like-minded thinkers was to provide the shock-troops of David Astor's revolution on the *Observer*. He saw that the 1941 Committee would not be able to achieve the end which he, displaying what was to become a highly cultivated sense of practical idealism, considered essential: "getting power for their ideas". In this he was right: the Commonwealth Party faded away as soon as the two-party system re-asserted itself in 1945. What was needed was a practical instrument for the expression of those ideas — a newspaper. In the new year David Astor turned his attention to

---

3. Acland to Crozier, December 9, 1940; *Guardian* Archive 145/40, John Rylands University Library of Manchester.

the *Observer*. In the letter to TJ criticizing the 1941 Committee he was already enlisting the great mandarin in his scheme to "begin the gradual change-over from the ancient regime to the one I hope some day to establish there".

The "core" of 1941-ers had already met for a weekend at Cliveden on November 30—December 2 to discuss their ideas. The names in the guest book for that weekend are Stephen King-Hall (editor of the anti-Nazi *King-Hall Newsletter*), Ronald Fredenburgh (a Canadian assistant editor of that *Newsletter*), Alastair Forbes (a writer whom David met on his first day with the Royal Marines in Portsmouth), General Mark McNaughton, Edward Hulton and Tom Hopkinson. Of those guests, Fredenburgh, Forbes and King-Hall, together with Michael Foot, were to be some of the new writers with which David Astor hoped to transform the *Observer*.

As has been noted, David Astor had deliberately kept away from the *Observer* throughout the 1930s, despite his interest in journalism. This was principally due to his instinctive mistrust of its famous but domineering editor, James Louis Garvin. Both Nancy and Lord Astor had been keen for David to go into the *Observer*, and Lord Astor in particular had tried to build bridges between him and Garvin. Writing to Garvin in 1937, Lord Astor had said:

> Do let me know what you think of David — I have always hoped that at some time he might train or come into the "Observer" — he went through a queer phase at Oxford — was v. socialistic (thank God he was not ultra Tory) — saw all the world's disappointments — now he is much more stable.[5]

These efforts were to no avail. However, by 1940 David Astor had both the confidence and the political purpose to try to encroach on Garvin's sacred territory. Once again, the impetus came from Trott. As David Astor put it to the author in 1990, "If Adam had the nerve to go back to Germany to fight for his ideas, the least I could do was to take on the *Observer* for those same ideas."

---

5. Lord Astor to J. L. Garvin, December 6, 1937; Garvin Papers, The University of Texas at Austin.

By 1940, Garvin was indeed a formidable figure, a Fleet Street institution. Editor of the *Observer* since 1908, he was not only the longest-serving editor in Fleet Street, but he dominated his paper in a way unmatched by any of his rivals. The *Observer* was Britain's oldest Sunday newspaper, having been founded in 1791 by W. S. Bourne. It had an undistinguished Victorian history, and by the turn of the century the proprietors, the Beer family, were looking around for another owner. It took them until May 1905 to find a purchaser. Sir Alfred Harmsworth, later Lord Northcliffe, a journalist of genius, was to say that he found the *Observer*, lying "derelict in the Fleet (Street) ditch". For the minuscule sum of £4,000 he bought a newspaper whose circulation oscillated between 2,000 and 4,000 a week and which was probably losing £15,000 a year. From the very start Northcliffe wanted Garvin to revitalize his new, but ailing, title, but he had to wait until 1908 before he got his man.

James Louis Garvin, born in 1868, had served a rigorous apprenticeship on the *Newcastle Chronicle* and as a leader-writer on the *Daily Telegraph*. He was a man of immense energy and industry with a near photographic memory and an enormous range of political, social and intellectual contacts, supremely confident of his own judgement. His relationship with Northcliffe, a man of equally strong views, was not likely to last and by 1911 editorial disagreements between the two led to Northcliffe's resignation from the paper. He gave Garvin three weeks to find a purchaser for the *Observer* — if he failed to do so Northcliffe would buy him out. Garvin found David's grandfather, as his White Knight. At the urging of his son Waldorf, William Waldorf bought the paper to add to the *Pall Mall Gazette*, for £45,000.

From the very start it was Waldorf Astor who took an interest in the paper, although he did not succeed his father as proprietor until 1919. It was in tandem with Waldorf Astor that Garvin enjoyed his golden age, increasing the circulation to 200,000 by the early 1920s. Indeed, it can be said that Garvin largely invented Sunday journalism. He described his own creation as "half a newspaper; half a magazine or serial".[6] Garvin's aim in journalism, like David Astor's, was to exercise influence amongst

---

6. Garvin notebook No. 88: Garvin Papers.

policy-makers and in the corridors of power. Under Garvin, the *Observer* achieved this influence by independent argument and criticism of a high order, most famously during the First World War. The Astors had bought the *Observer* not to make money, but, as Waldorf explained,

> to get certain things done [we] agree in fundamentals [that] to bring about what we want or believe in, some independent thought and the formation of sound opinion is essential. That is why I tried hard to get my father to purchase the Observer.[7]

Helped by a small but dedicated staff, Garvin made the *Observer* into a well-respected, influential paper. However, the First World War was his peak. From the mid-1920s onwards he not only mingled much less in political circles, but started to neglect the paper. This was mainly the result of his move to a new house, Gregories at Beaconsfield, formerly the residence of one of his great political heroes, Edmund Burke. Surrounded by a vast library, Garvin tried to edit the *Observer* from Gregories, twenty-four miles away from Whitehall, Westminster and Clubland – to say nothing of the paper itself, in Tudor Street. His physical distance was reflected in a gradual distancing of himself from new ideas and political personalities. David Ayerst, Garvin's biographer, has written that Tudor Street became "an outstation of his office.... [as] secretaries and messengers shuttled between Beaconsfield and London". John Stubbs, the paper's official historian, has written that by the mid-1930s, Garvin was "...a man living at the fringes of political influence – a man who hears only the echoes of his own voice and those of his friends of that generation".[8] Garvin added to his burdens by writing two volumes of a monumental three-volume biography of Joseph Chamberlain, which caused further neglect of his politicking and his journalism.

---

7. Lord Astor to J. L. Garvin, December 27, 1912; Garvin Papers.

8. Stubbs, *Appearance and Reality: a Case Study of the Observer and J. L. Garvin* in *Newspaper history from the 19th Century to the present day*, ed. J. Curran and G. Boyle, (London 1978).

In his heyday, Garvin's long, signed leader, the centrepiece of the *Observer*, was required reading for the politically aware. His clear, authoritative prose was somewhat rhetorical, but still the best editorial writing of its day. By the 1930s, however, as John Silverlight has observed, "the rhetoric was overshadowing the conviction...". Garvin had almost become a parody of himself. G. B. Shaw would talk to David Astor of "that mud Volcano".

Lord Astor was acutely conscious of the declining influence of the paper during the 1930s, but Garvin remained blissfully unaware of his fading powers. He became increasingly combative, self-important and opinionated as time went on — which led to increasingly acrimonious renegotiations of his contract with Waldorf Astor in 1929 and 1938. By 1940 he was seventy-two and his tiny staff had grown older with him, and smaller, but he still did nothing to prepare for the future of the *Observer*. Lord Astor, who was genuinely fond of him, tried by the gentlest of hints — such as getting Garvin to consult the physician, Lord Dawson of Penn — to make his editor aware of his own mortality. Garvin, however, treated such hints with imperial insensitivity. By May 2, 1940, Lord Astor was writing to TJ that his main aim on the *Observer* was:

> ...to keep JLG at work without a breakdown or backfire or misfire — it's a complicated bit of machinery — unlike the ordinary machinery — it's complicated further by age — health is a factor, as is mutual happiness — some parts of the machinery are now held together by bits of string — lately it has not slept well and is losing weight — I know by experience that if it gets out of gear or unbalanced things get much worse.... Suppose I were to force someone on to an unwilling G (or even David) the result might be totally inharmonious and unsuccessful....[9]

David, for his part, realized that Garvin could not share, or delegate, his responsibilities for the paper — which is why he had always kept away from it. To David, Garvin was making the *Observer* "moribund" and standing "in the way of all progress".

---

9. Lord Astor to TJ, May 2, 1940; Thomas Jones Papers.

Even before David had started writing for the paper in 1941, he was expressing his despair at "the old megalomaniac's behaviour" to TJ:

I find it impossible to achieve serious contact with him or the simplest degree of cooperation, no matter how patient I am. (My mother by the opposite technique is able to intimidate him momentarily but he returns to his old ways as soon as he's back at Gregories). The worst aspect of Garvin after his non-cooperativeness is his basic lack of principle. He changes his ground as shamelessly as Hitler but with this difference — he has no political objectives. His only purpose is to keep on with his Wagnerian outgoings. He never commits himself to anything beyond platitudes....[10]

Garvin's relationship with Lord Astor became even more strained in the late 1930s due to their first serious political disagreement, which concerned appeasement. Garvin has always been remembered as one of the cartoonist Low's famous "Shiver Sisters", dancing to the propaganda tune of Dr Goebbels. This is unfair. He was certainly an appeaser in the sense that he was highly critical of the Versailles Treaty and believed that if peace were to be preserved, the more punitive clauses of that treaty would have to be renegotiated — but he reached this conclusion, and worked for it, entirely independently, unlike some of his journalistic colleagues. And Lord Astor agreed with him until the Prime Minister, Neville Chamberlain, came back from his meeting with Hitler at Munich and announced that the meeting had ushered in a new era of European peace.

It was not that Garvin and Astor disagreed in their analysis of the situation. It was on the question of what ought to be done about it that they parted company. Astor looked on Munich as "a way to get out of a situation in which we have been caught unarmed", and thought Hitler had been revealed as nothing more that "a more heavily armed gangster", and Garvin shared this view. But whereas Astor reacted to the menace by pressing his political contacts to work for "a new and national government for

---

10. David Astor to TJ, August 8, 1941; Thomas Jones Papers.

defence with a striking programme for increased output and aero engines. . . to negotiate from strength", and urged Garvin to criticize the Chamberlain Government's deficiencies and complacency, Garvin insisted that to publish dissent in the midst of the tense situation of 1938—39 would be unpatriotic and could be exploited by the Germans. He knew the gravity of the crisis and the increasing unpopularity of Chamberlain in the country, but he was adamant that "it was not possible for us to enable the Germans to say or think that the PM has lost the confidence of the country and the nation is already split or splitting".[12] Editor and proprietor entered into an increasingly acrimonious correspondence, but Garvin refused to give way and Lord Astor had to look on impotently as the *Observer* supported Chamberlain right to the end, while the country went to its doom "united in silence".[13] The most that Astor could do was to use his Labour front-bench contacts to bring about some sort of political coalition against Chamberlain. Nancy Astor was one of the brave thirty-three Conservative MPs who voted against their party's three-line whip to bring about Chamberlain's downfall in the House of Commons on May 9, 1940. So much for the "Cliveden Set".

With the fall of Chamberlain and the arrival of Winston Churchill at 10 Downing Street the differences between Garvin and Astor increased. Garvin was a fervent supporter and lifelong friend of Churchill's and pledged the paper to unquestioning loyalty to the new Prime Minister, who was also Minister of Defence. This he did for much the same reasons as he had pledged undying loyalty to Chamberlain. Lord Astor, for his part, looked on the new administration with some dismay. Like many in the Conservative Party he had always wanted Halifax to succeed Chamberlain. He did not harbour any personal antipathy towards Churchill, but like many who had been schooled in the traditions of tidy, orderly Whitehall methods of government he was shocked by Churchill's assumption of near-dictatorial powers, and his way of riding roughshod over the finer points of cabinet government. In particular, Astor was troubled by the influx of buccaneering "irregulars" into Churchill's government: men like Brendan Bracken, Beaverbrook

---

12. Garvin to Lord Astor, July 10, 1939; Garvin Papers.

13. Astor to Garvin, May 3, 1940; Garvin Papers.

and Professor Lindemann. He would probably have agreed with another critic, Geoffrey Dawson of *The Times*, that with the departure of Lord Halifax to Washington in December 1940 the Government was reduced to "thugs and under-secretaries".[14] Once again, Lord Astor's doubts were shared by most of the press, but Garvin refused even to discuss them in the paper — unlike *The Times*, which began to regain some of the prestige lost through its blind pursuit of appeasement by its constructive criticism of the Government. Astor urged Garvin to "help Winston by constructive criticism"[15], but his editor construed this as "anti-Churchill". As the succession of British military failures continued through 1941, so Astor's frustration with Garvin mounted. The disasters in Greece, Crete and Libya continued through the early summer, and on July 31 Astor tried for the last time to use the paper to call for Government reconstruction and improvements in civil defence, munitions production and the quality of cabinet government. Yet again Garvin took no notice of him. By the beginning of August 1941 they were no longer on speaking terms.

Lord Astor was thus in a particularly receptive frame of mind in the spring of 1941 when David suggested to him a new feature for the *Observer*. A new column, "Forum", would be written by his "core" group of the 1941 Committee, and would express their ideas on how the war should be run. The central idea of "Forum" was to allow David's group of young writers to describe the new methods of war that were being neglected. The "Forum" had to

> preach the gospel of modern war. . . the actual business of making a modern army and above all, we must preach the word that this is no nationalist war but a crusade against a particular evil — a civil war with German enemies and German friends, English enemies and English friends, etc. Until this certain truth about the war is understood we will not have a chance of arriving at the new political creed which is needed to extirpate Fascism in the world.

---

14. Dawson Diary, May 13, 1940; Dawson Papers, Bodleian Library Oxford.

15. Astor to Garvin, June 21, 1941; Garvin Papers.

David found a willing convert to his ideas in his father, who had also, of course, sympathized with the position of Adam von Trott. Although David was still on Hayling Island, he went up to Cliveden and 4 St James's Square as often as possible. Lord Astor was becoming interested in the radical policies and ideas that were circulating in political circles — he was to become a staunch proponent of such reforming legislation as that proposed in the Beveridge Report — so he was naturally attracted to the youthful radicalism of David and his friends. The special bond between Waldorf and David became stronger, and increasingly important to the latter because Waldorf was an enthusiastic backer not only of David's political ideas but also of his ideas for the *Observer*. Waldorf was the key to the *Observer*, and his natural political sympathies would always lie more with David than with his more conservative brothers — or with Nancy. By April 1941, Waldorf was writing to Garvin in very un-Waldorf-like manner that the war "was no longer the Battle of Britain...it's the battle of the World. Will the USA realise this in time...this is a world conflict between the irreconcilable conceptions of Government or 'order' — the ideologies or philosophies of Democracy (liberty) and Dictatorship (tyranny)...".[16]

David's influence over his father was to be of enormous importance not only to the *Observer* but to the Astor family. For his elder brother Bill had fully been expecting to conduct the affairs of the *Observer*, but was in the Middle East during these crucial years, 1940–43. On his return to England Bill wrote to TJ in 1943 that his father had "seldom asked his views on any political subject" since he had arrived back — "...although he often sends me his which are often David's in origin".[17] As David and Waldorf moved to the "left" during the war, Bill — and Nancy even more — moved to the "right": and the *Observer* became something of a family battleground in-between.

On May 12, 1941, Lord Astor wrote to Garvin informing him that he should find space for articles of about 800 words below his own leader-page article. David wrote to Garvin to reassure him

---

16. Lord Astor to Garvin, April 22, 1941; Garvin Papers.

17. "Bill" Astor to TJ, April 7, 1943; Thomas Jones Papers.

that these "Forum" articles would be written by those "younger men who have been showing outstanding merit in thinking out the intellectual and internal political problems that face us and who have most successfully studied the enemy's methods. I want to get the cream of their thinking for the *Observer* and to give prominence to their vitally important subject."[18]

An initial list of subjects to be printed by the "Forum" included:

1. "Public Opinion"   by Tom Harrisson (founder of *Mass Observation*)
2. "Radio Power"   by Francis Williams
3. "Party Politics"   by Richard Crossman
4. "Martial Civilians"   by Stephen King-Hall
5. "Modern Guerrillas"   by Tom Wintringham
6. "Age and Leadership"   by Edward Hulton
7. "Anglo-Russian Politics" by Michael Foot

All these writers were young and working in the field of propaganda or journalism. Tom Wintringham had been a commander of the International Brigade in Spain, Crossman was deeply involved in "Black Propaganda" work for the Government and Francis Williams was in the Ministry of Information. The first "Forum" appeared on June 15; "Civil Defence", by TJ. Some of the "Forum" articles were initialled, others were completely anonymous. In the end many of them, eleven in all, were written by David Astor himself. The second "Forum" came out on June 22, written by David Astor, entitled the "Task of Propaganda", and on June 29 the direct influence of Cripps was apparent in the "Forum" entitled "The Four Fronts", which was written by Forbes after a lengthy conversation with Cripps at his Whitehall flat. Cripps divided the war front into four spheres — the strategic front, the home front, the propaganda front and the diplomatic front. Of these Churchill was interested only in the first front; it was the other three that Cripps and his young disciples on the "Forum" felt they should be addressing. The main administration of "Forum" was left to TJ (who had much influence on Lord Astor at this time) and to the invaluable Miss Kindersley, Lord Astor's personal assistant, a director of the *Observer* and the sister of the 1st Baron Kindersley.

---

18. David Astor to Garvin, May 26, 1941; Garvin Papers.

At first the "Forum" seemed to work well. David Astor wrote to Miss Kindersley: "I am terribly proud of the Forum to date (and I think Papa is too). Even the old ogre of Beaconsfield has been saying some reasonably nice things about it. . . ." The "ogre" of Beaconsfield did indeed *seem* to welcome "Forum" and even entertained David and what he liked to call David's "set" to lunch at the Ivy Restaurant in London. He wrote to Lord Astor: "As David and I get more accustomed to each other, his letters and surveys begin to impress me in a curious way. I have the feeling that he is growing every day and that he has the makings of a remarkable man. . . ."[19] Privately, however, Garvin saw the whole thing as an anti-Churchill ramp by the Astors, interpreting the "Forum" topics as anti-Churchill in an almost paranoid manner. On his own copy of the proposed "Forum" article "On Age and Leadership" by Hulton he wrote:

> Winston 67 30th November next. He is going to have more power than ever. He may select his own young men.
> Over 70 — Palmerston, Dizzy, Gladstone, Clemenceau, Bismarck.

Next to "The Modern Empire" he merely scribbled, "anti-Churchill" together with most of the others — relenting at the end by writing next to the proposed "One Man War", "Anti-Churchill?"

He was rather more frank in the privacy of his own notebook, writing of the ". . . carpers, crabbers, grousers, disappointed prigs-pedants, meddlers, moon-struck dreamers about war aims. The people who don't lift a finger to fight but are really skulkers in uniform."[20]

The inevitable collision came on August 24 when Garvin rejected a "Forum" article by Alastair Forbes on the subject of Anglo-American relations. He found Forbes's article ". . . an impossible contribution" on a number of grounds, not least because, in his view, the article would have caused a "rash injury to Anglo-American relations and a direct offence to President Roosevelt".[21]

---

19. Garvin to Lord Astor, June 3, 1941; Garvin Papers.

20. Garvin Notebook No. 78, 1942; Garvin Papers.

21. "Statement read to Miss Kindersley over the 'phone'", August 25, 1941; Garvin Papers.

Garvin described Forbes's article to David as "trash", a judgement reinforced by the poor personal impression that Forbes had made on Garvin. Forbes's article was undoubtedly a little unwise in its criticism of America, at one point asking for a declaration of war to prove to the British and Russians that America was serious about achieving "maximum production" for those two countries. But it is hard to see why this phrase could not just have been cut out. Probably of more concern to Garvin was the danger that Forbes's article represented to his own monopoly on the general surveys of the war situation. As Miss Kindersley put it to TJ, "I am afraid we are going to have a very difficult time with J. L. G...."[22]

The "Forum" resumed on August 31 with "Party Politics" by Stephen King-Hall, but relations between the two sides were now conducted in an atmosphere of barely concealed hostility. This atmosphere was worsened by the fact that Garvin's contract ran out on March 1, 1942. As he had done before, Lord Astor convened a tribunal to renegotiate his contract. The "tribunal" was a unique institution invented by Lord Astor over the years to handle negotiations between himself and Garvin over Garvin's contract. In setting it up Lord Astor sacrificed considerable proprietorial power by putting the responsibility for the negotiations in the hands of — usually — three independent "experts". This time, however, the word tribunal merited its slightly sinister overtones: the ensuing discussions, which lasted for five months, were conducted in an atmosphere of considerable hostility and bitterness. The tribunal this time was composed of Geoffrey Dawson (the editor of *The Times* who had retired from that position in September 1941), Sir Edward Grigg (an old friend of the Astors and a Conservative MP and minister), and Arthur Mann, David Astor's old editor on the *Yorkshire Post*, who was invited by Garvin to represent his interests. Throughout the winter of 1941—42 these three toiled away — Dawson and Mann were both a good deal less than fully fit — to find some common ground between Garvin and Lord Astor.

Lord Astor put it to the tribunal that due to Garvin's age and his neglect of the paper, he should relinquish some of his power in

---

22. Miss Kindersley to TJ, August 29, 1941; Thomas Jones Papers.

preparation for the future. Due to a clause in an earlier contract, Lord Astor was obliged to retain his services on the paper for life, so he proposed that Garvin should accept an associate editor who would be responsible for running the paper and its policy, apart from Garvin's signed leader-page article. Lord Astor later recounted what happened next: "When, however, I put forward my proposals for reforms he reacted very badly and almost drove the Tribunal off their heads." Lord Astor genuinely wanted to retain his services, which he valued, but Garvin refused to accept any encroachment on his authority. Furthermore, although Lord Astor was proposing reform principally for sound journalistic reasons, Garvin saw the confrontation as a straight political duel between himself, representing Churchill, and the anti-Churchillian Astors. At least, this is how he tried to tell it to the Churchillians who rallied to his side. Brendan Bracken, Churchill's "faithful Chela" urged Garvin to stiffen his sinews for the forthcoming battle:

> It would take a lot more than the decadent descendants of Wall Street toughs to fray your nerves. Stand like the rock you are, always remembering your friends are more embittered than you could ever be by the way you have been treated. You made the "Observer" and in good times also a lot of money for the Shareholders....[23]

Garvin's memos to the tribunal became increasingly shrill, almost hysterical, until he was accusing Lord Astor of trying to run "an autocracy in detail" on the paper, and "trying the rather Nazified procedure of treating my instinct for responsible editorship as a 'scrap of paper'...."[24] David Astor, for his part, supported his father's position, although he was not involved in the detailed arguments of the tribunal. His own submission to the tribunal supported the idea that Garvin should stay, but made it clear that the old man would only "be able to assist them if he assumes the role of elder Statesman in the affairs of the paper. If he were to be relieved of the very onerous organisational duties which he now fulfils and thereby were free to devote himself to writing and

---

23. Bracken to Garvin, November 4, 1941; Garvin Papers.

24. Garvin to Astor, August 14, 1941; Garvin Papers.

advising on general policy. This should be an advantage to the paper and Mr Garvin." This is not what Garvin had in mind at all, for he remained blithely unaware of the need for any transitional period ahead. However, much to Lord Astor's surprise, the tribunal inched towards a compromise whereby Garvin would retain the title of editor-in-chief, and continue writing, while relinquishing the day-to-day political control to an associate editor. This was, in fact, a very unsatisfactory compromise, inviting endless disagreements on matters of policy on the leader-page between Garvin's piece and the other, anonymous, leading articles. The tribunal edged towards a resolution in February 1942, but Lord Astor, as he later recalled, still could not quite believe that a new contract would really be signed. He was right.

It was over a matter of policy that Garvin's editorship came to an end at the end of February. Lord Astor had always argued that Churchill's system of highly personalized administration was unwieldy and ineffective. As a member of Lloyd George's cabinet secretariat, Astor was a firm believer in a small non-departmental War Cabinet on Lloyd George lines. This was a sentiment shared by many other observers of Churchill's government, but with Lord Astor it was part of a wider critique of the Government that he increasingly shared with David Astor and Stafford Cripps. Garvin was well aware of his proprietor's views, and Lord Astor made them quite plain in a letter on this subject to *The Times* in May 1941. Needless to say, Garvin dismissed Lord Astor's idea for a small War Cabinet as nothing more than part of an anti-Churchill plot, and wrote an article in the *Observer* in October rejecting his proprietor's views. Lord Astor drew the attention of the tribunal to this public rejection of his views. Just as Garvin looked to his past contracts to protect his association for life with the *Observer*, so Lord Astor drew the tribunal's attention to a clause in the 1929 contract stipulating that the "editor will... conform to the general lines and instructions...laid down and given by the Chairman of Directors [i.e. Lord Astor] as to the general policy to be pursued and advocated by the *Observer*". So Garvin was being warned, although Astor took the matter no further at the time. Garvin chose to ignore the incident, to his cost.

At the beginning of 1942 the war situation was at its bleakest.

After the series of defeats in 1941, the first few weeks of 1942 saw the rapid Japanese conquest of the British South-East Asian empire, culminating in the surrender of Singapore, probably the most severe humiliation in the history of the British Army. Add to that the sinking of HMS *Repulse* and HMS *Prince of Wales* in the East and the successful "channel dash" of the *Scharnhorst* and the *Gneisenau* in the English Channel, and it was not surprising that a feeling of anger and alarm began to grip Westminster. All the old doubts about Churchill's government began to surface again, and on February 15 the *Observer* published a "Forum" article by King-Hall called "What's Wrong", urging radical reform, and in particular the resignation of Churchill as Minister of Defence. This was written in consultation with Astor himself, as Garvin was duly informed. The piece was uncompromising:

> ...In this critical moment in our history we have not got a PRIME Minister. That office has been swallowed up and eclipsed by our energetic and pugnacious Minister of Defence.
>
> Mr Churchill must make the great personal sacrifice of abandoning the congenial task of Minister of Defence and devote his great talents to the job of being Prime Minister. Then he will be able to attend to the Home Front and inspire it with his own great qualities...The essential reform of a segregation of Prime Minister and Minister of Defence having been brought about, the way would be clear for a great crusade on the Home Front, a crusade which would include something more definite about war-aims as well as a tough but equitable wages policy.

However, the very next Sunday, February 22, Garvin chose to devote most of his own article to contradicting every idea in the previous week's "Forum". To ask Churchill to resign his main function as Minister of Defence was "an impossible proposition". He also advocated the return of Beaverbrook to the War Cabinet (he had recently been dropped in a reshuffle), knowing full well that Lord Astor was virulently opposed to such a course of action. In fact, the whole piece was a spectacular rebuttal of virtually every criticism that Lord Astor had ever made of Churchill's Government. Lord Astor was at Cliveden on the Sunday, and David Astor, who also happened to be there, could remember his father descending the stairs in a very dark mood and merely saying that this was "surely a breach of the contract". Lord Astor immediately wrote to the tribunal that it was now "impossible" to go on with the new contract, and Sir Edward Grigg was obliged to ask for Garvin's resignation. Garvin did not even bother to dispute the matter, perhaps conscious of the fact that he could not have expected a very sympathetic hearing from the exhausted Mann, Dawson and Grigg. He cleared his desk in midweek. His contract ran out on Saturday, February 28, and the following day's *Observer* appeared untouched by the guiding hand of Garvin for the first time since 1908.

The break between Astor and Garvin was painful on both sides. Garvin felt his life's work had been betrayed and there is no doubt that he received a sympathetic hearing in 10 Downing Street. Indeed, it is the view of Sir Edward Grigg's son, John Grigg, that Churchill held Grigg responsible for Garvin's downfall and thus excluded him from the Government until 1944. The Astors also suspected Garvin's malign influence when they tried to secure the release from Whitehall of a Treasury civil servant, Sir Wilfred Eady, to take over as editor later in 1942, and Eady's release was blocked. For Lord Astor's part, the struggle with Garvin was a severe drain on an already fragile constitution, which must have contributed to a mild heart attack that he suffered in the spring of 1941. The two never spoke to one another again. Garvin wrote, rather unsuccessfully, for Beaverbrook's *Sunday Express* for a while and then enjoyed a brief Indian Summer on the *Daily Telegraph* towards the end of the war. David Ayerst, his biographer, records that in 1946, the year before he died, Garvin was dining at a dinner of the Other Club at the Savoy and saw Lord Astor. He "went up to shake hands. Waldorf welcomed the gesture. Garvin drove home to Gregories and told Ursula (his youngest daughter): 'I think he meant it.' Waldorf did."

4

David Astor and the Transformation of the Observer

The departure of Garvin in such a precipitate manner threw the paper into chaos. As Lord Astor later recalled, he had made contingency plans for just such an eventuality, but these plans did not work out. "I had previously warned Geoffrey Dawson and Arthur Mann...that in case of a breakdown in the negotiations, I should look to one of them to help me editorially. Unfortunately, when the break finally came, they were both seriously ill."[1] The *Observer* was thus left with no editor and a tiny editorial staff consisting of Garvin's eldest daughter, Viola, the news editor Ronald Harmer and J. C. Trewin, a sub-editor and a very fine writer. It was perfectly natural that David Astor, having already contributed to the paper so much, should fill the vacuum; and it was in the chaotic weeks following Garvin's departure that David, still only twenty-nine, began to refashion the paper and earn his spurs as the editor-in-waiting of the post-war *Observer*.

Luckily he had managed to obtain a transfer from Hayling Island to London, where he joined Lord Mountbatten's new Combined Operations Headquarters at Richmond Terrace as press officer. He saw no action in this capacity: the four Commando

---

1. Lord Astor Memo, September 1, 1952; David Astor Papers.

cross-Channel raids he was attached to were all called off at the last moment. In London, he devoted all his spare time — which was often little more than a lunch-hour — to rescuing the *Observer*.

The first task was to find a temporary editor and here the Astors were lucky, because Geoffrey Crowther of the *Economist* agreed to help out on the first post-Garvin issue at very short notice. During the next few weeks Crowther and Barbara Ward, his colleague on the *Economist*, filled the role. Crowther came in and worked in the editor's office after editing the *Economist*. He wrote mainly the domestic political commentary, while Barbara Ward wrote the foreign editorials. TJ came to David's rescue by recruiting the authoritative Oxford historian G. M. Young (author of the widely praised *Victorian England: Portrait of an Age*) to write the leader-page article, which had always been Garvin's speciality. Young and David Astor would meet weekly, normally in Young's club, the Athenaeum, to discuss these articles.

Barbara Ward and Geoffrey Crowther were part of a vigorous journalistic culture that flourished in London during the war. They were both young and believed in the progressive political thinking of wartime Britain. They advocated a "peaceful revolution" in domestic politics after the war, producing a Welfare State and increased central government planning. They thus supported the Beveridge Report and nationalization of certain industries. This, in general, became the creed of a young generation of journalists who called themselves "Socialists" or "Progressive Tories" and who reflected and championed the gradual leftward shift of British wartime society as a whole. David Astor became closely connected with this group of journalists, not least through his membership of the "Shanghai Club". Named after a Soho restaurant, this was an informal dining club started by Edward Hulton and Gerald Barry, which met every Tuesday to discuss politics. It was composed of most of the younger left-wing journalists in London, many of whom worked for the *Economist*, *The Times*, the *News Chronicle* and the *Observer*. It was at the Shanghai that the communality of political feeling was built up that made the transfer of journalistic talent from paper to paper so easy, making it a useful recruiting ground for David Astor's *Observer*. The star attraction was probably E. H. Carr, the brilliant, academic Russophile assistant editor of *The Times* who was blamed by many for turning the organ of the establishment into "The Threepenny *Daily Worker*" during the war. Other regulars at the Shanghai included Barbara Ward, Crowther, Geoffrey Wilson (a Foreign Office official, and close confidant of Cripps), David Owen (Cripps's personal secretary), Norman Luher (of the BBC Talks department), Ronald Fredenburgh, Tom Hopkinson, Frank Pakenham (David's old family friend and secretary to Sir William Beveridge), Dennis Routh and P. Smollett (of the Ministry of Information), Ted Castle (news editor of the *Daily Mirror*) and Donald Tyerman (deputy editor of the *Economist* and later a key figure on the *Observer*). Sebastian Haffner, George Orwell, Jon Kimche, Isaac Deutscher and John Strachey, all to be intimately associated with the *Observer* and all of whom David met outside the Shanghai, also belonged to the club. The Shanghai's most famous meeting witnessed a ferocious argument between Guy Burgess, arguing an anti-communist line, and Isaac Deutscher, a redoubtable anti-Stalinist, arguing a communist one!

Both inside the Shanghai Club and outside it, David now demonstrated his principal attribute as an editor, his flair as a talentscout. His unique quality in this capacity was simple: he was looking for writers rather than journalists. Garvin's *Observer* was known for Garvin's own political writing, but David wished the new *Observer* to be known for its writers in the plural. Good writing was his chief criterion. He believed that carefully chosen *writers* would produce the fresh ideas and philosophies that the *Observer* — and the war — needed, and that they would learn to be journalists — a new kind of journalist — as they wrote. *Horizon*, the cultural magazine started by Cyril Connolly at the beginning of the war, was to some extent his model.

One of the first writers that David Astor found was Sebastian Haffner, who came to his attention through his book *Germany Jekyll and Hyde*, published by Secker and Warburg in 1940. The book, an account of Hitler's rise to power and his relationship with the German people, is still one of the best ever written about Hitler. For David Astor, Haffner's essential insight was that the Nazis, for all their apparent powers, were alien to the real nature of Germany, and that Germany was an organic community that would continue to exist despite Nazism and would have rights, like other nations, despite the sins of the Nazis. His message was much the same as Trott's, that the Germans were as much a "conquered" people as the French or the Dutch, and that the

British could — and must — appeal to the conquered Germans in the same way as they appealed to the French Resistance. In one of his most telling passages Haffner wrote:

> The Nazi leaders from the outset have ruled over Germany not as their Fatherland feeling the beat of its pulse and understanding its weaknesses, yearning to save the country they love. They have treated Germany like a conquered land, a colony to be used and abused without consideration. . . . The ground is not unprepared for a recognition of the fact that the Nazis are no patriots, that they do not work for Germany, that they are active nihilists and are consciously leading Germany into the abyss of nothingness. However, to cultivate it the statesmen outside Germany must themselves have perceived the fact. I am not quite sure that they have everywhere done so.

David, enthused by Haffner's remarks on the potential for propaganda, got his address from Secker and Warburg and found him to be a journalist working for a pittance on a British-backed German newspaper, who came from Berlin (although ethnically he was a Wend, a Slavonic tribe which existed in the middle of Prussia). Haffner's wife was Jewish, so they had to leave Germany. He could not write under his real name — Raimund Pretzel — because he still had family there. He took his pseudonym from his favourite composer J. Sebastian Bach, and his favourite piece of music, Mozart's Haffner symphony. He was still very German, with quite a thick accent, but David was attracted to his quiet sense of humour and the way he "did not take himself too seriously". The two became close friends, and Astor would often eat with Haffner's family in Wimbledon.

For someone in Haffner's position, working for the *Observer* was a great opportunity. His first article for the paper was a "Forum" article on mass politics, published in 1941, which argued for a propaganda offensive against the Nazis in Germany. When Garvin left, Haffner was taken on full-time and was soon writing leader-page pieces as "Liberator," as well as several of the new "Profile" features and some leaders. He would later write his column under the pseudonym "Student of Europe". He quickly established himself as the intellectual backbone of the paper. He was essentially a historian by training, and — unlike the other

Observer writers — a conservative in politics, although he normally presented a historical and philosophical perspective on current affairs that made the artificial division of left/right politics meaningless. He was a teacher and friend to David, and exercised considerable influence over the Astor household because Lord Astor became just as much his admirer as David was, and would often invite him to Cliveden for conversation. (Nancy Astor was not so fond of him, preferring Adam von Trott, the man of action.)

Another writer recruited at this time, who was to have less of an effect on the *Observer* but more on David, was George Orwell. As with Haffner, David was attracted to Orwell through his writing, particularly a celebrated essay called "The Lion and the Unicorn", written in 1940, expressing the character of the English at war. David secured an introduction to him through Cyril Connolly in the spring of 1941. They met in a café near the BBC off Portland Place, where Orwell was then working on broadcasts to India. David had never seen Orwell but recognized him at once: the truthfulness and simplicity evident in his writing were also visible in the man himself. Talking to him came as a surprising relief to the rather shy and diffident David, because Orwell was a man who put people at their ease almost immediately. They quickly became friends, recognizing each other's directness and simplicity, and David seeing him as an intellectual guide and companion. Much as Trott had given David political purpose, so Orwell showed him how to *express* and *articulate* that political purpose. After Trott, Orwell must have been the second most influential person in his life.

Orwell's sister Avril once said that the sort of person he admired most was the working-class mother of eight children; a comment revealing a straightforwardness that was notably absent from the other "intellectuals" of his generation. Unlike Haffner, Orwell was a socialist, but he was not a dogmatist or an ideologue. He was essentially a sceptic and a questioner, and this is what attracted David to long evenings at Orwell's Belsize Park flat, where he would often stay overnight during the black-out. They would have long discussions about politics and the war. Orwell's main interest at the time was India, for he was an anti-colonialist ahead of his time, partly as a result of his own experiences of Imperial rule in Burma; and it was on the subject of India that he made his first contribution of the *Observer* in the shape of a "Forum" article called "India Next" on February 22, 1942. This "Forum" appeared just below J. L. Garvin's last explosive article for the *Observer*; the whole page was thus an excellent, if unintentional juxtaposition of Britain's old, Imperial, Churchillian past and her new post-colonial future. In February 1942 Britain was finely poised between the two — but the future belonged to Orwell and Astor, not to Garvin and Churchill.

"India Next" argued for Indian independence as a part of Britain's war aims, and was, perhaps, the first article of the *Observer's* long campaign under David Astor against colonialism. It was Orwell who made David aware of the full importance of this, at that time neglected, subject. Orwell went on to write regularly for the paper, mainly book reviews but occasional editorial and "feature" pieces as well. His major journalistic contribution was to *Tribune*, the left-wing weekly, where he wrote the column "As I please". His contribution to the *Observer* was as much in his influence upon the young editor-to-be as in his actual writing for the paper. The nature of this influence and their friendship is more fully explained at the end of this chapter.

Another recruit from *Tribune* who was to become an *Observer* wartime contributor was Jon Kimche. Kimche was a Swiss of Jewish background whose family had emigrated to Britain at the end of the First World War, when he was aged twelve. A left-wing intellectual, he fought in the Spanish Civil War, where he met Orwell. Later he ran a celebrated left-wing bookshop, the *Socialist Bookcentre* off Fleet Street, which became a prominent meeting and discussion centre for the British left. At the beginning of the war he started work for the *Evening Standard*, then edited by Frank Owen, writing as the paper's military correspondent. At the same time he was also filling in as editor of *Tribune*. In March 1942, David walked into his bookshop with an introduction from Tosco Fyvel, a friend of Orwell's, to ask Kimche whether he could help out at the *Observer*, "as everyone had walked out". This was, of course, a slight exaggeration, but when Kimche arrived at the *Observer* he did indeed find the situation chaotic, with no editorial meetings at all, and a new editor almost every week. Haffner joked to David that when he first walked into the paper's offices in 1942 it reminded him of the Japanese entering Singapore — they entered with awe, but there was no one there to resist. Kimche immediately became the military correspondent, and in 1943 started the famous "Liberator" column (under which pseudonym Haffner also wrote). Although Kimche and Haffner differed politically, the column worked because Haffner wrote from a broad philosophical – historical point of view, while Kimche wrote from a strictly strategic point of view. They were both arguing on the same theme, but with the crucial difference that, as Kimche told the author, "Haffner was liberating Europe from the right, while I was liberating Europe from the left". Kimche, a gentle, thoughtful man, was surely unique in journalism in having worked for Astor, Beaverbrook and Nye Bevan simultaneously. It was also Kimche who introduced John Beavan, later Lord Ardwick, to the paper in 1942. Beavan became news editor and chief sub-editor of the paper and supervised the switching of news on to the front page in August 1942.

A surprise recruit to the paper at this time was Isaac Deutscher, who got to know David through Barbara Ward. A correspondent for the *Economist*, Deutscher was also writing under the pseudonym Major Rabski in *Tribune*. A Marxist intellectual, he was born a Jew in 1907 at Krakow in Poland and joined the Communist Party in 1927. In 1932 he was expelled from the Party for opposing the contemporary Stalinist alliance with the Nazis in Germany against the so-called "Social Fascists" (the German Social Democrats) – a piece of Stalinist *real politik* which was to have fatally injurious results for the Communists. He came to London in 1939 and built a reputation as the most famous Marxist anti-Stalinist writer of his generation, realizing earlier than most that Stalinism was a corruption of communism. He was also a gifted writer and began working for the *Observer* in 1943. In April 1945 he started a column called "Peregrine's European Notebook". Deutscher's own slogan for this column was "views not news", and the mysterious Peregrine's powerful views became widely quoted. Deutscher's Polish accent was as strong as Haffner's German accent, but while Haffner remained very German (speaking German at home), Deutscher integrated much more and spoke English a good deal. He was aggressively intellectual, quite without the sense of humour which leavened Haffner's seriousness.

Naturally it was the competition between Haffner and Deutscher that dominated the *Observer* office in the years 1943–46, after which Deutscher left the paper to pursue his book writing. Both were men of strong conviction, with irreconcilable "world views", as circumstances then stood. Deutscher was more of a dogmatist, writing from a Trotskyist, anti-Stalinist viewpoint, whilst Haffner, a much more flexible thinker, basically viewed the world through a more sceptical, analytical prism, but was principally a conservative. It was a measure of David Astor's breadth of vision that he could accommodate both men on the paper at the same time. This tolerance of conflicting views was, indeed, to become one of the hallmarks of the *Observer* under David Astor. Unlike many editors, he was never afraid to admit to doubt over an issue, rather than lay down the law in a Garvinesque manner. Thus, when Haffner and Deutscher could not be reconciled over the British intervention on the side of the monarchist forces during the Greek Civil War in December 1944, they were invited to publish the "case for" and "case against" intervention side by side on the leader page. Arguing for intervention against Greek Communist guerrillas Haffner (anonymously of course) argued that:

> This war would not advance the cause of democracy if we allowed left tyrannies simply to take the place of right tyrannies.

Whilst Deutscher, in the case against, argued that:

> ...the events that preceded the Athens disaster speak loudly in favour of the defendant, the Greek left.... In this civil war the aggression is not on the left but on the right....

This pair of articles, giving a choice of views in a genuinely difficult matter, was highly popular with the readers.

These writers were joined by others who were to become important components of the mature *Observer*. Donald Tyerman, crippled as a boy by polio, came as assistant editor from 1943—45 to help on the home political side. Two other very important men were "Fritz" Schumacher and Willi Guttman. Guttman had been employed as a radio listener for the "Europe Study Group" by David, but in December 1941, after a period of internment, he was invited to work on the *Observer* with the title of "assistant foreign editor" — slightly spurious, as Garvin did not have a foreign editor. He continued his monitoring duties and wrote a column under the title "A Listener" summarizing Axis broadcasting. His material was later embellished by Haffner and formed the core of a column called "Voice of the Axis", which became a regular feature until the end of the war. In 1942 he became the paper's librarian, a post he held until 1965. He was much more than a librarian, and has been better described as the backroom researcher "who started hares for the hounds to follow". With his encyclopaedic knowledge and warm, humorous personality he was, for most journalists, the core of the paper.

Schumacher began writing for the paper at the same time. He had been a Rhodes Scholar at Oxford in the year before Trott. David first met him on the football field at New College. Schumacher was both brilliant and original but did not enjoy Oxford at all. As he was later to write:

> Oxford has much of beauty and interest to recommend it but
> I fear that it damned easily leads one to intellectual enervation.

In Germany he worked as an economist, but being a fervent anti-Nazi left his country for London in 1937. Like many other foreign anti-Nazis he was interned in the summer of 1940. David came to his rescue, getting him a farm labourer's job on his Uncle Bob Brand's estate at Eydon in Northamptonshire after only a few months of internment. Brand, a Fellow of All Souls and an economist of considerable standing, took to Schumacher and was partly responsible for getting him a job at the Oxford Institute of Statistics in March 1942; Brand also had to vouch for Schumacher's credentials at Eydon as on one occasion suspicious local villagers threatened to denounce the German "farm labourer" in their midst as a spy. In 1943 Schumacher began submitting articles on economic subjects to the *Observer*. Although his ability as a writer in English was questionable, with a strong sub-editor he made a very valuable intellectual addition to the new *Observer* team. As a mark of his worth, Sir William Beveridge took him on as his economic assistant (on the recommendation of Frank Pakenham and David Astor) to write his 1944 *Report on Full Employment*. David Astor and Donald Tyerman both hoped that Schumacher would become one of the main planks in the post-war *Observer*, but at the end of the war decided he did not want the "semi-responsibility" of journalism and took a full-time economics post with the newly created National Coal Board.

Another émigré who joined the paper in 1944, to write about Spanish affairs, was Rafael Nadal, formerly a lecturer in Spanish at King's College, London. Spain was then of considerable interest to the British war effort, and Nadal adopted a challenging attitude towards Franco and was later one of the first correspondents to argue for a return of the monarchy to achieve a peaceful transition from Franco's Fascism.

This influx of new talent had a dramatic, almost revolutionary, effect on the *Observer*. By the end of 1942 it was already a very different paper from the one that Garvin had presided over. The "Forum" articles, now otiose, finished in June 1942, but there were many new features that marked the difference in the paper. As well as Haffner's and Kimche's "Liberator", Deutscher's "Peregrine" and Guttman's "Voice of the Enemy", David introduced a feature called "Mood of the Moment", a three-hundred-word essay in Mass Observation style on the state of morale in both Britain and Germany. The first "Mood" was written by George Orwell and the second by Sebastian Haffner — on fears in both Germany and Britain about the prospects of defeat. Another important feature introduced at this time, which was to become the most famous hallmark of the *Observer*, was the "Profile". This was a new idea in English journalism, borrowed by David from the rather longer *New Yorker* profiles of the time. The first "Profile" in the *Observer* was of the new War Minister, Sir James Grigg, by Lionel Fielden. Fielden, together with Forbes and Fredenburgh, was one of the original "Forum" writers who continued doing occasional pieces of writing for the paper after March 1942. This "Profile" appeared on March 1, and was followed on March 15 by a "Profile" of Sir Stafford Cripps, the *Observer*'s politician of the moment after his return from the British Embassy in Moscow in February 1942. The master of the genre soon proved to be Haffner, who could write with a detailed and very human understanding of individuals which was quite masterly. In his "Profile" of Hitler, entitled "The Crank", of May 3, 1942, he looked at Hitler from an entirely novel, psychological angle:

> The crank in his unhappy youth knocked at many doors; and was always refused. He tried his hand as an artist, but his sunsets in aquarelle did not sell. He worked on a building site, but was refused the fraternity of his fellow workers because he drank milk instead of beer, and made crankish speeches. He joined the army, but never got further than his

first stripe. He lived in Salvation Army shelters, under bridge-vaults, and in casual wards: he mixed with the *Lumpen-proletariat*, the nomadic outcasts in the no-man's-land society. This period lasted for several years; it was a unique experience for a future statesman.... He divined that the mentality of the crowd is not the sum total of the mentality of the individuals which form it, but their lowest common denominator: that their intellectual powers are not integrated by contact but bewildered by the interference of their minds — light plus light resulting in darkness; that their emotional vibrations, however, increase by induction and self-induction like the current in a wire coil. By descending into the bottom strata of society the crank made the discovery of his life; the discovery of the lowest common denominator. The master key was found.

This was innovative journalism in 1942. The "Profiles" were an attempt to understand the subject, and particularly the circumstances and forces that shaped the subject's mature political outlook. It was, perhaps, the first sustained attempt at a deeper understanding of public figures in the British press.

The new *Observer* immediately attracted the attention and enthusiasm of professional journalists and the public alike. After an initial dip in sales after the loss of Garvin, circulation began to rise — though wartime newsprint restrictions made the rise gradual. However, one section of the population did not view the new *Observer* with equanimity: the security service, MI5, which considered David Astor's connection with so many emigré Germans as distinctly suspicious, if not worse. David Astor was apprised of these suspicions by Lord Mountbatten, who called his young press officer into his office in the summer of 1942 to warn him that he himself had been warned by his security officer of Astor's circle of German friends. Astor answered that he was proud to know such anti-Nazi Germans. Much to his surprise, Mountbatten replied forthrightly, "You're perfectly right". No doubt Mountbatten, being himself of German ancestry, saw Germans as discriminatingly as David Astor did.

Lord Astor's attitude to David's somewhat unusual journalistic enterprise was one of wholehearted support. He was particularly generous with his time and money towards the often disorientated and destitute German émigrés whom David introduced to him. If it might have seemed ironic that this generation of left-wing intellectuals should flock to work for the arch Anglo-American capitalist Astors, it was perfectly explicable in the context of wartime London. Not only had the *Observer* broken from the Conservative faith in a meaningful way; but − more important − David Astor hired his writers to write as they wanted: once taken on, the writer was given his head. Even the Marxist Deutscher enjoyed the wartime *Observer*, later commenting generously: "The *Observer* is a courageous paper which allows its contributors a certain scope for the expression of their opinions...." Although Deutscher, like others, would eventually cite irreconcilable political differences with David Astor as reason for leaving the paper, the writers did enjoy an unusual amount of freedom. Under David the *Observer* also became intellectually exciting; the wartime *Times*, under the guidance of Barrington-Ward and E. H. Carr, was the only paper to rival its sense of intellectual excitement. They were both papers that had traditionally been loyal to the Conservative Party, but that now advocated new social, economic and international solutions to post-war problems that marked the foundations of the post-war consensus on the mixed economy and the Welfare State. The defection of the *Observer* and *The Times* from the traditional Conservative fold foreshadowed, and reflected, the collapse of the Conservative vote at the 1945 election. Lord Astor, the guiding hand of the *Observer*'s politics, defended the paper's alleged socialism in a letter to Arthur Mann in 1942. Defending Beveridge, Astor wrote:

> As to his alleged Socialism, ever since I got into the House I have been called a Socialist....So that does not worry me! The real danger when the war is over is from Communism. In order to avoid this we have to have a progressive policy.[2]

New features by young, talented writers were making the paper more readable and intellectually distinguished than it had been for years. However, as David could work for the *Observer* only

---

2. Lord Astor to Arthur Mann, September 3, 1942; Thomas Jones Papers.

during his lunch-hour and spare weekends, there was still need for an editor to give the new stable of writers some central direction. During the summer of 1942, as temporary editors such as Crowther and Barbara Ward grappled bravely with the *Observer* in their spare time, the Astors conducted a frantic search for a viable editor. Amongst the main candidates considered were Sir Wilfred Eady, chairman of the Board of Customs and Excise and a friend of TJ's. Eady was Lord Astor's favoured choice, but he could not be released from government service. David's favoured candidate for a time was Peter Smollett, head of the Russian division at the Ministry of Information; but he, again, could not be released. As it happens, neither of these choices was wise: Eady would not have had the intellectual flexibility to sympathize with the *Observer*'s new writers, and Smollett was later denounced as a Soviet agent by Chapman Pincher, a charge that has never been denied. Arthur Mann was also considered, but illness prevented him from assuming the responsibility. In June the ex-editor of the *Spectator* magazine, Wilson Harris, took on the role of temporary editor for five weeks, but it soon became obvious that he was too old and conservative for the new *Observer*. As TJ wrote to Mann:

> Under him the paper would be good...but I fear it would lack that "little bit" extra....He is too much of the old fashioned Liberal....His mind is too critical of the new world such as E. H. Carr and others put forward in *The Times*. He cannot see beyond the League of Nations. Unless we are bold in our post-war constructive policy we may be swept away by Communism after demobilisation comes.[3]

It was Garvin's old news editor, Ronald Harmer, who then suggested that they had "someone sitting in this office who could edit the paper". This was the drama critic, Ivor Brown, a man of wide interests and a shrewd sense of politics. Brown was fifty-two at the time, educated at Cheltenham and Balliol, and had served briefly in Whitehall before becoming a widely respected freelance journalist. He published some fifty books on literary and theatrical subjects during his life, and became drama critic of the *Observer*

---

3. TJ to Mann, June 13, 1942; Thomas Jones Papers.

in 1929. A quiet, pleasant man, he was famous for working on his editorial proofs while chewing on a handkerchief hanging out of his mouth. I.B. as editor? In the absence of any other likely candidates, he was appointed in August 1942.

From the start Brown seems to have been somewhat bewildered by the collection of exotic foreign nationals that now peppered the office, and he seems to have been extremely uncomfortable in the midst of the highly charged intellectual atmosphere that now prevailed. But it was acknowledged that the real force in the office was to be David Astor. Indeed, it was made clear that Ivor Brown was only "acting" editor and that David would be taking over eventually and, indeed, would be in charge of hiring the staff. This informal arrangement was confirmed by Lord Astor's transfer of shares to David Astor in 1942, which gave him 24,498 shares out of 50,000; his father retained an overall majority of 502 shares only. This was in recognition of David's skill in not only saving the post-Garvin *Observer* from a chaotic collapse, but in transforming it into a better, more stimulating paper.

Even as Ivor Brown was appointed editor in 1942, David Astor was taking over the position *de jure*, if not *de facto*. Periodically over the next few years questions were raised about Brown's shortcomings in the editorial chair; he seemed overawed by the gathering of Germans and others which now made up the *Observer* office, and was obviously out of his depth in the editorial discussions on international affairs — but then in fairness he had neither chosen these Germans nor had he ever specialized in foreign affairs. He could give no lead or firm directions to the staff. However, to the Astors there were advantages to his lack of political weight. As TJ wrote in 1943:

> What I feel about it is this. It took a major operation to get rid of a strong editor. If IB were much more positive than he is, he would clash, sometimes with you and frequently with David. There is at this juncture, until David takes over, much advantage as I see it in not having too strong a political personality.[4]

---

4. TJ to Lord Astor, February 15, 1942; Astor Papers 1066/1/1268.

So Brown stayed. But his weaknesses were amply compensated for by Donald Tyerman, the excellent assistant editor from 1943 to 1945, and later editor of the *Economist*.

If Brown stoically put up with the steady influx of émigré writers on the political side of the paper, he did draw the line when the newcomers affected his own predominance on the cultural side. His sensitivity on this matter led to the one failure in David Astor's new recruitment drive, his hiring of Cyril Connolly as "cultural editor" in December 1942. Connolly was in many ways a prize catch, as he was already an established literary critic and editor of the very successful arts magazine *Horizon*, on which David Astor was to a certain extent modelling the new *Observer*. The Old Etonian Connolly had also been very helpful in finding the *Observer*'s new writers, pointing David in the direction of George Orwell and introducing him to the Hungarian émigré writer and ex-Communist Arthur Koestler, who was to write for the paper after the war. The arrival of Connolly on the paper immediately added to the prestige and quality of the arts pages, and it was he who oversaw the first book reviews of George Orwell. The arrangement worked well until the summer of 1943 and the arrival of Tyerman to run the political side of the paper. Brown was persuaded by David to relinquish control of the political side in deference to Tyerman, the editor perhaps sensibly realizing his own limitations in this field, but in return Ivor Brown asked that he should be able to return to his first love and run the book pages as well as continuing as the drama critic. Connolly had one limitation, that he never did any writing for the *Observer* himself — but Brown had still put David in something of a dilemma as he could see that Connolly would not want to work as a mere book reviewer under Ivor Brown's direction. It was thus with some foreboding that he met Connolly in the latter's club, White's, in August 1943, hoping to talk him gently into relinquishing overall control of the arts page and writing reviews and other signed articles instead. Their conversation started amicably but, as Connolly began to go back over the promises that he thought the *Observer* had made to him in the past, the atmosphere deteriorated. After a time David Astor accused him of saying something which he thought to be untrue, at which point Connolly, without a word, got up and left the room, leaving the bewildered David sitting alone in somebody else's club with his host making for the door.

After this Connolly became uncooperative and he was sacked in August 1943. Even before he left, there started a bitter exchange of letters between David and Lord Astor and Connolly, trading recrimination with counter-recrimination. Connolly had some right to feel aggrieved and wrote to David Astor in August 1943 just after he had been sacked:

> ...I naturally however felt rather sore when the official reasons given.... are shown to be false — it would have been better to say "you go because there is no room for both of you and Ivor Brown is more important to us...." You call me utterly dishonest and then say I have been rude to you! You are the only person who has ever forced me to leave, once as a guest, once as a host, rather than remain and be insulted, just as you are the only person whose handwriting I dread because I know a letter from you will always contain recriminations. It is clear to me we are very bad for each other and should not meet.

Neither did they, although Astor became friends with Connolly again towards the end of Connolly's life. David Astor, for his part, was very disappointed at having to lose Connolly, writing a generous acknowledgment of his contribution to the new *Observer* to his father.

On the whole the new writers, bar Connolly, all proved a vital success. However, this transformation of the paper obviously did not suit Garvin's "old guard", and the most difficult task of the wartime *Observer* management was gradually to prise out some of the older staff. One of these was Ronald Harmer, the news editor, a very gentle man but not one who was completely reliable in his job, a point emphasized when the *Observer* failed to report the Allied landings in North Africa on Sunday, November 8, 1942 because Harmer had gone home when the news broke at the Ministry of Information at 2.25 a.m. The *Observer* was the only paper not to carry the story. Harmer's departure was unsettling, as he had for long been the mainstay of the office. He retired to run the *Wilts and Gloucestershire Standard* with his brother and sister. He was replaced by John Beavan of the *Evening Standard*, who oversaw the most obvious journalistic transformation of the *Observer* at this time, the shifting of news (rather than advertisements) to the front page in August 1942. Another old stalwart who had to go was Viola Garvin, the literary editor and J. L. Garvin's daughter. She was very heavily involved with her father so it was decided that rather than let any possible resentment or malice fester, it would be best to let her go. The situation was intensely embarrassing, but Harmer handled the affair expertly before he, too, had to leave. Congratulated by David after the war on the success of the *Wilts and Gloucestershire Standard*, Harmer replied, wryly, "Well, it's rather like having been a captain of a liner and you then have to take to a rowing boat."

With the departure of Garvin and the influx of new writers and new ideas, the *Observer's* politics underwent a radical transformation. The paper became a leading advocate of the "new and better" society that many people hoped would emerge in Britain after the war. In home affairs the paper shed its mainstream Tory politics and, as we have seen, became an enthusiastic supporter of the Beveridge Plan for social welfare and full employment, and for town and country planning controls, nationalization of the basic industries and greater redistribution of wealth. Lord Astor, with his long expertise in the field of domestic politics, became the main architect of the *Observer's* policy in these areas, and Beveridge became not only a regular writer for the paper but, together with Lord Astor, sat in on editorial conferences to steer the paper in the right direction. Sir Stafford Cripps figured importantly in their deliberations, as during the pivotal year of 1942 he seemed to represent all their aspirations, arguing, as he did, that the dream of the new and better society after the war would motivate the British, as well as the oppressed Europeans, to fight ever harder against Hitler. The *Observer*, together with *The Times*, backed Cripps's often coded campaigns and speeches against Churchill's conduct of the war during 1942 and fully expected Cripps to replace Churchill as premier during the anxious summer and autumn of 1942, when defeat after defeat of the Allied forces all over the world put Churchill under immense pressure. Churchill's position was only saved by the victory at El Alamein in November of that year, after which he felt strong enough to shunt Cripps out of harm's way into the Ministry of Aircraft Production. With that and the rapid success of the Allied forces in North Africa and the Pacific, and the Russian victory at Stalingrad, the need for a war of ideas in the absence of military success, favoured by Cripps,

David Astor, his "Forum" writers and Haffner in the manner of
Adam von Trott, faded. However, in domestic politics the drive
for a new vision of society, a new "idea" of a better society to
dispel the *need* for the radical solutions of Fascism or Communism,
had swept away all the old certainties, and would eventually sweep
Churchill away in 1945.

When the *Observer* advocated reforms and new ideas in terms
of domestic politics, it was acting as part of a gathering "new left"
consensus that would dictate the course of British politics up to
1979. It was in the field of foreign affairs, however, that the
Observer began to make its mark in a truly independent way, and
to distinguish itself from many of the more accepted points of
view that might be found, of an evening, at the Shanghai Club.
This independence of mind on foreign policy was largely David
Astor's own. From the beginning he took a special interest in the
paper's foreign policy, leaving domestic politics and economics to
his father and others — a division of interest that was to characterize
the whole of his editorship. His main interest was foreign affairs;
it was because he was so acutely aware of the need to solve the
problem of Germany and Europe that he had involved himself in
politics and journalism in the first place. It was not surprising
therefore that the future shape of Europe exercised David Astor's
mind to an exceptional degree, and that he saw one of his tasks on
the *Observer* as being to help evolve a European anti-Fascist
policy by using the paper to influence policy makers.

The test case for the future of Europe was, of course, France,
and it was in an attempt to define British policy towards Europe
that, in 1942—43, David Astor and his paper led a campaign
against de Gaulle whom the paper saw as the leader of a quasi-
Fascist regime in London. The official historian of the *Observer*,
Dr John Stubbs, has written that:

> In challenging de Gaulle, the *Observer* was challenging
> one of the central tenets of British wartime diplomacy. How-
> ever much Churchill, Eden and others might grumble to
> themselves and to de Gaulle himself about the near impossi-
> bility of working with the General, the British public revered
> de Gaulle as a symbol of a France that had not accepted
> defeat. Thus, any attack on him or his objectives raised the
> spectre of being accused of disloyalty to the Allied cause in

wartime. To David Astor and his friends, de Gaulle was a two-fold menace. He was an immediate threat to the war effort by virtue of his strained relations with the British and his potential for creating friction between London and Washington. In the longer view a Gaullist France, it was passionately believed, would never fit into the post-war vision of a federated democratic Europe.

Indeed, the *Observer* was remarkably prescient in its ideas on Europe, recognizing that British leadership of a democratic, federated Europe was the only "world power" role that the country could hope to play in the post-war world. In 1944, in a paper on "*Observer* foreign policy", Lord Astor wrote that:

> Britain must make sure that Europe becomes united under British leadership. Only as spokesman and trustee of a United Europe can Britain pull her full weight in the High Council of the Big Three. Only in attachment to Britain can Europe hope to play a part in world-politics consistent with her culture, industry and talent. The interests of Britain and Europe coincide.
>
> Technical developments have made the sovereignty of the European States unreal and the unity of Europe inescapable, the choice for Europe lies between becoming either the Europe of Germany or Russia, or of federating under the leadership of Britain.

This was an extension of Lord Lothian's ideas on federalism for which the *Observer* became the leading spokesman. In retrospect, it is tragic that Britain never took the opportunity to lead a federated Europe after the war, a role that was urged on the British by the Europeans themselves; it was the great "missed opportunity" of British foreign policy in the post-war era. At the time, though, the *Observer* saw it as perfectly possible. It targeted a France led by de Gaulle and Soviet expansion into Eastern Europe as the two great obstacles to such a course, and attacked both. In both cases, the paper was going against the grain of contemporary opinion.

David was heavily involved in the campaign against de Gaulle. By the beginning of 1942, the splits in the Free French Movement in London were an open secret, as many Frenchmen became increasingly suspicious of de Gaulle's politics and the manner in which he ran his organization in London. They alleged that he was an autocrat, ruthless with dissenters, and surrounded himself with near-Fascist cronies. The most notorious of these was Colonel "Passy". Passy was a member of the Cagoule (Secret Committee of Revolutionary Action), a pre-war Fascist organization which, *à la* Ku-Klux-Klan, sometimes donned hoods (*cagoules*) and carried out political murders. Passy later strenuously denied being a Cagoulard, but there were undoubtedly others in the Gaullist secret service, who, under Passy's guidance, carried out torture and interrogation in the basement of the Free French Headquarters in Duke Street. There were plenty of Frenchmen in London willing to talk about the iniquities of de Gaulle's organization in London, and it quickly became clear to David Astor that a Gaullist regime in post-war France could endanger everything that the democratic Allies were supposed to be working for. The main source for The *Observer* was Maurice Dejean, Commissioner for Foreign Affairs in the French National Committee from spring 1941 to October 1942, who was then demoted by de Gaulle. Another key informant and close friend was Denis Saurat, director of the Institut Français, who by 1943 had become a convinced anti-Gaullist, as had Raymond Aron, the philosopher then writing for *La France Libre*.

On the *Observer*, David found willing collaborators on the French question among his new writers. Those principally involved were Ronald Fredenburgh and Alastair Forbes from "Forum" days, and Jon Kimche. Fredenburgh became diplomatic correspondent in succession to Mallory Browne in 1943, whilst Forbes had studied French at Cambridge and had a considerable range of contacts in the French community, as did Kimche. Up to 1943 it was still an open question as to whether de Gaulle rather than Darlan or Giraud would be recognized by the Allies as the undisputed leader of the French, so as soon as enough facts were gathered the *Observer* launched into its campaign against de Gaulle, the first editorial (by David) on the subject appearing on November 1, 1942. It was entitled "Freedom", and argued that de Gaulle's "movement with its rather colourless national committee of little known Frenchmen, has failed to fulfil the great hopes placed in him — that he would recruit to his cause millions of men from France and her Empire". It added that far from being "liberal and democratic", de Gaulle's movement was "autocratic" and included men "who did not hide their approval of certain Fascist aspects of the budding reorganization of France". Furthermore, the responsibility for this was at least "partly British".

Believing that an alternative to de Gaulle, had, in mid-war, to be another military man, the *Observer* promoted the prospects of General Henri Giraud, who was the subject of a flattering "Profile" in November 1942. But more importantly the paper argued for the establishment of a provisional French government that would be *civil* and not military in nature, composed of a provisional parliament made up of the twenty to thirty non-collaborationist deputies still at liberty. This was not a definitive scheme, and the *Observer* devoted considerable space to the subject of the nature of a provisional government throughout the first half of 1943. With the success of Allied forces in French North Africa in 1943, the "French problem" became more urgent and on March 21 the paper published a very critical attack (by David Astor), on the Gaullist organization, accusing it of being an "autocracy".

The *Observer* quickly became noted for its outspokenness about de Gaulle. As Willi Guttman remembers of the campaign in his unpublished memoirs:

A more delicate subject [than the Beveridge Report] was de Gaulle, commonly supposed to be one of the heroes of the war, the saviour of at least the spiritual grandeur of France.... In the *Observer* office he was considered nothing short of an ogre, a tyrant and potential dictator, an enemy of Britain, a menace to a future better world, and, to say the least, a confounded nuisance. This was expressed in print only with an understandable degree of reticence and tact. But there was never any reluctance to devise schemes to get at him, and adversaries of his had always kept contact with the office....

The Government itself was angered by the *Observer*'s revelations on a subject that they wished to keep as quiet as possible. A Ministry of Information official minuted to his minister, Brendan Bracken, that his colleagues at the MOI and in the Foreign Office "despair of making any impression on the correspondents themselves". But, he asked, could not something be "done at the top" about "Captain Astor"? Bracken's private secretary replied, however, that the minister felt "he could not influence the *Observer*.... British papers cannot be browbeaten like foreign ones and the only way of getting them to modify their views is by personal influence, which in the case of the *Observer* we do not possess." Forbes, described as a "self-appointed adviser to the PM on foreign affairs", was reckoned to be "proof against guidance" — but the MOI officials scored a small victory against Forbes and the *Observer* by apparently blocking his appointment as Press Attaché to Harold Macmillan in Algiers when the latter took up his appointment as "Viceroy of the Mediterranean".[5]

In March 1943 David Astor wrote his father:

> I wish the *Observer* to do something very brave and of, I believe, very great importance. You have often told me how in the last war Garvin exploded with one article a man who was a national nuisance [Colonel Repington]. The task I wish to tackle is too big to be achieved by one article but it should be begun. In a word, I want the *Observer* to state plainly the facts about de Gaulle's movement.

During the course of the summer David collected facts and information for his exposé of de Gaulle, proposing that his "white paper" should take up a whole page in the paper. On August 1 a profile of de Gaulle appeared, but the big exposé of the man and his movement never appeared — for reasons that remain obscure. The most likely is that Lord Astor did not want seriously to inconvenience the Government at a time when Churchill was reluctantly agreeing officially to recognize de Gaulle's French Committee of National Liberation as the legitimate provisional government. As Churchill wrote to Roosevelt on July 21: "I am no more enamoured of de Gaulle than you are, but I would rather have him on the Committee than strutting about as a combination of Joan of Arc and Clemenceau." On August 27, 1943 the British and Americans, using slightly different formulae, both recognized de Gaulle as the leader of the provisional French government, paving his way to return as leader of France to liberated Paris in

---

5. Minutes in PRO INF 1/970. I am indebted to Dr Stubbs for his meticulous research on the *Observer* and de Gaulle.

1944. The *Observer*'s campaign had failed; partly, it must be admitted, because although the paper's doubts about de Gaulle may have been justified, there was no real alternative to him; a point that David Astor was willing to acknowledge at the time, despite the paper's attempts to build up Giraud. The *Observer* achieved nothing politically, but did raise its reputation for the independence of thought and boldness of action which were to characterize the Astor years.

For David Astor himself, his involvement with the Free French Movement was to win him the Croix de Guerre. The military commander of the Free French in London was General Koenig. He sought David Astor's help to gain greater French representation in the planning of the "D-Day" invasion of France in 1944, from which the French themselves were largely excluded. David and his colonel met General "Pug" Ismay, Churchill's most trusted military adviser, to persuade him of Koenig's case. Ismay cross-examined them "very severely", but in the end Koenig did actually get better treatment from Eisenhower, the Supreme Allied Commander of the invasion. Koenig was deeply grateful for this help and rewarded members of the liaison group with this honour.

David Astor's other contribution to the cause of Free France came in the early autumn of 1944, after the successful Normandy landings on June 6. During his time at Mountbatten's headquarters in London David had been ready to go on missions, but they had all been cancelled at the last minute. In 1944, he transferred to a unit liaising between the Special Operations Executive (SOE) in London and the *maquis* in France. He went on his first, abortive, raid for this unit in July. On the second occasion the mission went wrong. They landed in occupied South-East France where the Americans had recently landed on the coast and successfully made contact with the *maquis*, who produced cars to make a journey northwards. However, the convoy, heading north, was ambushed by retreating Germans. The *maquisards*, by now very over-confident, knew that there were Germans on the route, but claimed that they could go round them. They made the elementary mistake of stopping in the middle of an open crossroads to consult their map, at which point the convoy of cars was machine-gunned. Together with several of his colleagues, David was hit, his wound being in the shoulder. It was painful but not severe, and the convoy retreated south. David was eventually transferred to a hospital in Naples; it was there that he learnt of the fate of Adam von Trott, before being moved on to a hospital in Ischia for convalescence.

This ambush in France was to have one lasting consequence for the *Observer*, as David Astor shared the experience with Terry Kilmartin, who was then in the SOE. Kilmartin, uninjured in the ambush, was on hand to distribute bandages and cigarettes to the wounded British and French, including David. The friendship forged then was to flourish after the war, and Kilmartin became the literary editor of the *Observer* in 1951, retiring only in 1985 as the most distinguished literary editor of his generation.

The *Observer*'s concept of a democratic federated Europe was, of course, blocked by Soviet Russia's imperial ambitions in Eastern Europe. In identifying the danger from the Soviet Union to the post-war balance of Europe, David Astor parted company with many in the Shanghai Club, who, mesmerized by E. H. Carr, felt that wartime Soviet Russia could — and would — do little wrong. However, David proved to be as correct on the threat from total-itarianism of the left in the 1940s as he had been about totalitarianism of the right in the 1930s. The *Observer* became the first and leading advocate of the now commonly held opinion that there was precious little difference between the two — a novel idea in the period 1944—45, when admiration for Uncle Joe and all his works was at its height. George Orwell, then unsuccessfully trying to find a publisher for his satire on Soviet communism, *Animal Farm*, was very important in guiding the *Observer*'s — and David's — thinking in this respect. On June 7, 1944 David wrote to TJ:

> On Russia and Germany.... It is not a question of co-operating with *either* Russia or Germany. We have to co-operate with both if we are to know peace and security.
>
> You will notice that I do not talk about left and right in politics. What is Russia today; she is both extreme left and extreme right. And, after all, what is Fascism? It is also both extreme left and right in its politics and economics alike. These terms are beginning to lose their meaning. In matters of *liberty* we are to the "left" of everyone and Russia is extreme right.

Orwell's view on this is that soon all countries will have state planning and therefore a more or less degree of state ownership of property. The old Marxist struggle will thus be played out. The new struggle will be for more or less freedom within the planned state....[6]

Observer writers such as Orwell, Kimche and Deutscher were representatives of the anti-Stalinist left, and it was this school of thinking that David Astor was much influenced by — unlike most of the rest of the left who during the war tended to accept without question the Soviet Union's version of itself as the democratic liberator of Europe. In early 1945, David Astor wrote to John Pringle, then on the *Manchester Guardian*:

> ...I don't believe that "the left" in this country, whether informed Fleet Street intellectuals or less informed Labour Party members, will ever find the self-confidence and courage to face the situation that is developing, in which it is Russia that presents the totalitarian threat and that plays the Imperialist game. They will just bleat "down with the Tories", fight minor domestic issues and funk the larger international ones. The Tories will blunder along, more bravely maybe but with all the wrong ideas of how to deal with the new threat — the mixture of appeasement of Russia by underestimating her malefactions and support of reactionaries or of queer adventurers to be....

The litmus test for Soviet intentions in Europe was Poland, which was the first country that the Red Army re-entered in the long fight to Berlin. Isaac Deutscher and Jon Kimche were both very involved in the Polish question; Deutscher all the more so because he was from Poland and had a healthy suspicion of Stalinist intentions. The *Observer* was the first paper to raise doubts about Soviet intentions as they "liberated" Eastern Europe, in an editorial called "Britain and the Soviet Union" on May 30, 1943:

> ...certainly it is not in the interests of British-Russian friendship to invite Russia to claim a protectorate over wide stretches of Eastern Europe, whose populations would, in

---

6. David Astor to TJ, June 7, 1944; Thomas Jones Papers.

their majority, almost certainly react adversely....Politically such a solution, imposed on unwilling European nations, would inevitably lead to trouble, which Britain could not, morally or materially, view with equanimity.

The Polish case tended to go by default in the British press, partly because the old Polish government was widely perceived as being quasi-Fascist and thus not worth saving, and partly because, as Beaverbrook put it to Eden, the Foreign Secretary, "the friendship of Russia is far more important to us than the future of Anglo-Polish relations".[7] As well as this, the Polish armed forces in Britain acquired a reputation for anti-semitism which attracted a lot of press interest. The fate of millions of Polish Jews in the east did not. The Beaverbrook press was the most crudely anti-Polish and pro-Soviet of the lot, closely followed by *The Times* under the direction of the Russophile E. H. Carr. This bias was vividly illustrated by a report on the question of the Poles and the British press compiled by Mr McLaren of the Political Warfare Executive for Frank Roberts of the Foreign Office. McLaren wrote:

Last week I met the business manager of the Express Newspapers....I mentioned the point of the million Jews in Poland. He quite frankly said that such a matter was not news for his papers, but that the knocking down of Jews in Hyde Park was. I smiled at this, but pointed out that surely the blowing up of the bridges between Lvov, and Krakow (by Polish partisans) was news....and was not even mentioned in "Express Newspapers". His reply to that was even more frank. I give his exact words: "Look here old boy. The sub-editors of our papers are angry about the way the Poles have been knocking the Jews about and they usually look with a great deal of distrust on any pro-Polishness coming in." I then said: "Even if it comes from the Ministry of Information and the FO Press Department?" He replied: "Yes, the sub-editors of our papers just now think that Poland is the pus of Europe, and it is no good your trying to persuade them or me that it isn't".

---

7. Beaverbrook to Eden, August 26, 1944; Beaverbrook Papers, House of Lords Record Office.

Various other conversations I have had in a non-official way in Fleet Street support this attitude.[8]

It was thus with some courage that the *Observer* went against this consensus and took up the cause of the "pus of Europe". In December 1943 — January 1944 Anglo-Russian negotiations on the future of Poland began in earnest at the highest level. A Russian team came to London to contribute to the European Advisory Commission, and Churchill took a personal interest in the matter. The negotiations centred — and eventually foundered — on the post-war frontiers of Poland. The British wanted Poland's pre-war frontiers restored, as did the Polish government in exile in London, while the Russians wanted the Soviet border extended into Poland's eastern territories. As any concessions to the Soviets would have been politically embarrassing, the press was requested by the MOI not to write that such negotiations were going on at all. This was an informal D-Notice request with no legal sanction, but they were generally observed throughout the war. When the *Observer* heard about these negotiations, it was decided to give publicity to them; otherwise the Polish case would go by default and the country which Britain had gone to war for in the first place would be secretly carved up. Isaac Deutscher later told David that his source for the story of the contents of these "secret" negotiations was a member of the Russian delegation visiting London who passed the information on to an old Polish Trotskyist friend of Deutscher's. On January 9, 1944, the *Observer* printed Deutscher's first story based on this source under the headline "The Polish-Russian Triangle". The article went on to state that the Russians were demanding the inclusion of some eastern Polish territory into Russia after the war:

> It is to be hoped that Polish fears and misgivings are baseless. But Russian policy has so far done little to dispel them or to give the Poles that confidence in Russia's intentions without which the present breach cannot be healed. Only a few days ago a broadcast by the Union of Polish Patriots from Moscow hinted at the setting up of a new Polish Government in Warsaw after the entry of the Red Army....

---

8. PRO FO 372/39484. 6188.

This was followed on February 13 by another article revealing that the Russians were hardening in their negotiating position and were "no longer prepared to cede Lvov to Poland". This article and a further one on February 27 chronicled the sinister story of the setting up of the Communist National Council in Poland as an alternative to the London Polish Council, a move accompanied by the systematic denigration of the London Polish government-in-exile as a gang of Fascist politicians "...who live in a misty world of Nazi mirage".

The *Observer* was thus chronicling the unfolding story of the Soviet takeover of Poland, and was alone in trying to ensure that at least it did not happen in secret, so that the public could make its voice heard on the issue. The *Observer* broke the news embargo on the Polish-Russian issue in the full knowledge that the paper would become unpopular in Whitehall — and, sure enough, Whitehall was furious. The Foreign Office and MOI officials immediately began to speculate on where the leak came from, whilst Eden wrote to Bracken, the Minister of Information, that he had taken the *Observer* of February 13 "along with me to see the PM. I think that Cliveden should really be blamed. There was the original sin!"[9] On being told that the articles were probably written by one of the paper's selection of European émigrés, Eden minuted that: "The German émigrés should go home if they unduly muddy our waters."[10] Reading the *Observer* of February 27, Oliver Harvey, Eden's private secretary, noted in his diary: "Further leakage in 'Observer' today which in addition to giving circumstantial account of further negotiations between PM and Polish PM...reports that a new Polish C-in-C has been appointed in Poland by the pro-Soviet National Council there. This is news to us....All this makes any serious negotiations almost impossible."[11]

After seeing Churchill, Eden's next move was to send for Ivor Brown. Brown had the backing of Lord Astor in this matter, and

9. PRO INF 1/859.

10. PRO FO 371/39387. 1063.

11. *The Diplomatic Diaries of Oliver Harvey* (Collins 1970), ed. John Harvey, February 27, 1944.

David Astor had lunch with him, followed by a walk around St James's Park, to fortify him before he went into the Foreign Office. Awaiting Brown in the Foreign Secretary's room overlooking the park were Eden and Bracken. They grilled him for just under two hours, telling the increasingly despondent editor that the Russians were going to break off negotiations unless the British could tell them who had leaked the information to Deutscher. There is no doubt that Brown was very shaken by this ordeal — Bracken was especially good at mixing political attack with personal abuse — and he immediately went to Deutscher to demand the name of his source. Deutscher refused to give it, and was prepared to go to jail, which Eden threatened him with, rather than betray his sources. Ivor Brown's nerve, according to Lord Astor, was "rather shattered" by this experience and he wanted to resign and hand over to Donald Tyerman. However, just at this moment Tyerman revealed that he was going to *The Times* at the end of the war, so Lord Astor prevailed upon Brown to stay. Brown was understandably resentful at having to shoulder the responsibility for the journalism of a writer whom he had never wanted in the first place, and this sense of grievance spilled over towards the other émigrés as well. With dismay David reported to TJ "IB's partial collapse of morale". Writing on May 25, David continued that

Last week IB would allow no contentious material to appear.... and cut out Deutscher's piece altogether. Deutscher was very upset...he formed the impression that IB thought he was more trouble than he was worth. IB later...started denigrating Haffner ("requires too much supervision") plus Kimche ("he's just a little political spy"). Altogether he showed himself to be in full retreat and ready to take out of the paper all that has made it distinguished, brilliant, informative and bold. He has this yearning for a quiet life and a quiet newspaper which is a constant danger....Despite both you and WA [Lord Astor] telling him to back Deutscher in the trouble with Eden he has not done so....DT [Tyerman] tells me that in the interview he "grovelled" and lost his nerve completely.[12]

---

12. David Astor to TJ, May 25, 1944; Thomas Jones Papers.

Lord Astor was also "disappointed" at Brown's back-pedalling and treatment of Deutscher, "...because I have told him twice, and told him in the presence of Tyerman, that I would back him a hundred per cent in taking an *independent* line".[13] Ivor Brown's lack of enthusiasm for this particular cause did, to a certain extent, diminish the *Observer*'s support for Poland, but by the end of the year the paper was finding its voice again. Bracken and Eden, having failed to browbeat Deutscher into revealing his sources or keeping quiet, handed the matter over to the Foreign Office news department, where Peter Loxley called in Brigadier O. A. Harker of MI5 to investigate the leaks. William Ridsdale of the FO news department was particularly ready to see sinister reasons behind the *Observer*'s Russian-Polish revelations:

> The common characteristic of most of these stories is that they all seem to be designed to provoke or exaggerate disagreement among the Allies and it is mainly because of this fact that I cannot help wondering whether some deliberately inimical influence might not be at work....[14]

Shades of the "Cliveden Set" conspiracy theory were revived here.

The *Observer*'s campaign on Poland developed into a growing journalistic fight to present a more objective picture of the Soviet Union than appeared elsewhere in the British press during the war. At a time when both *The Times* and the middle-market Express Newspapers were endeavouring to apologize for and explain away almost every conceivable Soviet wrongdoing, the *Observer* was alone in subjecting the Soviet Union to proper critical scrutiny. Both on the subject of de Gaulle and Russia the newspaper demonstrated a spirit of robust independence and intelligent writing that made it noticed, and it began to regain the influence which Garvin had given it earlier in the century. David Astor's golden age can be said to have started in 1942, for the new

---

13. Lord Astor to TJ, May 23, 1944; Thomas Jones Papers.

14. Minute in PRO FO 371/39399. 5597.

post-Garvin *Observer* was well established even before the end of the war.

There was no doubt in anyone's mind that the architect of this transformation in its fortunes was not the proprietor, Lord Astor, nor any of the succession of post-Garvin temporary editors, but David Astor, who as yet had no official position on the paper at all. Lord Astor generously acknowledged this and, as we have seen, transferred almost half of his shares to David in 1942. Before the year was out, Lord Astor had settled the question of the identity of the post-war editor in his own mind. David Astor's achievement on the wartime *Observer* was indeed remarkable: bringing about an intellectual and journalistic reformation on the paper at the age of twenty-nine, while serving fulltime in the Royal Marines, was a considerable feat.

This success was at the expense of his elder brother, who returned from the Middle East at the end of 1942 to find David firmly in harness at the *Observer* with a "complete ascendancy...over Papa".[15] Bill had worked on the paper before the war and had fully expected to be in charge of it after Garvin. On his return to Britain he lobbied his father and TJ to secure him his rightful place whilst David resisted Bill's overtures as best he could on the grounds that Bill was too conservative for the new *Observer*. As David put it to TJ on December 9, 1942:

> The...big subject which I have been discussing with my father is Bill's connection with the paper. My father suggested that Bill should have twenty per cent of the shares, become a director and then have a permanent connection with the paper, while it being made clear that I would have the majority of the shares and therefore the major control of the policy. I feel very mean cavilling at this arrangement which is most generous to me, and which is the least that Bill might reasonably expect, but I must add that I feel very uneasy about this suggestion. You will no doubt guess the reason for my misgivings. I am perfectly in agreement that the type of Liberal-Conservative attitude of my father and of yourself (and also of Arthur Mann, Mallory Browne, etc.) should always be strongly represented. Left completely to myself in

15. Bill Astor to TJ, May 12, 1942; Thomas Jones Papers.

the years to come I would definitely invite people to become directors who represented this point of view. My anxiety about Bill is that I don't think he does represent this point of view. I fear that he has always been a Right Wing Tory with a certain amount of impatience with mild progressives and an almost violent antagonism towards radical progressives.... I feel that if he owned twenty per cent of the shares he would demand twenty per cent of the paper representing his opinions. If I and the rest of the *Observer* staff could not agree with this I fear that there would be nasty clashes rather than a compromise.

Bill, for his part, was dismayed by David's new prominence in the affairs of the paper, writing to TJ:

I think it is very dangerous to leave it entirely in the hands of one person, David, who is brilliant, but emotional and some-times erratic.... If the general line of the paper is to be that of the last six months I am sure it can't work.... [16]

To complicate things further Nancy Astor now started to grow alarmed at what she saw as the new "leftward" trend of the *Observer* as guided by Waldorf and David. As they moved further to the "left" during the war, Nancy moved further to the "right", embarrassing herself and her family by her not-infrequent Parliamentary references to the supposed Roman Catholic conspiracy that threatened England. On May 23, 1944, David wrote to TJ:

I learn today re: the *Observer* and Bill.... that part of the trouble is my mother. She apparently says (a) I am too "Bolshie" and (b) she resents the way my father and I have got together to her exclusion. Egging Bill on and advising my father to take him into the *Observer* is apparently her reply...." [17]

Lord Astor's solution to this family problem was to create a Trust that would run the *Observer* on non-profit-making, non-party lines. The idea of a Trust actually came from David, whose

---

16. Bill Astor to TJ, April 7, 1943; Thomas Jones Papers.

17. David Astor to TJ, May 23, 1944; Thomas Jones Papers.

model was the BBC, but to Lord Astor such a scheme not only
had political attractions but would serve to "ease the family situation". Having made up his mind that David should take over
the *Observer* after the war, Waldorf also saw the creation of the
Trust as a means to curb him, for, as he explained to TJ, much
as he admired David's journalistic skills, he also felt him liable to
be too impetuous and impulsive; in his own words, "If the editor
is also the proprietor there is practically no check upon him".[18] Sir
William Haley, then director-general of the BBC, was very important in advising TJ and Lord Astor on how such a Trust could
be operated. The Scott Trust that controlled the *Manchester
Guardian* also served as an example.

It was constructed out of Waldorf and David's shares in the
Observer company, which went into the new *Observer* Trust in
1944. It was to consist of three or four trustees who were to be
responsible for the overall control of the paper, with powers to
hire and fire both the editor and the general manager. There was
also a board of directors who met more regularly to regulate the
detailed financial and commercial concerns of the paper. Bill Astor
served loyally as a director for some years, as did Jakie in the
1970s. The first chairman was Lord Astor, and his two fellow
trustees were Arthur Mann and TJ. Any profit accruing from the
Trust's administration of the paper was to be ploughed back into
the paper, or given to charitable and educational causes associated
with the newspaper industry. In a statement of policy drawn up
on June 14, 1944 it was stated that:

> The *Observer* should not be a Party paper. It must be tied to
> no group, no sect, no interest. It should belong to no combine
> of journals. Its independence must be absolute. But merely
> to stand alone...is not enough. One must also stand for a
> system of ideas and for a pattern of constructive reform. Not
> to be bound by Party or personal ties makes allegiance to
> declared principles all the more necessary.

Those who upheld these principles and policies "would be
supported without distinction between political parties". These

---

18. Lord Astor to TJ, August 14, 1943; Astor Papers 1066/1/1268.

principles were defined as practical "tasks" facing Britain in 1945:

> The first task is to end the mad competition of nations by a world-wide organic control, a control not based on dictatorship but on the principles of representative authority and liberty. The second is to destroy the social injustices of an ill-balanced society without creating a sluggish conformity and a dull inertia.

This was, indeed, the basis of the political *via media* that the *Observer* embraced from 1945 to 1975.

In practice, the Trust solved the problem of David and Bill. Accompanying the first deed was a memo by Waldorf Astor on "The *Observer* and Family". In this he set out the roles that he saw the two brothers playing:

> I hope that the trustees and directors will give David a main share in the control of the paper and that at some stage he will be appointed editor...in general I support the political objectives that he has in mind.... I have a high regard for his capacity, judgement and public spirit....
>
> I have shown my confidence in Bill by giving him most of my British real estate. I have also looked to him largely for the supervision of my American property.... As to the *Observer*, if he desires to have some connection.... Then in my judgement he should be asked to assist on the business side....but not to the exclusion of David.

Bill did indeed serve as a loyal director for David. He was undoubtedly disappointed with the fate of the *Observer*, but he showed no lingering resentment. Not so Nancy Astor, who was alarmed at the paper's "leftish" politics during the war and horrified at the idea of its leaving the Conservative fold to become independent — for she knew only too well what that meant under David.

To exacerbate the situation, while the Trust was being drawn up, Lord Astor (supported by David) had to persuade Nancy to stand down as MP for Plymouth at the forthcoming general election. For Waldorf it was a painful thing to ask of her, but by 1945 her public performances had so deteriorated that she had become a serious liability to herself. Nancy Astor refused to acknowledge her declining powers, and she never forgave Waldorf for "forcing" her to give up her favourite activity. As a conciliatory concession to her, Waldorf inserted a clause in the Trust which was to haunt the *Observer* in later years: the trustees "must be of the Protestant religion interpreted in the widest and most literal sense". This was, of course, a sop to Nancy's anti-Catholic prejudices, but it was so worded as to be meaningless — in law there was no such thing as the Protestant religion. However, this clause caused considerable embarrassment to the supposedly "liberal" *Observer* for its alleged hypocrisy and bigotry. In fact, it was ignored; but this did not deter Beaverbrook, who was pleased to continue an old vendetta against the Astors with fresh ammunition. In 1960, when his mother was too old to mind, David had the clause deleted.

So in 1948 David Astor took control, as editor, of a paper already fashioned in his own image. The only shadow over him was the family rift, for Waldorf and Nancy became almost totally estranged over their political differences and lived the last years of Waldorf's life (he died in 1952) on very strained terms. The gulf between Nancy and David became greater than ever before. Her antipathy to his *Observer* and its politics became legendary, and she became the paper's most savage critic, both in private and in public. Her motives were both political and emotional; her possessiveness could not have allowed her to view with any equanimity David's making a success of the editorship *on his own* and not under her direction. The pain went deeper in that she had wanted him to be a journalist — but on her terms and not on his. In its own way David Astor's struggle to build the *Observer* independent of his mother was as difficult as building its political independence. In 1947 Nancy Astor went on a trip to America on her own, pursued by letters from Waldorf, pleading with her to be reasonable. The letter of June 17 gives a flavour of the rupture in the family:

Tho' you may not believe it David needs your help more than any of the others and secretly wants it — so why not try to help him instead of malpracticing [sic] and running him down....remember that you have repeatedly told me and your family that you were going away because you could not direct the *Observer* — or *because you could not bear to see your son make a success of the paper* — or because you were not in Parliament. You had said you might be away months or a year or even longer but that under no circumstances would you return if I had anything to do with the unfortunate David. I told you then and I repeat now that if you insist on this choice naturally I come to you and leave David to do as best he can — I think it would be a pity because oddly enough I can influence him more than either Bill or Jakie — I think he needs and wants our help but it must be done tactfully and lovingly and not by telling everybody that he is the worst judge of everything and is bound to make a mess of everything — that is not very C.S....[19]

Unfortunately, tact was not Nancy Astor's strong suit.

The family rupture was hard enough to bear, and now David Astor was also to lose the man who more than any other had helped to shape the new *Observer*: George Orwell. Orwell's health quickly deteriorated after the war and he lived as a virtual invalid during the post-war years, dying on January 21, 1950, aged forty-six. This was a cruel blow, as Astor's friendship with him had blossomed into a close intellectual kinship. Orwell's biographer, Bernard Crick, has written:

[David Astor] became a true and helpful friend, ever sensitive that Orwell might resent even the suspicion of patronage. Some people would have exploited the opportunities of friendship with the future proprietor and editor of a great newspaper, and would have tried to become an *éminence grise*. Not Orwell who behaved to Astor much as he did to any other of his friends — speaking with frankness, making no demands, treating ideas on their merits, not for their suitability to the image or mission of the *Observer*[20]

This was exactly why David liked him. Although Orwell stuck to book reviews for the *Observer*, together with the occasional "Forum" or "Mood of the Moment", David was constantly trying

---

19. Lord Astor to Nancy Astor, June 17, 1947; Astor Papers 1416/1/3.

20. Bernard Crick, *Orwell: A Life* (Penguin 1980), p. 426.

to get his friend more involved in the paper, particularly by sending him to report from areas of the world which would be bound to interest him. The *Observer* tried to get Orwell sent out as a correspondent to Algiers and Sicily in August 1943, in the wake of the Allied landings, but the attempt failed in the face of official obstruction. A far more intriguing prospect was the idea of sending him to South Africa in 1947—48 to report on the election contest between Dr Malan's National Party and Jan Smuts's Unionists. Unfortunately Orwell was far too ill by then to undertake the journey.

Orwell's contribution to David Astor and his paper took several forms. As a political guide, he was important in confirming Astor's suspicion of the Soviet Union and in equating totalitarianism on the left with totalitarianism on the right — the thesis of *Animal Farm* and *Nineteen Eighty-Four*. More importantly, perhaps, Orwell was instrumental in making David aware of the post-war problem of decolonization in Africa. Orwell had always taken an interest in Indian independence — the subject of his first "Forum" — and towards the end of the war he persuaded David that the next great challenge to British post-imperialism would come in Africa, a continent which then excited little interest, apart from the fighting in the desert. Orwell argued that Africa would become the greatest challenge for decolonization, and it was there that Britain could avoid the mistakes made during the course of the struggle for Indian independence. The *Observer* was thus the first, and for a long time the only, British paper to focus on the problems of decolonization in Africa and in particular the plight of Africans on their own continent. The *Observer*'s interest was intensified by the political victory of Dr Malan in the South African elections in May 1948 which swept his National Party to power. Dr Malan thereafter began to institutionalize the apartheid system, and the *Observer* began its campaign of drawing the facts of the oppressive regime to the attention of the world — a campaign for which it was to become better known than anything else. Orwell looked on in admiration as the *Observer* started to write about Africa, writing to David Astor on November 19, 1949: "I am so glad the Obs. is taking up Africa."

Orwell's contribution was not only political but journalistic. It was he who taught David the merits of clear, simple English prose as the best vehicle for communication. In April 1946 *Horizon* magazine published an essay by Orwell called "Politics and the English Language", which David had circulated to every new writer on the *Observer* while he was foreign editor from 1945 to 1948. Orwell's message was simple: that precise English leads to precise thinking, and vice versa.

"A man may take to drink because he feels himself to be a failure, and then fail all the more completely because he drinks. It is rather the same thing that is happening to the English language. It becomes ugly and inaccurate because our thoughts are foolish but the slovenliness of our language makes it easier for us to have foolish thoughts. The point is that the process is reversible.[21]

This remained the yardstick for *Observer* writing throughout David Astor's time as editor. There were to be no rhetorical flourishes or purple prose. Orwell again:

The inflated style is itself a kind of euphemism. A mass of Latin words falls upon the facts like soft snow, blurring the outlines and covering up all the details. The great enemy of clear language is insincerity. When there is a gap between one's real and one's declared aims, one turns as it were instinctively to long words and exhausted idioms, like a cuttlefish squirting out ink.[22]

David's contribution to Orwell's life in the post-war years was to help the ailing writer in any way, big or small, that he could. He suggested that he should spend a summer on the Isle of Jura off the coast of the Scottish Western Highlands, part of which was owned by Lord Astor, in the hope that it would be good for his health. Orwell, who had long dreamed of such a retreat, leaped at the idea and set out for the island. Much to Astor's surprise, instead of being content with one summer holiday, Orwell rented a desolate farmhouse called Barnhill on the northern tip of the island in which he intended to try to live the whole year round. It

21. *The Collected Essays, Journalism and Letters of George Orwell*, Vol 4. (Penguin 1980), p. 157.

22. Ibid, p. 166.

had never occurred to David that a seriously ill man would elect to live on Jura all year, let alone at Barnhill, which was at least fifteen miles away from a telephone or any other outpost of civilization. It was indeed in many ways an unwise decision, but Orwell warmed to Barnhill and stayed there continuously — with winter breaks in sanatoria — until he was too ill to live on his own. He sent David a series of letters reporting on his life on the island and his struggles against nature in the garden. It was on Jura that he wrote *Nineteen Eighty-Four*, and he related to David the ups and downs of composition. Orwell was living at Barnhill, out of contact with the outside world, during the beginning of the Cold War, the Berlin Airlift, the stationing of American bombers in England and the explosion of the Russian atomic bomb. On October 9, 1948, he wrote to Astor with the outside circumstances very much on his mind.

> I'm a bit out of touch with the news, partly because the battery of my wireless is getting weak, but everything looks pretty black. I don't personally believe an all-out shooting war could happen now, only perhaps "incidents" such as used to occur all the time between Russia and Japan, but I suppose the atomic war is now a certainty within not very many years. This book I am writing is about the possible state of affairs if the atomic war *isn't* conclusive.... I am still worried about our politics in Africa and South Asia. Is Crankshaw still going to Africa for you, I wonder? I keep thinking, shall I get such and such a book done before the rockets begin to fly and we go back to clay tablets.
>
> There is an eagle flying over the field in front. They always come here in windy weather.

Orwell continued to do occasional book reviewing for the *Observer*, and on the eve of the publication of *Nineteen Eighty-Four* the paper also carried a "Profile" of him.

During 1948 he had to spend a considerable amount of time in hospital but by the end of the year his health had declined to the point where it was no longer possible for him to continue living on the island and he moved to Cranham Sanatorium in the Cotswold Hills. In 1948 David Astor had been able to help him by obtaining the drug Streptomycin from the United States. Streptomycin was soon to end tuberculosis as a fatal disease, but it came too late to save Orwell. Throughout his time in hospital, David Astor used the Astor Estate in New York to send him food parcels (rationing in Britain was still very strict) in hospital, and even managed to procure for him a pair of hand-made size twelve boots, which Orwell always found very difficult to find. David was in constant touch with Orwell's doctor, Dr Bruce Dick, and helped in any way that he could. But all the doctors could advise was quiet and rest. Bernard Crick has written:

> Only the occasional review now for the *Observer* — less for the money than to express his gratitude to Astor who kept sending him little comforts, anxious enquiries and helpful suggestions. "Have you ever considered the idea of using the wire-recorder machine?" he asked when they took Orwell's typewriter away....since he seemed to be overworking. No more articles but his correspondence with his agent got ever longer and more complex.[23]

In July 1949, David Astor was surprised to get the following letter from Orwell, then at Cranham, dated July 18:

> When I am well and about again, some time next year perhaps, I intend getting married again. I suppose everyone will be horrified, but it seems to me a good idea. Apart from other considerations, I think I shall stay alive longer if I were married and had someone to look after me. It is Sonia Brownell, the sub-editor of *Horizon*. I can't remember whether you know her, but you probably do.

On September 3, 1949, he moved from Cranham to his last bed at University College Hospital in Gower Street, London. David visited him frequently there, as he had done at Cranham, and found that although Orwell was almost skeletal in appearance, he never lost his sense of humour or his dignity. On October 13 Orwell married Sonia in the hospital. It involved getting a special licence from the Archbishop of Canterbury, and David Astor handled the necessary correspondence with Lambeth Palace and was a witness at the ceremony. It was kept short, so as not to tire

---

23. Bernard Crick, p. 553

Orwell, and afterwards David entertained Sonia and a few friends to a wedding lunch at the Ritz.

Orwell died on January 21, 1950. A memorial service was held in London, but Orwell presented his friends with one last, rather puzzling request — that he, the avowed sceptic, should be buried in a churchyard. He had no connections with any church, so it was David who came to the rescue again by finding him a small plot in the church courtyard of All Saints, Sutton Courtenay, opposite the country house that David had bought just after the war. Sutton Courtenay is a small village near Oxford; now it is dwarfed by the nearby cooling towers of Didcot power station and immediately adjacent to the churchyard is a testing laboratory for the Atomic Energy Commission. It was a suitably Orwellian resting place.

The small gravestone was inscribed simply with his real name, Eric Arthur Blair 1903—1950. In the same graveyard is the rather more substantial tomb of H. H. Asquith, Prime Minister from 1908 to 1916, a resident of Sutton Courtenay. However, it is to find George Orwell's last resting-place that the pilgrims come.

5

The Golden Age

The golden age of David Astor's *Observer* has often been described as lasting from his appointment as editor in 1948 to the Suez Crisis in 1956. In fact, as we have seen, the paper had been responding to David's particular blend of politics and ideas long before '48 − even before the departure of Garvin − and it was less damaged by Suez than is commonly supposed.

The *Observer* at the end of the war was a very different paper from the *Observer* at the war's beginning. Its average yearly sale in 1942 had been 241,613, whereas in 1947, just before David became editor, it was 359,912: he had already got his revolution moving before he was officially in charge − and even more so in terms of influence than in terms of circulation. And once he was in the saddle this rise in circulation and widening of influence continued steadily. In September 1956 the *Observer* overtook the *Sunday Times* for the first time, with a circulation of 568,969, and it did not start to level off until 1960.

The paper also made a reasonable profit during those years, rising from £12,855 in 1949 to £76,249 in 1955. But to keep this success in perspective it must be remembered that conditions for newspaper publishing in the 1940s and 1950s were very different from what they were in the 1960s − not to mention the post-Wapping 1980s. The most important factor in this difference was newsprint rationing, which was in force for seventeen years, from

1940 to 1957. Throughout the war the *Observer* was limited to eight pages, and even by the time of Suez, when rationing was much less severe, it was still only a sixteen-page newspaper.

This suited the *Observer*, because it meant that advertising space in its pages was at a premium and could be sold at a relatively high price (before commercial TV got under way in 1955, newspapers were the favoured advertising medium). Furthermore, safe in the knowledge that the advertisers had few other outlets, it did not have to worry about becoming "an attractive advertising medium". The only competition up to 1960 was the *Sunday Times*; the *Observer* and its rival exercised a cosy duopoly on the nation's Sunday morning reading habits; moreover the *Sunday Times* was going through one of its more torpid phases under the uninspired direction of Viscount Kemsley, who ran his newspapers to climb the ladder of the peerage as much as anything else, and thus required them to be as inoffensive and unexciting as possible. The official historians of the *Sunday Times* acknowledge this problem. There was

> too much nagging attention to detail and no full-time reporting staff to gather or analyse news.... There was painstaking effort but no real strength, nothing exceptional in political authority and nothing to compare with the fresh assessments of things such as were attracting the young to the *Observer*.[1]

The *Sunday Times* was stuffy, archaic and establishment-minded; it had its own constituency — clarified by its editor as "say a small shop-keeper in Swindon, doing rather well, a lad just about to go up to university", but the paper did not seem to be able to broaden its base during the 1940s and 1950s. The success of the *Observer* during its golden age was thus achieved in a somewhat artificial commercial environment. This is not to say that it would have found it impossible to thrive if those artificial market conditions had not existed, only that if a paper was going to experiment and take risks, as David Astor's *Observer* did during the 1940s and 1950s, there was no better time to do it. Immediately the insulating and comfortable artificial trading conditions of the

---

1. *Pearl of Days: An intimate portrait of the Sunday Times, 1822–1972.* Hobson, Kingley, Russell: (1972), p. 287.

1950s were removed towards the end of that decade — commercial TV was introduced in 1955, newsprint rationing lifted in 1957 and increased competition began with the *Sunday Telegraph* in 1960 and continued with colour magazines — the *Observer* found itself in difficulties that it was unable, ultimately, to resolve. But while the prevailing winds of newspaper economics were blowing his way, David Astor certainly made the most of them.

The *Observer* was also exactly in tune with the spirit of the age; it was the product of a thoughtful, serious generation which had fought through the Second World War, and had also seen — and in some cases experienced — the miseries of Depression and the failure to combat Fascism in the 1930s. To this generation ideas about politics, disarmament and world peace were serious issues. Such ideas were also in a considerable state of flux, which gave this generation the opportunity for constructive thinking about the world and its difficulties that had been denied to an earlier generation, and was to be denied to a later one brought up on the fixities of the Cold War. The *Observer* spoke for that generation of the middle classes which searched for ideas about and solutions to the problems of their earlier life. When this gave way to the hedonism of the 1960s and the cynicism of the 1970s, the *Observer* would begin to sound high-minded and self-righteous.

So what was David Astor trying to do with his paper during these golden years? He had come to it with the ideas of Adam von Trott and had honed his journalistic and political instincts with the help of George Orwell. It was not surprising, therefore, that when he tried to answer this question in a confidential memo in December 1959, entitled "On the Soul of the Paper", he started off with Hitler:

In the character of this paper, ethics matter more than politics. The particular ethics could be roughly defined as trying to do the opposite of what Hitler would have done. In fact, that may be their historic origin, as the paper's present personality was established in and just after the last war by people drawn together more by being "anti-Fascist" than by anything else.

Personally, I admit to being haunted by what Hitler showed to exist in all of us ordinary people, and therefore to being especially interested in antidotes to the kind of thinking he stimulated in people and they so readily adopted. I don't think that kind of thought and behaviour is specifically German, and believe that those who do are themselves unconsciously thinking in his terms.

In the same memo he described himself and the staff as "liberals, as internationalists"; David was indeed an ethical liberal, believing strenuously in the classic liberal maxims of toleration and freedom. Like Trott, he was an internationalist in the sense that he believed ethics transcended national boundaries, that the fight for tolerance and freedom was just as pertinent in the British Empire as anywhere else in the world. To Anthony Howard, a journalist doing a profile of David Astor for the *New Statesman* in 1975, David wrote:

> My aim has been to be militant in fighting for tolerance, freedom of expression, non-prejudice — all causes of moderation — here and abroad. What's wrong with moderates is that they lack militancy.

The *Observer* was certainly extreme in moderation, and fought for tolerance, democracy and freedom of expression in, for instance, South Africa as early as 1948, years before any other paper took up the cause of Africa. At the time it was accused of radicalism, subversion and worse, by the right-wing in Britain as much as by the whites in South Africa. In advocating equal rights for the Africans the *Observer* was doing no more than arguing forcefully for the hallmarks of moderation and liberalism to be applied to Africa. For its pains the paper was attacked by the Conservative Party and even by some in the Labour Party. In the 1970s the *Observer* attacked Arthur Scargill and union militants in Britain on the same grounds — that their activities were prejudicial to freedom and tolerance in Britain — for which the paper was attacked by the left-wing of the Labour Party for having "deserted the fold". It had, of course, never been part of "the fold"; in attacking Arthur Scargill it was merely identifying the same elements of intolerance and authoritarianism that it had earlier identified in the British colonial empire and South Africa.

When the *Observer* claimed it was "independent" of political party, this was no idle boast: its principles were indivisible and transcended the party boundaries drawn up in Britain by the arbitrary forces of historical circumstance. Indeed, David Astor's politics, reflecting his ancestry, had more in common with the modern American Democratic Party than any British political party. There would be jibes of "Socialism south of the Sahara" when the millionaire Astor took up the cause of the black Africa. But David was never a socialist anywhere, nor did the *Observer* ever advocate Socialism, which David always saw as inimical to freedom. He saw the freedom to own private property as going hand in hand with freedom of expression and racial toleration — private property was a bastion against the overlordship of the State. He could be best understood in terms of the American democratic tradition; Sam Beer, his Balliol contemporary, compared him to John F. Kennedy, another man who used his wealth and privilege to gain for others the "rights" that he enjoyed for himself. The nearest the British political tradition comes to this is with the conservative paternalist tradition — with the crucial difference that the liberal democrats of the Astor ilk did not expect any deference in return for their help. Indeed, a characteristic often noted in David Astor was his lack of deference and acute embarrassment at being deferred to. Like his father, he was a true "American democrat", and as such was often incomprehensible to the English.

David was therefore first and foremost an idealist, running his paper on a system of principles. He was probably the only real idealist to edit or own a major British newspaper this century. The paper was not run to make money or to curry favour with a political party or with the establishment. David had no interest in money, other than in giving it away; he was disdainful of party allegiances; and he was born into the establishment (although he lived at arm's length from it). The *Observer* was run much as though it were a public service — which was fitting, the role model of the Observer Trust being the BBC. This is what made the paper unique. Not being driven to chase a higher readership, it left popular or sensational stories about subjects that were well-known to the public to the rest of the press, and became involved in reporting political, cultural and ethnic movements which were under-represented — which often made its coverage eclectic. This involved an interest in minorities that was a direct reflection of its editor's long-standing interest in the disadvantaged and the oppressed: they would always find a voice in the *Observer*.

Above all David Astor's *Observer* was a paper of ideas. The office was originally staffed with thinkers and writers, not reporters — they became reporters later on. In picking his writers David was careful to ensure that within certain broad parameters the quality and nature of their thinking chimed with his own, and that the way they expressed their ideas would appeal to the readers he wanted to attract. He has described these readers as "the question-asking, scientifically minded readers among all three political parties; people who liked a reasoned approach, not a declamatory one; who wanted to extend their knowledge and were willing to hear new propositions". He was looking, therefore, for writing of honesty and clarity, rather than for journalistic cleverness. And having found writers who suited his ends, he then — within a clearly defined ideological context — gave them their heads. If that context became uncomfortable for a writer, then it was the writer who had to give way: both Deutscher and Haffner reached a point in their *Observer* careers when they could no longer work within the context, and they had to leave.

It was already apparent during the war that David was trying to create a "writers'" newspaper, along the lines of the more literate French press, or of Cyril Connolly's *Horizon*. (The contemporary equivalent of his ideal newspaper is the *New York Review of Books*.) He finally collected round him probably the largest and most distinguished selection of intellectuals ever to have graced a British newspaper office, including at different times Haffner, Deutscher, Orwell, Schumacher, Koestler, William Clark, Alastair Buchan, Edward Crankshaw, Neal Ascherson and many others. As David Astor told the author, the *Observer* was "the Balliol I never had".

The *Observer*'s emphasis on ideas rather than on news, together with David's preoccupation with foreign affairs and defence matters, meant that those who saw themselves principally as news-gatherers, or who were concerned with domestic affairs, such as the excellent foreign and political correspondent Nora Beloff, would always feel comparatively neglected. Cyril Dunn, one of the few professional journalists imported from the *Yorkshire Post*, later recalled the perpetual competition between "ideas" and "news":

> Not every Saturday was as fraught as the day in 1952 when a stand collapsed at a Bolton cup-tie match, killing some 60 spectators. A natural splash if ever there was one. But the editor put his foot down, firmly. This spat was so traumatic

for me that I could never remember exactly what happened. For years I believed that I'd got the first edition away before the editor stepped in, but the files disprove this. In EVERY edition the cup-tie tragedy is a discreet single-column story at the end of Page One, and the splash is a diplomatic piece from Robert Stephens.

In this distribution of emphasis the *Observer* was following a strict house rule: subjects must be put in order of what was perceived to be their *real* importance, so the paper usually favoured the foreign crisis as against the details of domestic affairs that might be of less long-term importance. The principle behind this was to avoid the mistakes of the 1930s, when British newspapers had tended to favour the doings of Stanley Baldwin and the Abdication crisis, and had not adequately reported the realities of Fascist Europe.

The *Observer* also concentrated on what Willi Guttman called "the scoop by interpretation". This was based on the idea that there was no longer any such thing as "exclusive news" for a newspaper. A paper could present an "exclusive story" as a result of its own investigative journalism, but in an age when all news reached the public first by radio or television, "news exclusives" no longer occurred — or did so very rarely. Therefore, although David Astor had nothing against "news exclusives", he preferred his paper to concentrate its efforts on explaining what the events that flashed by on radio and television actually meant. *Observer* writers were seeking for the scoop of new arguments or new interpretations, and it is for such "scoops of interpretation" that the paper is remembered: for example, its presentation of Khrushchev's speech to the Twentieth Party Congress, and of the Marshall Plan. On such subjects a new and challenging perspective would often be offered: the "scoop by interpretation" was what made David Astor's journalistic pulse race.

The opposite was true of economics, which would remain one of his blank spots. On receiving the *Observer* accounts in July 1941 he had written to Miss Kindersley: "The accounts you sent me stunned me by their weight. I am allergic to figures." This was true. He had never had to take an interest in money, which was always taken care of for the family by teams of lawyers and accountants; he was only ever interested in money when he could give it away. Anthony Sampson has written of arriving at the *Observer*:

> David's range of interests and curiosities seemed limitless: one day I was involved with urging Herbert Morrison to re-plan the whole of London; the next day I was writing a series reassessing Freud. Only when economics and industry loomed up did David's eyes begin to glaze over; he delegated them thankfully to successive economics editors – Susan Strange, then Andrew Shonfield, then Sam Brittan [infact Shonfield came first] – but hardly anyone else seemed to notice Britain's industrial decline. It was the discussions about traffic which revealed the full detachment from industry. David could never understand why he could not park his car in the middle of Oxford; and when the new motorways were soon congested Philip Toynbee suggested that they should be banned to all lorries. But it was part of the prevailing political mood in the fifties, to be too preoccupied with Britain's role in the world to notice that she was losing her economic means to have much of a role.

However, this blind spot of the *Observer*'s was shared with the rest of the British press.

In practical terms, David Astor stood closer to the right-wing of the Labour Party than to any other section of the political spectrum. The *Observer* agreed with the Labour Party on a wide range of issues from the abolition of capital punishment to the Suez crisis. Attlee, Gaitskell, Crosland and Jenkins were natural political allies, and David was closer to Hugh Gaitskell himself than to almost any other politician. Indeed, Attlee wrote occasionally and Roy Jenkins wrote regularly for the paper. In domestic politics, the *Observer* supported the mixed economy and the political consensus between moderate Conservatives and moderate Socialists that prevailed in Britain from 1945 to 1979, and which the *Observer* had done a great deal to bring about during the war. When Jim Rose joined the paper as literary editor in 1948, David sent him a leader from the *Observer* of May 23, 1948 entitled "ONE PARTY", which he claimed would tell Rose "where we stand". The editorial was a commentary on the Labour Party conference at Scarborough, attacking the "fiery spirits" of the Labour left for wanting to impose what they conceived to be the true creed of Socialism on everybody else. The *Observer*, however, took pride in the balance and continuity that the two-party system was giving Britain:

> The two-party system is no result of accident or theory. It has its roots in human nature. There is a broad temperamental division between natural reformers and natural conservatives; they tend to gravitate into two parties, one wanting to go fast, the other slow. But the system will fail unless the two parties agree on the fundamentals of the good society not to wish to wreck each other's work.... Until lately the system worked smoothly in this country. Liberals and Conservatives differed sufficiently to give the country a choice, and agreed sufficiently to maintain the continuity of national life. Is a similar harmony possible between Socialists and Conservatives? Yes, it is possible; modern Conservatives and moderate Socialists have a good deal of common ground. They could alternate in office without vast, destructive reversals of legislation.

These were the words of the "middle way", and as Anthony Crosland, the high priest of Socialist revisionism, told Terry Kilmartin, the literary editor, in 1957: "The *Observer* is our bible".

In one respect, however, the *Observer* was out ahead of the Labour Party, and that was in the field of foreign policy. It was taking an interest in Africa and decolonization long before the Labour Party establishment began seriously to consider the issue. Attlee, Party leader until 1955, "liberator" of India, seemed particularly immune to the *Observer's* coverage of Africa. The paper also advocated the abandonment of the British nuclear deterrent in the late 1950s as the means towards establishing a nuclear duopoly of the USA and USSR, which might encourage a degree of dual policing and responsibility between the two superpowers, whilst Gaitskell – and Nye Bevan – were staunchly defending the nuclear deterrent. Even Tony Benn, the 1980s radical but the 1960s apostle of "White Heat" as the Minister of Technology in Wilson's government, looked on Astor's ideas for the bomb with amused condescension. Benn noted in his diary of a dinner with Astor in July 1966:

> We talked about prices and incomes, and the Labour Government and de Gaulle's view of the world. Astor is a

sentimental old liberal who thinks that we ought to give up the bomb altogether and try to persuade de Gaulle to do the same, and that the prices and incomes policy wouldn't succeed − generally speaking not incisive or effective. But he is a fundamentally nice guy.[2]

Roy Thomson, the Canadian press baron who bought *The Times* and *Sunday Times* during the 1960s, put it in a nutshell when he compared the *Observer* as a "question-asking paper" to the *Sunday Times*, which was a "reassuring, establishment paper". The *Observer* set out to ask questions of the world, to challenge the prevailing wisdom and to search for the new. Sir William Haley described it as "beacon for the young and ardent in the heart and for all who cared".[3] The paper's natural readers were the young, students, teachers and academics, intellectuals, writers and members of the liberal professions. It had a special affinity with students, the most enthusiastic question-askers, and was the natural sponsor of the first national student debating competition, the *Observer* Mace debating tournament. One Oxford student and future correspondent of the paper, Tony Howard, compared it with the *Sunday Times* in *Isis* on February 16, 1955:

> For when all has been said. . . it remains true that the *Sunday Times*, finding its inspiration in Lieutenant-General Sir Brian Horrocks, belongs to the establishment, and the *Observer*, deriving its ethos from Father Trevor Huddleston, to the barricades. Between the two, students − if that's not a dirty word − have never had much difficulty in choosing.

If this marks the distinction between the two papers, a conversation between David Astor and Roy Thomson at a dinner party given by the International Press Institute illustrates the distinction between David Astor as an editor and the more run-of-the-mill press barons. Thomson asked David how much money the *Observer* was making, to which David replied, "I don't deal with that side of the

2. Hutchinson 1987 *Out of the Wilderness, Tony Benn Diaries: 1963−67*, July 4, 1966: p. 444.

3. Haley to David Astor: October 21, 1976; David Astor Papers.

paper, you will have to ask the general manager." Roy Thomson was somewhat bewildered by this but after a pause he asked what the *Observer*'s circulation was, to which David replied "I am not sure, but it isn't as big as the circulation of the *Sunday Times*." As Thomson had recently bought the *Sunday Times*, this pleased him immensely. After some moments, David Astor then asked "What's your policy on Berlin, Roy?" Thomson was taken aback. "I don't know," he replied. Then, after a few seconds' reflection, "But I am sure I could buy one."

The quality that David Astor brought to the paper that was to be both the source of its strength during the golden years and its weakness during its declining years was amateurism. The year he had spent on the *Yorkshire Post* in 1936 was the sum total of his professional journalistic experience before he took over in 1942. He was not a professional journalist; he was involved in journalism to promote and advance certain principles and ideas, and the rules of journalism came second to this. David Astor was never bogged down by convention or habit — he had never been on an orthodox paper long enough to acquire either conventions or habits. This made the *Observer* innovative and daring.

His principal talent as an editor was his ability to identify and cultivate talent. It was on this that the fame of the *Observer* ultimately rested. As he has said to the author: "My aim was to find people of talent...people of real power as writers and then turn them into journalists and this was really what I was consciously doing." To allow these writers to flourish on the *Observer*, the paper was run in a relaxed fashion, with few rules, time schedules or other encumbrances: the writer was god and office life revolved around him. This could disorientate the new arrival. On re-joining the paper in the late 1950s, George Seddon tried to raise the matter of his salary with the general manager:

> ...but he was out of the office, wandering around Soho looking for antiques, and I had to leave with nothing finally settled. In the end I was offered £75–£150 more than originally suggested. I wrote to ask the administration editor what the office hours were and he said "If you ever find out, I would love to know."

At the core of the paper were the wartime recruits, Haffner, Orwell, Deutscher and Kimche. Of these only Haffner survived into the mid-1950s. Kimche ceased writing for the paper in 1945 and Orwell died in 1950. Deutscher left the paper in 1946 to concentrate on his writing — he was soon to write the best-selling biography of Stalin and later of Trotsky—but he also resigned because of the irrevocable difference between his own Marxist outlook and David Astor's liberal democratic political world-view. They parted on good terms, although by 1946 Deutscher found the paper "...too bourgeois...which on the whole tends towards the right and has a very militant anti-communist slant."[4] Haffner remained until 1955, and David always thought of him "as the *Observer*". Haffner remained undoubtedly the quintessential *Observer* figure, intellectual, liberal-minded, tolerant but with a very serious, stern combative streak to him. It was he who wrote most of the think-pieces from 1945 to 1955, although political disagreements with Astor at that time (which will be discussed later) forced his return to Germany in 1955. But as David Astor wrote to Haffner in 1953:

> I regard you as the most valuable member of the firm...and as a person I have the highest admiration for your courage and integrity, as well as for your intellect and artistic gifts, and have no illusions that you owe your success to me — you only owe me for the means and place of producing a success that you would have produced anyway, somewhere, inevitably.

Haffner won enormous admiration from the rest of the office. Cyril Dunn, who joined the paper in 1948, has written:

> Haffner struck me as easily the greatest in the [office], a typical high-domed Herr Dokter...He laid things on the line at editorial conferences with god-like authority. He showed the same kind of iron concentration as Charles Davy did; when he sat down at his typewriter to compose one of his massive leader-page pieces about world politics it was as if he had turned to stone; nothing could disturb his terrible composure...off duty Haffner was the kindest of men; he

---

4. *Isaac Deutscher* by Ludger Syre, p. 161; translation supplied by Tamara Deutscher.

went out of his way to give me, for instance, enormous and flattering encouragement in my early Obs. days, when I seemed to be getting nowhere.

Another German who was very influential was "Rix" Lowenthal, a member of the "Neue Beginnen" group whom David had met during the war. An ex-Communist, Lowenthal worked on the paper just after the war and then returned for a few years after Suez. He was as intellectual as Haffner, but without the human warmth and twinkling sense of humour that endeared Haffner to his English colleagues. Lowenthal was much more of a dry and inflexible intellectual.

To replace Orwell, Kimche, Deutscher and others, David began to recruit a new generation of writers that would prove to be the mainstay of the *Observer* during the golden age. His recruiting ground was the universities and his own circle of family friends. Very rarely did his gift for talent-spotting go astray. He sought mostly descriptive writers, to complement the core of intellectuals and foreign-policy specialists. One of the most important new arrivals was William Clark, who joined the paper on a full-time basis in May 1949 as an editorial assistant, but really made his mark as the diplomatic editor before leaving to become Eden's press secretary at Downing Street in May 1955. He resigned from that office in 1956 over the Suez Crisis (see Chapter 7) and then served as the paper's India correspondent from 1957 to 1960, after which he set up the Institute of Overseas Development. On a personal level Clark became David Astor's closest confidant on the paper during this period. In contrast to Haffner and Lowenthal, he was extremely gregarious and talkative, as well as very intelligent. After Oxford, he had served as an information officer in the British, diplomatic service during the war, in America, mainly in Chicago, and it was then that he began to build up the wide range of contacts for which he would become legendary. After the war he worked briefly in London as editor of the *Encyclopaedia Britannica*. He came to David Astor's notice through his voluntary contribution to the *Observer*'s large article on the Marshall Plan in 1947. At the time Clark was worried that the voice of Germany would be ignored in discussions about the future of Europe, "but I need not have worried about hearing the voice of Germany, for when I arrived at the *Observer* for my first ever editorial meeting there I found that more than half of the editorial group was German or central European".[5]

Clark was not just the diplomatic correspondent and confidant of David Astor, he was also the "court jester", who made a habit of standing on his head when he got to the office in the morning. He was ostentatiously brilliant — with the academic qualifications to back him up — and very witty. His voice was loud and educated and with his constant name-dropping he could appear pompous to those who did not know him well, unaware of the fact that he laid his name-dropping on with a trowel to enhance his image as a joker. The story which he most liked to tell against himself concerned an occasion when someone remarked to him that he was "the most terrible name-dropper". "That's odd," Clark replied after a pause. "The Queen Mother was telling me that just the other day." A glimpse of Clark at editorial conferences was recorded by Cyril Dunn in January 1948:

> The Conference passed on to Profiles. T. S. Eliot, who's just got an OM in the New Year's Honours List, was suggested...Ivor Brown couldn't understand why *Eliot* had been given an OM; why not Shaw for example?...IB asked outright *why* Eliot had got it and who had put him forward, to which Clark replied: "I've heard it was the Ministry of Agriculture because he'd written a poem called 'The Waste Land' and that it was the Archbishop of Canterbury, who's hoping for another murder in the cathedral".

Another stalwart was Hugh Massingham, the political correspondent from 1945 to 1961. Son of one of the most famous editors of Fleet Street, W. H. Massingham (editor of the *Nation*, 1907–23), Hugh was a brilliant writer, and the founder of the modern political column. One of his many admirers and imitators, Alan Watkins, has written that: "the change Massingham introduced was not of reporting convention or technique but of manner, tone, style. He refused to accept politicians at their own valuation." In his own description of his work he went back to the "irreverent, laughing, sardonic dimensions of Grub Street" for his inspiration, and was not prepared to treat politicians as sacred cows. His

---

5. Clark: *From Three Worlds* (Sidgwick and Jackson 1986), p. 94.

writing was inventive and exciting, though often rather too devoid of political content for David Astor's liking. In Watkins's words, "the idea of painstakingly guiding the readers of the *Observer* through, say, the latest White Paper on housing filled him with not the least enthusiasm".[6] A nervous man, with a stammer, he was probably more a novelist *manqué* than a journalist. None the less his column had a fanatical following at Westminster, for its wit and inside gossip. He was essentially a Bevanite in outlook, but he seldom allowed this to colour his judgement. He cultivated the friendship of only a few politicians, but these included Rab Butler and Bevan himself, both famously garrulous. His prime source remained a mystery until he was spied having tea with Lady Isobel Cripps at the Ritz on a Friday afternoon in 1949 — this was, apparently, a weekly ritual.

However, the two most gifted writers to emerge on the *Observer* during these years were John Gale and Patrick O'Donovan. John Gale was a feature writer, who was taken on by David on the strength of one article that he sent the paper entitled "In Defence of Suede Shoes", which was duly published. Gale worked for the paper for twenty years, before committing suicide in 1974, aged forty-eight. He was a perfectionist who would spend hours putting his pieces of prose together, and then polishing them until they were absolutely perfect — in contrast to O'Donovan. Gale was very emotional and got totally involved with his stories. He was a good interviewer, always conducting the interview standing up, with a clipboard, but would only continue to interview people if he liked them; he was famous for walking out of an interview with Fred Astaire after five minutes. His speciality was doing features on unusual subjects or unusual people, such as tramps — unknown people with something to say. This type of story entered the journalistic lexicon as a "John Gale Story". He suffered a mental breakdown after witnessing and describing scenes of horrendous violence during the Algerian war in the late 1950s, and never fully recovered. He turned this experience to great literary effect however, describing the experience with great wit and honesty in his autobiography, *Clean Young Englishman*.

The best writer on the paper, however, was probably Patrick

---

6. Massingham — *Brief Lives* (Hamish Hamilton 1982), p. 114.

O'Donovan, a product of Ampleforth and Christ Church and the youngest major in the wartime Irish Guards. Like Gale, he had no journalistic experience. He was recommended at the end of the War to David Astor by Nicholas Henderson of the Foreign Office. Astor asked O'Donovan to write a short piece on anything he liked and he chose to write on Anne Brontë. Astor and Ivor Brown liked it and the *Observer* took him on. David recruited talent even if there was no particular opening for the person in question at the time, seeing it as his own task to find a niche for them. He was clearly at a loss to know what to do with O'Donovan initially, because the latter wrote to his old schoolmaster at Ampleforth in July 1946:

> After a few unsettling weeks I have landed a job as a journalist here. The pay is exiguous and my position could hardly be more humble. I get about 6 pounds a week and they call me an apprentice. They tell me it is a good paper to start on and it looks as if I shall soon be sent to report on the fringes of the Iron Curtain...I have only been at it a couple of days and seem to have spent most of the time sitting in a large leather chair in the library...[7]

However, his talents were soon put to use and he became the paper's most celebrated foreign correspondent, crowning his career with five years in Washington from 1955 to 1960, during which time he twice won the award for the best reporting of America by the foreign press. But he was equally at home covering domestic events and issues, and was just as good on Churchill's funeral as he was on the Six-day War. Indeed, his article on Churchill's funeral showed O'Donovan at his best, and his description of the procession moving along Fleet Street to St Paul's is worth quoting from:

> The procession...was beautiful in the way that great works of art are beautiful. It obeyed secret rules. It was dignified and cast a dignity about it. There were the familiar and expected surprises. There was the Earl Marshal walking alone

---

7. Patrick O'Donovan *A Journalist's Odyssey* (Esmonde Publishing 1985), p. 12.

and worried in the centre of a great space like any man lost in a high street, but carrying a gilded sceptre. There was Lord Mountbatten pacing behind the Chiefs of Staff carefully manipulating his sword and, like any trooper, trying to keep pace with the band. There were the officers with their trays of Churchill's medals, held out like ware for sale. There were the heraldic banners of the Cinque Ports and the Spencer-Churchills, too stiff to wave in any wind, carried like trophies before the coffin. And there were the marshals with their batons held on their hips in a baroque gesture that Marlborough would have known. There was the family looking lost and human and trying to keep up. There were the anonymous coaches filled with women. But the central, the overwhelming fact was the dead body in a box made of oak. There was no getting away from that. It was trundled into the City on a huge and impractical gun-carriage. It was pulled by a great phalanx of lusty young men. It moved, huge and red with the Union flag, past the hotels and the steamy restaurants and the newspaper offices and the pubs, surrounded by this extraordinary silence that could not be broken even by the bands and the rhythmic feet. It was a silence, not of grief but of respect. In fact the City was stopped and was turned into a theatre and it was all performed as a drama that all men understand. Commentators all over the world have reached for their explanations. This was the last time that such a thing could happen. This was the last time that London would be the capital of the world. This was an act of mourning for the Imperial past. This marked the final act in Britain's greatness. This was a great gesture of self-pity and after this the coldness of reality and the status of Scandinavia.

O'Donovan was a supremely gifted writer. David Astor liked to call him "a poet", and he became one of his favourite sons on the paper. Unlike Gale, who had to work for his prose, O'Donovan was an instinctive writer, for whom it all seemed effortless. He was best at short pieces without too much research — indeed, he was almost too instinctive a writer for his own good, as he did not spend much time interviewing people or reading up. Jane Bown, the photographer, travelled widely with Gale and O'Donovan and noted that while Gale conducted scrupulous research, on one memorable trip to Ireland O'Donovan tended to draw a line at the publican and the parish priest. He was a gift to news editors, as Bill Millinchip recalls:

> One Saturday when news was slow and we had nothing to fill the page and it started to snow, a sudden fall of thick flakes — the start of a weather story. I rang Patrick at home — he hardly ever came into the office — and asked him if he could give us a little colour piece about the blizzard. It wasn't snowing in Hampshire, but Patrick left his lunch guests and in not much more than half an hour we had a seven-hundred-word feature about strange weather he had encountered on his travels round the world.

His technique was vividly illustrated by his account of an interview with a Greek minister. He sat pretending to take notes and was then asked by Isaldoris to read back to him what he had said. "Which was awkward," Patrick wrote, "because all I had in my notebook was a drawing of a cat, the address of an Athens barber I'd just remembered and one line saying 'UN Important'." If O'Donovan caught himself out on that occasion, there was one famous instance when the *Observer* was caught out by his special talent for inventive prose. Due to an inability to reach the Arlington Cemetery he filed a report of the burial of Robert Kennedy before it happened. Amongst other descriptive passages, was "and priests knelt in the sun". The train carrying Kennedy's body had been held up and the burial took place at night.

Another recruit at this time, who was to become David Astor's deputy editor, was Michael Davie. He came to the notice of Astor through Martin Wight, his teacher at Haileybury, who had written a much admired pamphlet for Chatham House called "Power Politics" which attracted the attention of Haffner, after which Wight was for a time the paper's UN correspondent. Wight mentioned Davie to Astor, who asked if he could write. Wight produced a letter from Davie about his holidays. Astor was impressed and asked Davie to write an 800 word "notebook" of his recent holiday. He was then interviewed by Ivor Brown, who published the notebook and gave Davie the sum of £8.00 — princely, considering that Davie was still a student at Oxford. This was in 1948, and he was more surprised still to be invited to dinner by Astor at

Boodles, and asked whether he would like to join the paper. Unfortunately, Davie had to wait until after his final exams, but when he turned up for his first day, like O'Donovan, he found that no one had any idea what he was supposed to do. However, at the behest of the news editor he was asked to be "religious correspondent", then a post unknown to Fleet Street. Upon asking what this might involve, Davie was advised to go and see Lord Astor at Cliveden. On lunching with Lord Astor, he learnt that the religious minorities were not well enough represented on the BBC. After this hesitant beginning to his career, Davie went on to do a variety of jobs for the paper, including spells as sports editor and editor of the colour magazine, before becoming deputy editor.

David's unerring sense for talent, little more than a "hunch" that a writer was worth trying out, worked again with Gavin Young, author of *A Slow Boat to China* and many other successful travel books, who became the *Observer*'s Peter Fleming in the 1960s and 1970s. Staying in Algeria in 1960, Gavin Young sent a letter to Astor asking if the paper would like him to report from Algeria, as he, like the *Observer*, was in sympathy with the Algerian side of the war. Expecting nothing in reply, Young was asked to come to London to discuss his proposals. He has written what happened next:

> At the *Observer*'s Dickensian offices in Tudor Street, Robert Stephens, the paper's Diplomatic Correspondent, grilled me very sweetly about recent events on the Arab scene, and evidently my replies were not unacceptably idiotic, because shortly afterwards the Editor himself received me. A floppy haired shy-voiced man, popping multicoloured sweets into his mouth from a tin on his desk, David Astor told me I would be taken on as a "stringer" — that is, a locally based correspondent paid a small retaining fee and so much extra for every word printed. Astounding...I had suddenly embarked on a new career.[8]

Gavin Young quickly proved his mettle by reporting from Nagaland, on the borders of north-east India, trekking for three

---

8. Gavin Young, *World Apart* (Hutchinson 1987), p. xiii.

weeks through very hostile Burmese jungle to get there — a journey that took great courage and ingenuity. Jim Rose had a similarly unusual introduction to the paper. Rose had been at Rugby and Oxford and worked at Bletchley during the war together with Alan Pryce-Jones, a friend of David's and an occasional reviewer for the *Observer* during the war. After the war Rose worked for Reuters, which he did not enjoy, so Pryce-Jones, who knew Astor was looking for a literary editor, advised him to consider Rose. Astor liked him and offered him the literary editorship. Rose said that he did not know much about the subject, which David Astor said was exactly what they were looking for: Rose would not be in the clutches of any particular literary coterie or movement. Somewhat to Rose's own surprise he took up this position in 1948 and stayed for three years. This was a conscious attempt to employ people to write on subjects outside their own field of expertise, to afford the reader a novel view of the subject.

Three other writers recruited to the paper in the late 1940s also had long and successful careers on the paper. Robert Stephens joined the paper in 1946, like Gavin Young, as a "stringer" in the Middle East. He returned to England in 1947 to become the *Observer*'s Middle East correspondent, and became diplomatic correspondent in 1957. Edward Crankshaw, author of several books on Russian history (as well as studies of Conrad and the Gestapo), had served from 1941 to 1944 on the British military mission to Moscow and was spotted for the *Observer* by TJ. He became the doyen of Kremlinologists; and his intellectual jousts with Deutscher, Lowenthal and Haffner at the editorial conferences were amongst the highlights of the week, as Crankshaw and Deutscher usually took diametrically opposite lines. Alastair Buchan, the son of novelist John Buchan, joined the paper from the *Economist* in 1951 and served as the Washington correspondent of the *Observer* before becoming diplomatic and defence correspondent in 1955. In 1958 he left the paper to become the first director of the Institute for Strategic Studies. On the *Observer* he virtually invented the study of nuclear and strategic thinking. Another correspondent who joined the paper in 1948 was Anthony Sampson, who together with the South African Colin Legum was recruited to specialize in African affairs. Their careers with the paper are discussed in more detail in the next chapter.

Economics was taken less seriously; but because he was aware of his own lack of interest in the subject, David acquired a string of very eminent economics correspondents.

In 1958 a young journalist from the *Financial Times*, Andrew Shonfield, recognizing this deficiency in the *Observer*, invited David to lunch in Fleet Street and told him that, excellent as the paper was, it did not have a good economics page. Up to that point, papers had City pages, but the discussion of economic questions was relatively ignored. Shonfield proposed himself as the man who could remedy this, and so he did during his three years on the paper from 1958 to 1961. He later became director of Chatham House and a professor at the European University in Florence. The Andrew Shonfield Association was named after him. Having established the tradition of economic journalism, he was followed by three equally distinguished economics journalists, Susan Strange, Samuel Brittan and Alan Day.

Good though these writers were, there can be no doubt that the *Observer* was chiefly known for its dazzling array of foreign correspondents. David Astor's own interests were focused on foreign affairs, and from the beginning of his spell as foreign editor from 1945 to 1948 he concentrated on building up the paper's foreign coverage, which under Garvin had been virtually non-existent. He founded the *Observer* Foreign News Service (or SERVOB) in 1946, to syndicate the dispatches of the its foreign correspondents, thus helping to pay for the cost of maintaining staff correspondents rather than relying on stringers. Ronald Harker was the first editor of SERVOB, and a service catering for six subscribers in 1946 could boast nearly a hundred subscribers by the late 1950s. The SERVOB correspondents were the young lions of the paper, and several of them became household names overseas. The reputation of the *Observer*'s correspondents was enough to cause panic in the novice Gavin Young, just taken on by the editor in 1960:

> Where on earth, I asked myself, would I scavenge enough information to compose an article authoritative enough to publish? Another thing; *Observer* correspondents were the cats' whiskers of Fleet Street, famous for their lucid, lively prose. How was I going to write like that at the drop of a hat?

Having made the grade, Young would later experience the value of being an *Observer* correspondent when he arrived in America:

"It was in New York that I realized the *Observer* was a newspaper of international and not merely national repute. I would tentatively introduce myself as its representative and watch doors fly open."[9]

Two of the most successful *Observer* correspondents were, of course, Young himself and Patrick O'Donovan. Some of the other correspondents were as unusual and exotic as anyone ever recruited on to a Fleet Street newspaper. One of the most celebrated was Philip Deane, whose real name was Gerassimos Gigantes; the *Observer* chose the pen-name. Gigantes was the son of a revered Greek general. He escaped to England after the invasion of Greece in 1941, served as a sublieutenant in the Royal Navy during the war, and returned to Athens to become an *Observer* stringer in 1945 at £25 a month. When the Korean War broke out he left at once for the front, filing dramatic stories for the *Observer* and three Greek papers, obviously regardless of his own safety. An Astor cable telling him to avoid danger was almost immediately followed by news that Deane had been wounded. He was hit four times in the thigh and marched off into captivity for almost three years by the North Koreans. In prison the North Koreans tried to brainwash him, giving up just as he thought he was going to break. A fellow prisoner was George Blake, with whom they probably had more success as on his return to the Secret Intelligence Service in London he spied for the Soviet Union. Deane arrived back in 1953 and, after working for a few more years for the *Observer*, went on to work for the United Nations and subsequently became a Canadian politician. Lajos Lederer was equally romantic: a strikingly handsome and well-connected Hungarian who had come to know Britain – and most of its eminent families – through his help to Lord Rothermere in the press baron's bizarre attempt to become King of Hungary in 1938. In 1934 Lederer escorted Lord and Lady Astor on a tour of Hungary, and it was Lord Astor who recommended him to his son David at the end of the war. Lederer was a maverick journalist; never a member of the *Observer*'s staff, he none the less spent the next forty years supplying it with journalistic scoops and stories from the Balkans and Eastern Europe. He was a great friend of President Tito of Yugoslavia, and it was through Tito that he was able to file some of his most

---

9. Gavin Young, p. xix.

important "exclusives" such as Tito's break with Stalin in 1948 and Tito's subsequent decision to re-establish diplomatic links with Moscow in 1953. He was usually around the *Observer* office, dropping juicy morsels of information on Central Europe that were often, coming from an anonymous source, impossible to check. But more often than not he would be right.

The *Observer* was the first national paper to appoint a Latin American editor. Jock Halcro Fergusson applied to the paper in 1947 as a Latin American expert, having served in South America during the war with the Foreign Office. David took him on to the staff in 1948. He stayed on the paper until his death in 1968. The *Observer* was also well served in Washington by a succession of distinguished correspondents. Kenneth Harris, a member of the famous Oxford Union debating trio (together with Tony Benn and Edward Boyle) which toured America in 1948, came to David's attention through Harold Nicolson's review of Harris's account of that debating tour, *Travelling Tongues*. He served as Washington correspondent from 1950 to 1953, before becoming the paper's chief interviewer throughout the 1960s. Nora Beloff joined the paper from Reuters in 1949. She was Washington correspondent from 1949 to 1951, after which she covered the fall of the Fourth Republic in Paris, ending as the *Observer*'s political correspondent from 1964 to 1975. Harris was succeeded by Alastair Buchan, and his successors included Patrick O'Donovan, Godfrey Hodgson (later foreign editor of *The Independent*) and Anthony Howard from 1966 to 1968. In the Middle East the paper was represented by Patrick Seale; and Dennis Bloodworth reported from South-East Asia. Neal Ascherson joined in 1960 and became staff correspondent in Bonn, later making regular visits to the East European capitals. Although some of these correspondents were professional journalists, many — such as Gavin Young and Patrick O'Donovan — were "created" by David Astor. However, most were young journalists who were given their first real chance on the *Observer*. It is an indication of David's judgement that very few of these young correspondents failed.

The *Observer* was sometimes criticized for its appointments, on the grounds that several of the staff were there only by virtue of their personal friendship with David Astor — men such as Pierre D'Harcourt, Philip Toynbee, Nigel Gosling, and (most controversially of all) TJ's son, Tristan Jones. David took the view that he was raised and educated among interesting people and should make the most of his contacts. Nigel Gosling was at Eton with David, and became a painter. He was persuaded by David to become the paper's dance and ballet critic, at which he was outstandingly successful. Gosling was the first British journalist to spot the talent of Rudolf Nureyev, and it was Gosling and the *Observer* who paid for his first trip to Britain when he was still a recently arrived and penniless defector. Philip Toynbee was the eldest son of Arnold Toynbee the historian, a colleague of Lord Astor's at Chatham House. David took Philip Toynbee on to the paper because he was "in trouble and brilliant". In 1949, when Arnold Toynbee asked David whether the *Observer* could do anything for his son, Philip, recently divorced, was already drinking heavily. His first assignment for the paper was to become his most notorious: he was sent to the Middle East and became Donald Maclean's drinking companion before the latter's defection to Russia. But David had read Toynbee in *Horizon*, and it was because of his literary ability that he became the paper's chief book reviewer during the 1950s and 1960s, complementing the more urbane and sober Harold Nicolson. One good judge of writing who encouraged David to take Toynbee on was George Orwell, who wrote from Cranham sanatorium just before his death:

> I think Philip Toynbee is a good idea. I don't know him well, but he seems to me to be quite gifted and politically o.k. I don't suppose he has much *editorial* experience, though he did have something to do with the editorship of a monthly, Contact or something.
> . . . One advantage of having Toynbee would be that he would bring you in contact with the younger writers, which is important.

Toynbee did make a good second life on the *Observer*, and grew into a literary critic of stature, to rival Desmond McCarthy on the *Sunday Times*. He also enlivened Tudor Street considerably on his occasional visits to the office. John Pringle, who joined the paper as deputy editor in 1956, remembered Toynbee as:

> . . . a tall, gaunt figure with a pale, craggy face and a loud and boisterous laugh. He only came up to London from the country once a week but the moment he entered the office in

Tudor Street everyone seemed to be smiling. He had a boyish enthusiasm for life which was infectious and was always longing to have a drink or a party where he could tell his marvellous stories. More important, however, he had developed a depth of humanity and wisdom which distinguished all his criticism. No one was more sensitive to real talent. No one was quicker to detect — and denounce — the phoney, the pretentious and the dishonest. He was one of the few men I have known who was always absolutely honest.[10]

His daughter Polly Toynbee was to follow him on to the paper in the 1960s.

If David Astor's sympathy for Toynbee paid off from the paper's point of view, another correspondent who was taken on for much the same reason certainly did nothing of the sort: Kim Philby. With the defection of Maclean and Burgess (a contemporary of David's at Eton) to Soviet Russia in May 1951, Philby, then serving as a senior officer in the Secret Intelligence Service (SIS or MI6), immediately came under suspicion and despite a public clearance by Foreign Secretary Harold Macmillan swiftly became *persona non grata* in the public service. The Foreign Office contacted David to ask if the *Observer* would employ Philby as a journalist on the paper. The Foreign Office official who called in on David told him that Philby had been cleared, and was employable, but needed a helping hand. David, who knew as much about Philby as anyone could read in the papers, sympathized with him because he felt "an injustice was being done against Philby", as he had been declared innocent but could not find employment. Astor, together with the *Economist*, took him on as a stringer in the Middle East on a joint retainer of £500 per annum. Ken Obank, the *Observer's* then chief sub-editor, advised Astor that he was "mad", but Philby stayed in the Lebanon as the paper's stringer until his own defection to Moscow in 1963. His dispatches were, in David's opinion, tidy and professional but — ironically — too pro-British Government in tone. When Philby *did* disappear, the *Observer* was severely embarrassed. Unknown to Astor, and the

10. John Pringle, *Have Pen Will Travel* (Chatto ampersand Windus 1973), p. 148.

Foreign Office, a clique within SIS had still believed in Philby and had reactivated him whilst in the employ of the *Observer* and the *Economist*. Nobody thought to tell the papers. But the *Observer*'s embarrassment was nothing compared to that of Edward Heath, who, as Lord Privy Seal in 1963, had the responsibility of summoning Astor and Donald Tyerman, editor of the *Economist*, to his office to apologize for the Foreign Office's clearance of Philby and to reveal the fact that Philby *had* been using the *Observer* as a cover whilst operating for a faction of SIS. SIS had clearly been in the wrong, and David felt understandably cheated by the Government.

Another man who might well be considered "a mistake" was Tristan Jones, the eldest son of TJ. He was at Balliol with David, where he joined the Communist Party and became an enthusiastic party organizer, before leaving over the Nazi-Soviet pact of August 1939. He served in the Horse Guards during the war, and his father, like Arnold Toynbee, approached David at the end of the war to enquire whether there was anything his son could do for the *Observer*. Tristan was taken on as a sub-editor, before moving to the *Observer* Foreign News Service. In 1953, with the retirement of John Berridge as general manager, David ran Tristan as Berridge's successor, a position which he occupied until 1975.

If ever there was a case of putting a square peg in a round hole, this was it. On a paper of eccentrics, Tristan was one of the most eccentric of all. A warm man with a great talent for friendship, he was one of the great collectors of his age, building extensions to his house in Kent to shelter his collection of political ceramics — probably bigger than the Victoria and Albert Museum's — as well as everything else from medical implements to royal carriages. His chauffeur drove him to Bermondsey market at six o'clock every Friday morning, where he would spend hours haggling with the dealers. He also constructed his own plywood coffin which he would proudly display to guests, to be drawn on its pram-wheeled carriage, complete with a plastic hand waving "bye-bye". When George Seddon was negotiating his salary with Tristan, in the middle of a particularly delicate part of the conversation Tristan suddenly paused, reached under his chair and produced a Victorian fireman's helmet, which he proceeded to wear for the rest of the interview. "I just got it from Camden Passage", he announced.

Tristan was very intelligent; he had won a Brackenbury

Scholarship from Stowe to Balliol. He took his responsibilities on the *Observer* seriously and impressed everyone with his professional dedication to the paper. But he was not qualified to be general manager; a point he cheerfully admitted to the author; "Guilty, my boy! Guilty!" David's reason for appointing him to the post was because he wanted someone willing to work for the same ideals as the rest of the staff. The fear was that a "pushful manager" would unbalance the paper. David admits that he chose him for the job of general manager on the wrong criteria, and Tristan's lack of technical or business qualifications severely hampered his effectiveness in that role. During the golden age it did not matter, as the *Observer* prospered effortlessly and Tristan could act as a bailiff rather than as a financial manager. He was extremely good at saving money, and to the staff his main function in life seemed to consist of curbing the editors' excessive spending. "He doesn't only say no like Molotov," David Astor said to Anthony Sampson one day, "but he *looks* like him too." Tristan Jones cultivated a negative and deadpan style behind his moustache which made him effective in that role. But the absence of any strategic financial planning or foresight in this vital position meant that when the competition hotted up in the late 1950s, the *Observer* was left cold, with no plans to take on the opposition. The number of commercial staff during the golden age was tiny, but this had not seemed to matter in the days of easy prosperity.

David Astor's talent-spotting was largely vindicated, and on occasions he did tactfully discourage the journalistic aspirations of other members of his extended family when their amibitions were not matched by real quality. None the less, with such a collection of writers, intellectuals, eccentrics and neurotics in the office, of at least five different nationalities, many people wondered how the paper was produced at all. Most *Observer* journalists put this phenomenon down to the presence of a small number of hardened professionals who kept the creative chaos on the rails. These "professionals" were mainly recruits from the *Yorkshire Post*, David's own training ground. Amongst them were Charles Davy, Cyril Dunn and Ken Obank.

Davy, former assistant editor of the *Yorkshire Post*, became a leader-writer for the *Observer*, and the letters editor. He was an aloof character, but wonderfully witty and incisive at conferences. He was famous for literally living at the office; his house was miles away in the country, so he used to spend several nights a week at Tudor Street, where he had his own fold-away camp bed and would often wander around the office in slippers and dressing gown. Cyril Dunn has written: "He lived physically in his own world of thought, and often passed you in the corridor or shared the lift with you without a word or even a nod." He was meticulous in his work; he was responsible for insisting on replying to every reader's letter. Although the *Observer* could be arrogant in its intellectual self-confidence, Davy none the less made a point of explaining the paper to every perplexed reader. Cyril Dunn was the professional reporter, who joined the *Observer* from the *Yorkshire Post* in 1947, starting as its home reporter and moving on to become one of the paper's finest foreign correspondents. Dunn, who bore more than a passing resemblance to George Orwell, was a professional journalist to his fingertips, neurotic about his copy — every page had to be typed without error — and had Orwell's unrelenting passion for honesty.

However, if there was one professional who held the paper together it was Ken Obank, a Yorkshireman who joined the *Observer* in July 1945 after sub-editing on the *Yorkshire Post* and *Daily Herald*, and served as the *Observer*'s chief sub-editor and then managing editor until his retirement in 1979. Most of the office, unsure as to how they ever actually produced a paper, put it down solely to the sturdy professionalism of Ken Obank on a Saturday afternoon and evening. On Obank's retirement, Patrick O'Donovan paid him the following tribute in the *Observer*:

> In the years after the war, Ken Obank had to hold together the most eccentric and exciting newspaper in Fleet Street. It seemed a weekly miracle that the paper ever emerged on the streets to be sold on Sunday. That it did so was largely due to him. He was the supreme professional who made sense out of the creative chaos....

As production editor from 1955 to 1962, Obank was also responsible for the design of the paper during a period when it won six awards for newspaper design organized annually by *Printing World*, and also (in 1956, 1957 and 1962) the award of "best-designed newspaper of the year". He could also give bold editorial advice — it was he who suggested devoting an issue to the publication of Khrushchev's "secret" speech denouncing Stalin on June 10, 1956.

However, at the centre of this paper of many talents stood David Astor. By the late 1940s, apart from a few survivors of the Garvin era such as Alison Settle, fashion editor from 1937 to 1959, and the film critic C. A. Lejeune, David had refashioned the *Observer* almost completely in his own image. All the writers that he chose reflected his own ideal of what the paper should be. His greatest gift as an editor − after his genius as a talent-spotter − was his ability to create, and to tolerate, a working environment for the host of outstanding intelligences he had recruited. They were not all easy to accommodate. There were those, like John Gale, who suffered from mental disorders, and there were some (as there are on many newspapers) who drank too much. (That puritanical scourge of the liberal press, Malcolm Muggeridge, once called the paper "the Astor home for intellectual drunks".) David recognized that this was a price he would some-times have to pay for good writing; alcohol could be a symptom of an emotional vulnerability which often ties in with creativity. Some of the drinkers were famous, such as Philip Toynbee, Patrick O'Donovan and Clifford Makins, the sports editor from 1962 to 1972, truly a "legend in his lunchtime". On his death in 1990, Julie Welch described a Makins day in *The Independent*:

> The *Observer* Sports desk under Makins was a kind of anarchic and eccentric heaven, unthinkable in today's cost-effective and circumspect times. At 11 o'clock, he arrived. At 11.20 he went out to lunch. Often, he did not return. He dealt with correspondence by sweeping it into the wastepaper bin and organised the pages in brief moments of marvellous lucidity between visits to the pub, where his deputy would bring him the page proofs. The filing cabinets were used to store champagne and Scotch. Even now, classic Makins-isms are still circulating, like his penchant for taking taxis from Ludgate Circus to El Vino (all of 200 yards).

The secret of the Astor style was extreme tolerance; everything in the office was left as informal and familiar as possible to allow the writers their full freedom of expression. This, of course, suited David's own temperament: even when he was wearing a jacket and tie his jacket would hang loosely on his shoulders without his arms in the sleeves, his collar button would probably be undone and the shirt sleeves, too, would be unbuttoned: however formal the occasion he would find some way of creating his own sartorial informalities. As he explained to Alastair Buchan

> ...I have a weakness for keeping office life informal and familiar. This tends to make all the office relationships a bit more personal and intimate than is usual. Why I find things easier that way, I don't know....

For those schooled in a more disciplined journalistic environment, this could come as quite a culture-shock. Nora Beloff later wrote:

> When I first joined the *Observer*, having been trained in the well-disciplined and, under Harold King, harshly regimented Reuter's Paris office, I found it almost impossible to adjust myself to the easy-going confusion of the *Observer*. Sent, young and eager, to be the paper's Washington correspondent, I was driven to distraction by the muddle and conflicting instructions. I once asked Astor why was it all so chaotic? He replied, after reflection, "Well if we had a more conventional office we couldn't employ geniuses like Philip Toynbee".[11]

Kenneth Harris, arriving from the well-ordered newspaper machine of the Kemsley empire was similarly amazed by the amateurism and informality of the *Observer*. John Pringle, who took a pay cut to move to the *Observer* as deputy editor in 1958 because it was "the best-written and most exciting paper in Fleet Street..." came from the highly disciplined environments of the *Manchester Guardian* and *The Times*. Arriving at the *Observer* expecting its brilliance to be a product of the editor's iron will, he was quickly disabused: "On the contrary, I found the *Observer* to be more like an experiment in participating democracy or even a Maoist commune. Every decision was discussed, interminably, by everyone."[12]

---

11. Nora Beloff: *Freedom under Foot* (Maurice Temple-Smith 1976), p. 59.

12. John Pringle, p. 56.

Rather than a "Maoist commune", most writers on the paper liked to think of the *Observer* as a "family", with, as Dinah Brooke has described it, "David Astor as a benign paternalist". The editor's office door was always open, anyone was welcome to drop in and discuss what was on their minds. David became heavily involved in the lives of some of his journalists, supporting them both financially and morally in their hours of need — but with the kind of people that he recruited, this had to be part of the job. Some observers commented, unkindly, that he hired people *because* they had some emotional weakness which would put them in his power; but, more to the point, he was prepared to tolerate weakness, and to help people whenever they got into difficulty in a personal or professional sense. One such sufferer wrote to David Astor at the lowest point in his life:

> I was deeply touched by your letter which arrived this morning. I am so thankful that at this crisis in my life I am working for a man of civilization and humanity instead of a mere brain box.

Few misunderstood his motives; John Pringle wrote that, despite all their differences, "one could not work with David for a month without realising that the essential feature of his character was an almost simple goodness".

The paternalist atmosphere of the office was supported by the office visits to Cliveden every year, when the whole of the *Observer* staff, from editor to cleaning ladies, would be entertained for the day, complete with brass bands and swimming in the Thames. Every Christmas there would be a dinner-dance at a London hotel, the highlight of which was David Astor's speech, a considerable trial to one who was always shy on public occasions. David also presided, rather more willingly, over the Wednesday office lunch at the Waldorf Hotel for important guests and selected members of staff. The Astors' own home was often used for long office discussions about politics, or for engagement and wedding parties. David Astor married Bridget Wreford, a sculpture student, in 1952, and Bridget was an unfailingly supportive hostess.

At the heart of the "Maoist commune", or "the family", was the conference. The *Observer* was a newspaper of endless conferences. Pringle again:

> David Astor could not have too many opinions and was never

happier than when surrounded by his staff talking, talking, talking. If Mao Tse-Tung invented the permanent revolution, the *Observer* in those days invented the permanent conference.[13]

This, once again, reflected David Astor's own way of absorbing information. Having been brought up at Cliveden, he had learnt to acquire information and sort out ideas through talking. As the journalists soon noticed, he read comparatively little. If this was a rather startling paradox, that the only "intellectual" editor of his generation, or any other, was not a great reader, this was partly explained by his love of listening. He was a rare character on the paper in that he saw his task at conferences as listening rather than giving everyone else the benefit of his views. It is a rare, and precious, quality. The conference week began on Tuesdays with a small meeting of senior staff, maybe eight or nine people, who would map out the major trends of the forthcoming week. The Wednesday conference was the general "news conference", open to everyone who wanted to air their views — at times there would be up to thirty people around the table. On Thursday afternoon was the "culture conference", presided over by the literary editor Terry Kilmartin, together with the "editorial conference" that decided the subjects of the leaders and "comments" on the leader page. The last was at 5.30 pm on Saturday, where only one bottle of sherry was produced to celebrate the paper's going to press, and where some senior staff discussed the outline of the following week's paper. Conspicuous by its absence, however, was the postmortem conference, which most other "Sundays" had on the Tuesday. The *Observer* ignored the *Sunday Times* and refused to contrast and compare; this gave the paper its communal self-confidence and intellectual arrogance. David Astor liked to say that he was editing the paper for himself and a few friends — he was not concerned with what the *Sunday Times* had to say.

The conferences were open-ended and of extraordinarily high quality in terms of intellectual debate. This is partly because of the calibre of the writers and intellectuals present — they were often joined by experts from Oxford or Cambridge — but also

---

13. Pringle, p. 145.

because of the editor's obvious sense of responsibility for the world's problems that they were discussing. Cyril Dunn observed the discussion of the Korean War, commenting in his diary on December 4, 1950:

David has been overwrought about the situation (Korea) — not excited about it the way an ordinary journalist would be, but genuinely distressed and anxious, as if he were carrying a grave responsibility and finding it too much. The stress has expressed itself in a bad and jumpy temper. I suppose this is the real difference between David and an old fraud like Andrews of the YP [*Yorkshire Post*], who would *claim* a heavy responsibility as editor, but who's really enjoying it as a newspaperman and for the public importance it gives him. (It's significant that lots of people still don't know who's editor of the Obs., whereas if there's *anybody* who doesn't know who edits the YP it's not Andrews's fault.)

William Clark, himself no intellectual slouch when he arrived at the *Observer*, was suitably impressed by a conference attended by Schumacher, Arthur Koestler, Haffner, Lowenthal, John Kimche, Edward Crankshaw, William Beveridge, O. M. Green, Colin Legum and Isaac Deutscher. Clark later wrote that

The intellectual content of the *Observer* editorial meeting and its mixture of national origins made it one of the most fascinating places to listen and learn and perhaps not remain entirely silent that I ever knew until I went to the World Bank.

. . . . Never had I heard argument so free based on principle and the long-term results that we hoped to achieve in the world over the next twenty or thirty years, or so well informed about the difficulties for the country or procedures that we were trying to put forward. There was a lot of disagreement and quite a lot of hurt feelings, including my own, when we did not succeed.[14]

Over these conferences David Astor would preside with silent authority, saying little and tolerating any interjection, however

14. Clark, p. 116.

irrelevant. As John Pringle noticed, it was the fact that everyone could speak at the conferences which meant that "everyone on the Staff felt that he had a say in the policy and running the paper. Their enthusiasm and loyalty were enormous." Astor ". . . listened attentively, with a smile on his handsome, boyish face, occasionally brushing his fair hair off his forehead with a characteristic gesture, and sometimes intervening shyly but effectively".[15]

These long, brilliant discussions produced the rarefied intellectual oxygen in which the *Observer* could breathe; but to those who had to distil them into a paper in time for Sunday they could be an exercise in frustration. Very little was actually *decided* at conference. It was Katherine Whitehorn who coined the expression "the editor's indecision is final". This style of conference used to drive Pringle "nearly frantic because of the difficulty of getting a decision". For David Astor, this created the atmosphere of creative tension, and Ken Obank was always there on Saturdays to make miraculous sense of "the editor's indecision" on the page. David Astor himself was aware of the limitations of the atmosphere of "creative chaos", and brought in a series of "assistants to the editor" to try to bring a little more structure and organization to his place in the office. Sampson originally tried to fill this role, and Edward Mace was recruited in 1955 specifically to bring some order into the editor's life. He even took notes at conferences, but his efforts were to little avail and he found his true niche as travel editor in the 1960s.

It is easy to see these conferences as the Balliol that David Astor had missed out on: most of the participants enjoyed them enormously. A few were more critical: John Pringle, for example, who would be itching to get on with producing the paper and who had been accustomed to the hushed, almost academic atmosphere of *The Times*, has said that he found them "a gigantic bore".[16] Often, however, it was the seasoned journalists who responded most enthusiastically to the *Observer*'s liberating way of life after years in the provincial press or Fleet Street. This was certainly the experience of John Silverlight, who came to the paper from the

---

15. Pringle, p. 135.

16. ibid.

Daily Mail in 1959; while Cyril Dunn was to write that discarding, as soon as you entered the doors of the *Observer*, the "censoring machine built into the frontal bone of the skull" of every reporter working on the predominantly Tory provincial press of the 1930s was "an unbelievably liberating experience".

David Astor's other exceptional quality with his journalists was to give them their heads. Once writers were hired, trouble was taken to let them find their *métier*, even if the first few months could mean a writer being under-employed or without any firm assignment — the experience of Michael Davie and Patrick O'Donovan. As part of the cult of the talented amateur, David Astor also encouraged writers to tackle subjects which they might have seemed unsuited to. The sports pages were as eccentric as any — often too much so for David — as Michael Davie and Clifford Makins brought in a selection of unusually highbrow writers to report on matches, to bring freshness and a new approach to the subject. In the 1950s and 1960s the philosopher A. J. Ayer wrote about football, as did the poet and subsequent Professor of Poetry at Oxford, John Jones. John Sparrow, of All Souls, Oxford, and the lawyer Louis Blom-Cooper also reported soccer matches. David Sylvester, an art critic and friend of Francis Bacon, wrote about soccer and cricket; Clement Freud also wrote on cricket. Clifford Makins transformed sports reporting by cultivating a generation of sports writers who were noticeable for their eloquent literacy, departing from the platitudinous, uncritical sports reporting of the time. His young apostles like Hugh McIlvanney, Chris Brasher, Richard Baerlin and Ronald Atkin proved that sports writing could be as much a matter of intellectual satisfaction as any other form of journalism. Makins himself was a bizarre choice for the job of sports editor — a lover of theatre, literature, music and conversation, but not of sport. However, it was Astor's willingness to take the risk of appointing him to the job that produced this revolution in sports writing.

The same boldness extended to the features pages. The "Profile" had been introduced in 1942 and continued as one of the most popular features. Arthur Mann, one of the trustees, suggested a "gossip or personality column" which would be of a different character from and lighter than the editorial "comments", but dealing with the same subjects. The column was called "Pendennis" and the first editor was William Clark. The most successful editor of this column was probably Anthony Sampson, and it was during the years on Pendennis that Sampson developed the style of a more gossipy, intimate yet informative coverage of politics and business that was to serve him so well in his *Anatomy of Britain* series of books. The *Observer* also became famous for occasionally devoting itself entirely to one subject that seemed to be of over-riding importance. Virtually the whole paper was cleared to accommodate the paper's own "Marshall Plan" of 1947, the "Secret Speech" by Khrushchev in 1956 and the Devlin Report on riots in Nyasaland in 1959. These decisions could only be justified on political grounds; they not only demonstrated intellectual confidence – that the readers would be sufficiently interested in reading Khrushchev's speech in its entirety – but they also showed commercial confidence: to accommodate Khrushchev Ken Obank had to lose seven columns of advertisements and almost all the usual features. The original speech had been given by Khrushchev in February 1956, but up to June 1956 only scrappy accounts of it had appeared in the Western press. A slightly longer version of it appeared in the *New York Times* on June 4, 1956, but on the following Thursday (June 7) Crankshaw revealed that he had obtained a full transcript. It was Ken Obank who suggested publishing the whole speech, all 26,000 words of it. It was a tremendous journalistic risk, as it would offend all the advertisers who would be excluded, and would also preclude the possibility of reporting any "hot" news over the weekend. It was the ultimate commitment to the "scoop by interpretation" over the obligation to reporting news, as the speech covered the entirety of the first eight of the *Observer*'s fourteen pages. On the front page of June 10, beside the speech, the paper justified itself:

> ...we believe that Mr Khrushchev's exposure of Stalin's rule, delivered to the Twentieth Party Congress in February and only now available in full, should be read as a whole to grasp what has been happening, and is now happening in the USSR. A momentous and fascinating document, it shows where single-party rule can bring them and nations.

Despite odd rumblings of complaint and angry letters from the Garrick Club protesting about "political tracts", the issue was a triumphant success, selling out and having to be reprinted. Seventeen years later it was described in Harold Evans's manual *Editing and Design* as "an example of classic layout resulting from powerful content and an outstanding value judgement".

Another most significant journalistic innovation on the *Observer* was the paper's use of photography. David found a picture editor in the extraordinary Mechthild Nawiasky, an utterly eccentric ex-art editor of *Lilliput* magazine. Astor and Mechthild conceived the idea of using photographs as stories in their own right. *Picture Post* had pioneered photo-journalism in the 1930s, but the *Observer* was the first national newspaper to use images often unrelated to the news on the front page, and write copy to complement the photograph. One of the first such photos was "Cow's eyes" — with accompanying copy by Cyril Dunn. The photos would often bear no relation to any of the news in the rest of the paper, but would illustrate more enduring themes, such as the changing of the seasons or the beauty of landscape. In 1950 Mechthild recruited Jane Bown, who became the *Observer*'s long-serving chief photo-grapher. Bown was an amateur, with no press training or the like, when she was phoned "out of the blue" by Mechthild to photograph Bertrand Russell and his new wife. Mechthild and David liked the result and Bown was given a permanent position on the paper. A similar spirit of spontaneity saw the creation of Fleet Street's first "education correspondent". Dinah Brooke, who was working part-time for the paper, went to the Isle of Wight for a holiday in 1955 and happened to become interested in one particular educationalist who was trying to introduce some innovative practices in the island's secondary modern schools. She wrote a three-hundred-word article on the subject which David liked, and it appeared in the paper under the by-line "Education Correspondent" — which she now became. As she was bringing up a family at the time, Dinah Brooke was allowed to work for only one day a week in the office.

The paper was also the first to have a science correspondent: John Davy, the son of Charles Davy. He joined the paper in the early 1960s, almost straight from university, where he had read science, and he transformed the coverage of science in the British press. Davy acknowledged that it was difficult to get science on to the news pages because "news" was thought of in terms of political events which occurred on particular days, while scientific develop-ments were gradual and long-drawn-out. So he worked out ways of translating long developments into comparatively short revealing episodes. He was very successful at raising the standard of scientific writing, and (as later became apparent through market research) the *Observer* became the most favoured paper among the scientific community. Davy was also partly responsible for the *Observer*'s being one of the first papers in Britain to mention the threatened exhaustion of the earth's resources and the danger to the environment from the continuing pollution of the seas and the atmosphere.

Another subject ignored by the rest of the British press which the *Observer* attempted to cover in some depth was psychology and psychoanalysis. This, which almost amounted to breaking a taboo, arose out of David's own emotional history and his daily analysis with Anna Freud in Hampstead during the years of his editorship. Robert Shields became the paper's — and Fleet Street's — first regular correspondent on psychological matters, and the *Observer* also serialized Dr Spock's work on the upbringing of children: Lydia James occasionally wrote on the subject of adolescents; and the Profiles might also be seen, to a certain extent, as an exercise in "understanding" people psychologically through studying their background and development. Those of Nye Bevan and Bertrand Russell were classic psychological mini-portraits, the former drawing praise from Jennie Lee, Bevan's wife. Whenever appropriate, the paper dealt more expansively with psychological subjects. On the centenary of Freud's birth in April 1956 it ran a series of commemorative articles on Freud by distinguished psychologists and writers, including such subjects as "Medicine since Freud" and "Freud and Religion". On the occasion of the sentencing of Ian Brady and Myra Hindley, the moors murderers, in 1966, the paper carried a long article by Maurice Richardson, (a writer of short stories and a weekly columnist on crime literature for the *Observer*) on their emotional and psychological characters, in an attempt to explain how they could have committed such crimes. Whether Richardson's conclusions were right or wrong, this did represent an unusual attempt to understand the nature of a crime before the mass hysteria of the popular press dulled the senses. David Astor always saw the paper as searching for "sense" in a world ruled by "nonsense" and insanity. By recognizing the importance of psychology, the *Observer* was acknowledging the relationship between the twin forces of the "conscious" and "unconscious" in man — its writers were acting as "the enemies of nonsense", a phrase much cherished by some of the paper's foreign correspondents. A good example of this concern was the leader written by David Astor himself on the trial of Adolf Eichmann, the Nazi mass-murderer, in Jerusalem in 1961. The leader, entitled "The Meaning of Eichmann", which originally appeared in the paper on March 26, 1961, and was later reprinted as a pamphlet, was a dispassionate and patient explanation of the permanent and universal issues involved in the trial. It was also an attempt to acknowledge the forces in everyone that could have driven Eichmann to commit the hideous crimes he did commit. It was a highly praised leader and attracted the attention of a psychological writer and historian, Norman Cohen. Together, Astor and Cohen set up the Columbus Trust, funded by Astor, to study the psychology of mass murder and mass persecution, with a chair at Sussex University. The Trust was initially chaired by R. A. Butler. Concerned about the neglect of Freudian studies in Britain, David also established a lectureship in Freudian Studies at University College London, and on retirement became a trustee of the Anna Freud Centre in Hampstead.

Psychoanalysis is a search for understanding, and the *Observer*, overtly and covertly, tried to be a paper of psychological understanding. However, not every application of psychology to journalism had the desired results. On one occasion Charles Davy suggested bringing in a renowned psychoanalyst, Edward Glover, to look at the front page to see if he could suggest any improvements in its make-up. The great man entered the office one day, and the front page was laid out before him for inspection. The senior staff gathered around in expectant silence. Glover pondered, then stabbed at the headlines with his finger, and murmured that they were "cheesy". After a pause while they attempted to digest this comment, the puzzled onlookers asked for enlightenment. What did the great man mean by "cheesy"? Glover looked taken aback, then explained that the headlines were, literally, "like cheese". He departed, leaving the staff none the wiser.

David was hardly less interested in the *Observer*'s coverage of the arts than he was in politics and foreign affairs. This was under the direction of firstly Jim Rose, then − from 1951 to 1986 − Terry Kilmartin. Also well known as a translator of Proust, Kilmartin built up the best 'culture' pages in Fleet Street. The critics he employed were a mixture of the tried and tested and the new and unconventional. In the former category were Harold

Nicolson and Vita Sackville-West. Vita Sackville-West wrote her famous gardening column from 1946 to 1961, probably doing more to change the face of the English garden through her writing than any other writer. So valuable was her contribution to the paper that in the early 1950s she was its highest paid correspondent. Her husband, Harold Nicolson, was chief book reviewer from 1945 until 1965, when he retired. Nicolson was a reviewer of great distinction, but always erred on the cautious side. He became famous on the paper for accompanying his book reviews, sent from Sissinghurst, with covering notes damning the writer he was prepared to praise in print. Having reviewed A. L. Rowse's book *Raleigh and the Throckmortons* as "valuable and readable", Nicolson sent the following accompanying note to Kilmartin: "Herewith a kind review of the Rowse book. My word how badly he writes! But he is a sensitive soul and I do not wish to wound him."[17]

It was with no irony that the less sensitive Toynbee, who succeeded Nicolson as one of the *Observer*'s chief critics, described Nicolson in an article to commemorate his years on the paper as "the gentle critic". The paper helped the career of several writers by giving them useful exposure, none more so than Muriel Spark, the novelist who won the *Observer*'s first short story competition held in 1952 with a story called "The Seraph and the Zambesi". The prize was £500, but more important was the fact that she got published. David Astor also involved himself in the personal support of artists, such as Brendan Behan.

Amongst the new and unconventional critics were A. Alvarez, who became poetry critic in 1956, and Nigel Gosling, ballet critic from 1955 to 1965. Philip Toynbee was the paper's main book reviewer, supported by regular contributors such as Angus Wilson and Kingsley Amis. Penelope Gilliat replaced C. A. Lejeune as film critic. As in other sections of the paper, the unusual and the unpredictable were encouraged. The match of reviewer to subject was often eclectic; for the first volume of Churchill's war memoirs, whilst the rest of the press wheeled out a cross-section of well-known British admirals and field-marshals, the *Observer* invited Paul Reynaud, leader of the French Government at the time of

---

17. Nicolson — Kilmartin: April 9, 1962; *Observer* Archive.

the fall of France in 1940, to review the book. A "Gallery Guide" was introduced as the first arts "listing".

Probably the two most famous reviewers were A. J. P. Taylor, the historian, and Kenneth Tynan, the drama critic. Astor did not always enjoy reading Taylor, as he felt he sometimes wrote more for effect than for anything else. He wrote to Kilmartin, on October 29, 1957:

> I want formally to record the fact that I regret the closer association with [Taylor] that we are engaged in and look forward to the time when we can only use him infrequently for things that he is specially qualified to do. I know it was me who suggested taking him on fully, but that was in the phase that K. P. O. [Obank] epitomised with the phrase "we are all businessmen, aren't we?" I was influenced by the idea that A. J. P. would give us circulation, but I really think that he is rather a terrible little man, although brilliant.[18]

Tynan's appointment as drama critic in 1953 was also originally David's idea; the boldest − and bravest − appointment he ever made. It was also the most difficult, as it meant replacing Ivor Brown, who had carried on happily at his first love, theatre reviewing, after relinquishing the editorship of the paper in 1948. By 1953, however, Astor knew that he wanted someone younger and more in touch with contemporary theatre than Brown. He had read Tynan's first book on the theatre, which he considered "brilliant", and determined that Tynan was his man. Tynan at that time was the *enfant terrible* of drama criticism. Young and ambitious, he had earned a fearsome reputation as a hard and merciless critic of unmerited theatrical reputations during his few years on the *Evening Standard*, from which he had been sacked; he was now writing for an obscure popular paper. He was a maverick, bold and passionate about theatre, but virtually unemployable because of his outspoken views. Ironically, it was Tynan who first approached Astor in July 1953, and at first he was employed on occasional articles. His first piece in the *Observer*,

---

18. David Astor − Kilmartin: Memo of October 29, 1957; *Observer* Archive.

"A Bunch of Comics", appeared on September 20, 1953. Warming to his writing, Astor then asked Ivor Brown to retire — the most difficult interview of his life. Ivor Brown accepted his fate with dignity, but was shocked to find that Tynan might succeed him. He regarded the young man as little more than a show-off, and warned David that he would not get away with the appointment because Tynan would provoke "too much of a row". Which he did. Astor was subjected to a ferocious anti-Tynan lobbying campaign by the theatrical establishment, afraid of what might happen to their reputations once Tynan had a chance to attack them from the prestigious platform of the *Observer*. The chairman of the trustees, Dingle Foot, was approached by Peggy Ashcroft, who claimed to be speaking on behalf of others, to warn the *Observer* that Tynan would wreck the theatre. "Brilliant but impossible" seemed to be the general opinion as individual actors also petitioned Astor. Even his next-door neighbours in Regent's Park, the thespians Michael Dennison and Dulcie Gray, invited themselves round to protest at the idea of employing Tynan. This campaign of opposition merely strengthened David's conviction that Tynan should join the paper, and, backed by Dingle Foot and Terry Kilmartin, he was duly appointed in December 1953; but David Astor was not to arouse such hostility against the paper again until the Suez Crisis three years later.

Tynan stayed as drama critic from 1953 to 1962, returning as film critic from 1962 to 1964. He made his name as Britain's pre-eminent theatre critic, largely for his support of new playwrights such as John Osborne. David, who sensed that they would not get on personally, avoided Tynan; but he also allowed him his head however passionately he might disagree with Tynan's views on politics (in the late 1950s) and sex and drugs (during the 1960s). Kilmartin was very good with the volatile young critic, filtering some of the more impossible notions from his copy, but Astor still, on occasion, found much of Tynan's writing wrong-headed. None the less, Tynan would probably never have survived under any other editor — the *Observer* certainly made his reputation.

Although David Astor was such a benign editor, in the sense of letting the people *he* had chosen follow their instincts, he was also a very strong, often stubborn, one in his control of the politics and the presentation of the paper. He took infinite pain over *how* the paper was written. Words mattered. His greatest journalistic skill, next to his gift for talent-spotting, was his ability as a sub-editor. Unlike some other editors, he did not write much himself, but he was a master of sub-editing other people's copy. Anthony Sampson has written that Astor "had skills as an editor which taught us all much...He took little notice of the conventional rules, like how the first sentence must tell you what, when, why and how, or how every piece must have a peg....He would stand at the long desk in his office, alongside the writer, mumbling, grunting, hovering, looking up questioningly as his fountain pen hovered. When I anxiously tried to write my first profile, about Albert Schweitzer, I agonised for hours over a first paragraph which could capture the essence of the man, and nervously submitted the draft profile to David. He liked it, but simply cut the first paragraph. 'It's like a cough before a speech, isn't it?' he said, 'you have to get it over with, before you begin'."

David personally edited all the anonymous leaders, comments and Profiles on the main pages. This was the heart of the paper, to which he devoted most of his time — often, others thought, to the neglect of the rest. Writers were given time to compose their pieces. A Profile could take anything up to three weeks to write. John Heilpern, who joined the paper in 1965, interviewed Henry Moore three times — once in Florence — for his Profile. David Astor cared passionately about good writing and this filtered down. John Heilpern's piece on Moore ended with a telling reference to Moore's appreciation of soccer, which served to humanize the great sculptor; Astor was congratulating him on this touch for weeks afterwards. On one occasion, though, when Heilpern did a Profile of a childhood hero of his, Max Wall, the last of the great clowns (who returned to the stage in 1975) he was summoned to the editor's office and was told that he'd got Wall "completely wrong". David Astor then got up and did a Max Wall imitation, including the famous walk, while talking about the clown's art, and Heilpern saw that his portrait had, indeed, been too senti-mental. Similarly, David came to blows with John Pringle over a Profile that the latter wrote of Roy Thomson whilst Astor was on holiday. Pringle said of Thomson that he was a "cracksman", breaking in through the floor of British public life. David was very annoyed at this Profile, and at what he saw as its loose use of language: Pringle was never to regain his former standing in the eyes of the editor. It was with good reason that Pringle later wrote that it was because David Astor "cared so passionately about his paper that he could not bear to let a single article or photograph appear without his approval."[19]

Just as David Astor was a strong editor in matters of detail, so he was a strong editor in the way he defined the political and moral objectives of the paper. There was much discussion about politics in the office, but — for all Katherine Whitehorn's joke — the final decision was always David Astor's. The trustees might sometimes complain about individual policies — such as decolonization in East Africa and the paper's objection to Eden's Suez policy — but David, by virtue of the fact that he always picked a chairman of the trustees who would support him, ensured that the policy was always his. After Lord Astor died in 1952 the chairmen were, successively, Dingle Foot, Sir Ifor Evans and Lord Goodman. Foot was a liberal barrister, elder brother of Michael Foot; Sir Ifor Evans was an academic of similar political inclinations, and Lord Goodman was a celebrated lawyer and *éminence grise*, also of broadly liberal political views. In all matters of policy, David Astor could always be assured of the support of the chairman of trustees. No one in the office was in any doubt as to where the real power on the paper lay. When it came to the crunch over Suez in 1956, it was the trustees who resigned, not the editor.

David resisted the word "campaigning" to describe the *Observer*. He explained to Lionel Curtis what he was trying to do:

> ...a newspaper cannot pursue a political doctrine as can and should a pamphleteer. What a newspaper can and should do is to cultivate a certain viewpoint in its readers (which is something different from advocating a policy).[20]

It was a fine distinction, but at the heart of the distinction lay the point that the *Observer* was primarily interested in explaining and exploring new issues, not in being right.

The first and most drastic campaign (*pace* David Astor's distinction) — the first major "scoop by interpretation" — was for

---

19. Pringle, p. 145.

20. David Astor — Lionel Curtis: February 18, 1937; Curtis Papers, Mss. Curtis 77, folio 37, Bodleian Library, Oxford.

European integration and the Marshall Plan. The *Observer* argued for a British-led federalist Europe at the end of the war, and as such became the first public advocate of the Marshall Plan for European recovery. On June 22, 1947 the paper, under the guidance of Sebastian Haffner, devoted most of the issue to an explanation of how such a plan could work, a few days after General Marshall had made his first tentative proposal in Boston. Following on from this the paper became a firm advocate of NATO and the Anglo-American alliance. If there was to be one durable, fixed point in the *Observer*'s foreign policy under David Astor, it was the Anglo-American alliance, seen as the bedrock of security and safety in the post-war world. This reflected David's own political inheritance — which marked him out from his fellow British editors — and was to be decisive at the time of Suez. Following its outspoken attack on Soviet Russia's designs on Poland at the end of the war, the paper was firmly anti-Communist, although always urging the building of bridges between East and West. For this reason the *Observer* welcomed the reforms of Khrushchev in the Soviet Union, although David Astor was a good deal more enthusiastic about Khrushchev than was the *Observer*'s Soviet specialist Edward Crankshaw. Ironically, it was over the issue of NATO that Sebastian Haffner split with the paper. Having been the main architect of the paper's principled advocacy of the Marshall Plan and NATO, in 1950 Haffner visited America to study policy-making at first hand. It was the beginning of the Korean War and the McCarthyite era, and over the next two years Haffner developed an increasing antipathy towards American militarism and extreme anti-Communism. As a result he started arguing for a strong, neutral Europe to stand between the USA and USSR. This was, of course, incompatible with the whole concept of NATO, and journalists in the office began to notice an increasing tension between Astor and Haffner, occasionally spilling over into the paper. Towards the end of 1953, Kenneth Harris, who had entertained Haffner in Washington, dined with him in Wimbledon. After dinner Haffner told him boldly that "David and I find now that we don't see eye to eye over some things, particularly the role of America in the world. In order to preserve our friendship, it would be better for me to go back to Germany for a spell." The break was inevitable, but left David "shattered". Haffner left the paper in 1955. However, the *Observer* lost little of its intellectual verve with his departure. As David Astor developed his own intellectual self-confidence, he could run the paper without his "gurus". He learnt from Haffner, but proved in the end that he was never ruled by him.

On its customary principles of freedom and toleration, the *Observer* became famous for launching campaigns against censorship and political imprisonment. On May 28, 1961 it devoted all its review front to an article by the lawyer Peter Benenson on "The Forgotten Prisoners" — those imprisoned around the world because of their political or religious views. Out of this grew Amnesty International. Twenty-five years later, Benenson wrote that:

> The *Observer* was largely responsible for the extraordinary sequence which transformed a call for an international, apolitical, humanitarian one-year campaign into a permanent organisation within two months.

David Astor was also largely responsible for setting up "Index on Censorship" in 1969, to monitor the abuse of the freedom of expression around the world. A magazine, *Index*, was founded and two years later the Writers and Scholars Educational Trust was set up to help banned or suppressed authors. The *Observer* attracted a lot of publicity to this cause.

In the 1950s the *Observer* was outspoken in its campaign for the abolition of capital punishment. This was directed largely by Arthur Koestler, who had met David in émigré circles during the war. Koestler had been imprisoned and under sentence of death during the Spanish Civil War, and this experience made him a passionate opponent of capital punishment. Koestler was never on the staff of the *Observer*, but was a powerful presence in the office, occasionally attending editorial meetings. In February and March 1956 the paper carried extracts from his book *Reflections on Hanging*, which started its campaign against the death penalty. It was through Koestler that David and the *Observer* got drawn into the whole area of prison reform, and David became a trustee of the Arthur Koestler Awards Trust, founded to reward artistic creativity by prisoners. Out of this grew the Butler Trust, founded to reward prison officers for outstanding service. The *Observer* also supported the campaign by the lawyer Louis Blom-Cooper for a change in society's attitude towards those who broke the law. Blom-Cooper wrote several articles on this subject and helped to launch the organization "Justice".

Like Koestler, Schumacher was another intellectual who wrote occasionally for the paper. It was in the *Observer* that he first advanced the ideas that were to gain a wider audience in his book *Small is Beautiful*, published in 1973. His first article, published in August 1960, was entitled "Non-Violent Economics", but his later article "How to Help Them Help Themselves" in August 1965, on Third World economic needs, produced such an enthusiastic response that the Intermediate Technology Development group was founded to put Schumacher's ideas into practice, supported by David Astor. The exact context of the Intermediate Technology Development Group in the paper's overall attitude towards the Third World will be looked at in the next chapter.

David Astor resembled an actor-manager in the way he presided over the writers, campaigns and politics of the *Observer*. He himself kept firmly in the background; his job was to create a suitable working environment in which his multi-talented, eclectic cast could perform. His greatness as an editor lay in the central paradox of his personality: that he was tolerant of his writers, and yet could never be indifferent either to their writing or to their characters. It was the fact David Astor could not be indifferent that gave the *Observer* its commitment, its sense of political purpose and its liberalism.

6

Africa

Of all the *Observer*'s campaigns, none was more important than that against British and European colonial rule in Africa; a cause with which David Astor himself also became closely identified and in which he was to invest a great amount of time, commitment and finance. Indeed, the *Observer*'s consistent and outspoken support for the cause of Black Africa was to bring the paper perhaps its greatest glory.

As we have seen, it was George Orwell who first aroused David's interest in the question of Africa. Having observed India's long and bitter struggle for independence, sometimes from close quarters, Orwell saw one of Britain's most important post-war tasks as ensuring that British governments did not make the same mistakes in Africa as they had in India. The *Observer* welcomed the independence of India (in 1947) and of other South-East Asian states, but it was Orwell who warned that this *must* be only the beginning of a longer process, and that the main battleground for this process of decolonization would now be Africa. Even during Orwell's lifetime, there were ominous signs that the liberal instincts inspiring Attlee's colonial policies would not necessarily be present in other British governments in relation to Africa, let alone in the white settlers there. The most conclusive evidence of this was the victory of Dr Malan's National Party in the general election in South Africa of May 1948. With the election defeat of

Jan Christiaan Smuts, the man partly responsible for drafting the Charter of the United Nations, the course of South African history took a savage turn. The new government began to pass legislation setting up the system of institutional apartheid that effectively made the country a two-tier state, debarring blacks from any political role in the country and separating them in almost every other conceivable way from the white settlers, the Boers and the English. This was, of course, an extreme reaction against the trend of independence movements around the world. Malan, a former "predikant" or preacher, believed the apartheid system to be founded on scripture and thus made no bones about what his intentions were. To David Astor, alerted to the dangers by George Orwell, the election of the Nationalist Government in May 1948 was a decisive victory for the forces of intolerance and racism, the two ugliest attributes of the Nazis that Britain had just spent six years fighting to overcome. It was David himself who wrote the famous *Observer* leader of May 1948, entitled "The Meaning of Malan". Explaining Malan's pro-German sympathies during the war and his ambitions to buttress white supremacy in South Africa, the leader warned of the deleterious world-wide repercussions that such a policy could have and ended with this thought:

> It is ironical, but not impossible, that an elderly Afrikaner gentleman, a Doctor of Divinity, pursuing an ideal of clean Dutch homesteads and simple-minded Negro villagers (in their allotted territory), the whole set in a remote extremity of the world, may start a chain-reaction in the relation of race to race that in the years to come will injure fatefully "everything that is holy and dear to a Christian nation and a white race".

For David Astor, the cause of the blacks, and South Africa in particular, was a particularly emotive one and struck an immediate chord. It united the strands of anti-imperialism and political freedom that were most marked in his political character. As a liberal of the American Democrat school, he was to fight the same fight against prejudice, bigotry and segregation in the British Empire as some of his fellow Democrats were to fight in the Civil Rights movement in the American South during the 1960s. In a letter to the journalist Anthony Howard on October 11, 1974, Astor wrote that:

My aim has been to be militant in fighting for tolerance, freedom of expression, non-prejudice — all causes of moderation — here and abroad.

Nowhere in the western world, in the late 1940s, were tolerance, freedom of expression and non-prejudice being trampled more obviously than in Africa. Emotionally, David Astor would always side with the underdog, or the "lame", as Nancy Astor liked to put it. Once again, there were no people in the world more obviously in the position of the "underdog" than the blacks of South Africa, or of the rest of colonial Africa.

David also became involved in black issues because, unlike most Englishmen of his background who held positions of power and responsibility, he had, to a certain extent, been brought up in an atmosphere in which the presence of black people was taken for granted. Nancy Astor had been brought up in the American South entirely surrounded by blacks. Most of these would have been her servants in some capacity, but she retained an instinctive sympathy and affection for the individual blacks that she met — if not for the cause of black liberation in general, as she was later to make quite clear to David. David saw his mother's attitude to blacks as "benign". She did not regard them as equals, yet would always warm to them; she would always lament the stiffness of English butlers compared to her black American ones who would feel free to join in the family conversation. Paternalist and patronizing as this was, it still made David aware of black culture and issues at an early stage, and he found that he always enjoyed an easy, unselfconscious relationship with blacks that was denied to many of his white contemporaries. One of his earliest thrills was being taken backstage by his mother to meet Paul Robeson when he was singing in *Showboat*.

There were compelling journalistic grounds for the *Observer*'s involvement in Africa, in addition to David Astor's personal attitude. As has been noted, a vital ingredient of the paper's *modus operandi* was the reporting of issues that were neglected by the rest of the press. In the late 1940s, Africa was just such an issue. Even in the field of foreign affairs, which seldom made much impression on public consciousness anyway, the affairs of Africa seemed to be of little interest beside the quickening Cold War, the conflict in the Middle East and the end of empire in Asia. Yet, as

William Clark enters the office

photo Tony McGrath

Edward Crankshaw

Charles Davy and his son John Davy, science correspondent

photos Tony McGrath

Nora Beloff

photo Tony McGrath

Gavin Young

Cyril Dunn

Michael Davie, deputy editor

photo Tony McGrath

Robert Stephens, diplomatic editor

photo Tony McGrath

Clifford Makins, sports editor

photo Tony McGrath

Jane Bown

photo Tony McGrath

Kenneth Tynan

Terence Kilmartin

photo Jane Bown

Philip Toynbee

photo Tony McGrath

Vita Sackville-West

photo Jane Bown

Colin Legum

photo Tony Prince

Anthony Sampson

photo Tony McGrath

Nelson Mandela outside the House of
Commons, 1962

photo Mary Benson

Michael Scott

The Chairman: Lord Goodman   The General Manager: Tristan Jones

photo Jane Bown

Ken Obank (left) and Donald Trelford

photo Jane Bown

Announcing the sale to Atlantic Richfield, 1976. Left to right: David Astor,
Douglas Cater, Lord Goodman, Donald Trelford

Robert Anderson inspects his new paper

David and Bridget Astor in 1991

photo Jane Bown

the *Observer* pointed out, Britain had enormous responsibilities in Africa which were, by 1950, without equal anywhere else in the world. In that year, Britain was still directly responsible for fourteen African states with a total population of fifty-six million. In addition, the Union of South Africa was also in the British Commonwealth, with strong ties to Britain. As David Astor realized, Britain had a wonderful opportunity to give independence to the African states while retaining their goodwill; but if public interest on the subject was not aroused, there was also a dreadful prospect that in some parts of Africa, for example Kenya and Rhodesia, clones of Dr Malan might take over, with all the bitterness and bloodshed that could easily be foreseen, to say nothing of the disastrous damage to any goodwill towards Britain on the African continent. The fact that Dr Malan's victory in 1948 went virtually unreported in the British press — save for the natural interest shown in the defeat of the legendary Smuts — only demonstrated the magnitude of the task ahead.

In the years after 1948, David Astor gathered together a collection of people who were to form the core of the early anti-apartheid movement in the British press, with the *Observer* offices at its centre. The first and most vital recruit as far as the paper was concerned was Colin Legum. A white South African, Legum had worked as a journalist for various labour publications in South Africa such as *Forward*, and had for a time acted as general secretary of the South African Labour Party. However, with the victory of Malan, he decided that there was no future for democratic socialism within South Africa, and that he could best advance the cause of democracy there by publicizing in the outside world what was happening. Legum had read the *Observer*'s leader on Malan's victory and, coming to the conclusion that it was the only British paper "breaking new ground" in its coverage of foreign affairs, he wrote to David Astor to offer his services. In August 1948 the two men met in Tudor Street. David had recently made his dispositions for reporting colonial problems around the world — O'Donovan had begun his travels to South-East Asia and Denis Bloodworth had been sent to Singapore — but there was as yet no correspondent to cover Africa. Now Cyril Dunn was sent out as "field" correspondent — it was the first time a Fleet Street paper had appointed a resident correspondent in Southern Africa and David made Legum the London-based "Africa editor" of the paper. Again, this was the first such post in Fleet Street, followed closely by Oliver Woods at *The Times*. Legum's post was later transformed into the "Commonwealth correspondent", but his interests always centred on Africa. He stayed on the paper until 1981. He became the premier "Africanist" on Fleet Street, and the doyen of Western African correspondents, making the *Observer* an unrivalled centre of intelligence and enterprise on African issues. The office became a mecca for foreign journalists seeking to inform themselves about Africa. The celebrated American correspondent John Gunther, whose series of "*Inside....*" books were internationally popular, wrote in "*Inside Africa*" that:

> ...London is the best centre for informed journalism about Africa. One might almost say that the "capital" of Africa is the office of the London *Observer*.[1]

Another recruit to the *Observer* who was to play a crucial role was Anthony Sampson. Sampson went out to South Africa straight from Oxford, to work on the magazine *Drum* from 1951 to 1955. It was during this period that he got to know David Astor, through their shared interest in South Africa. They had lunch together in 1953 and Sampson joined the *Observer* as "assistant to the editor" when he returned from Africa in 1955. Sampson was never a permanent African or diplomatic correspondent, but, because Colin Legum was forbidden to return to South Africa, he frequently covered major events there for the paper, including the historic African tour by Harold Macmillan in 1960 and the trial of Nelson Mandela and his co-defendants in 1964. He became close friends with Mandela and other African National Congress leaders such as Oliver Tambo and Walter Sisulu.

Soon after meeting Legum, David was introduced to the Reverend Michael Scott, who was to become not only his mentor on Africa but the first anti-apartheid campaigner to attract international attention. Scott was born in 1907 and went to South Africa at the age of nineteen. He came back to England, and also spent some time in India before returning to South Africa at the end of the war. As an Anglican priest in South Africa, he had

---

1. Gunther, *Inside Africa*, (Hamish Hamilton 1955), p. 532.

been horrified at the treatment of Africans even under Smuts, as well as their economic and political plight. He had spent several years agitating against the oppression of the black majority and in the course of exposing near-slavery conditions on farms in the Transvaal had nearly been lynched by angry white farmers. However, what brought him to the notice of the outside world was his effort in 1946 to present at the United Nations the case of the tribes of South West Africa who were fighting against the South African government's attempt to incorporate their mandated territory into the Union. He was the first man to ask for a debate on the apartheid policy at the United Nations, asking for it to be referred to the Security Council as a "threat to peace and racial harmony". David first met Michael Scott when he was brought to the *Observer* in 1946 by Bob Stephens, the paper's Middle East expert, who had met Scott through Quaker connections. David was immediately struck by him and they quickly developed an important and close friendship. Indeed, after Adam von Trott and George Orwell, Scott probably made a greater impression on David Astor than any other of his contemporaries.

Scott was, as Astor put it, "...a very striking person to meet". It is not difficult to understand why. Together with Colin Legum, who had known Scott in South Africa, David wrote an *Observer* Profile which appeared in the paper in December 1949. As Astor and Legum wrote:

> The impression that this controversial figure makes on those who know him best is one of diffidence and reserve. He is hesitant in speech, temperate and restrained in argument and respectful of other people's views. But he is totally uncompromising where he believes that principles of justice and humanity are involved, and he is unmoved by considerations of what may or may not be regarded as practical, even by his supporters.
>
> In appearance he is still youthful, with a strikingly handsome face that has something about it of the saint and something of the rebel. He is careless of food, clothes and all material pleasures. For some years now he has had no regular income, and has lived and travelled on the alms of those who wish him well; he has lived exiguously.

The immediate mutual understanding and sympathy that

developed between Scott and Astor is very understandable in the light of this Profile, for this — apart from the last sentence — could pass for a profile of David Astor himself. In Scott, Astor saw a man who was making great personal sacrifices for human causes comparable to those that Trott had made.

In America, a young South African woman who had also left her homeland in disgust at apartheid read the *Observer* Profile and was, in her own words, "spellbound" by the description of Scott. Her name was Mary Benson. She immediately flew to London and put herself at the service of Scott, helping to arrange a meeting at Westminster Central Hall, organized by Christian Action, on African reconstruction. Theirs was to be a fruitful partnership, and she became an essential element in the growing movement for Black Africa in London. Her experiences of working with Scott and Astor on African affairs are recorded in her admirable auto-biography, *A Far Cry, the Making of a South African.*

Scott influenced Astor "a lot", not only regarding the politics of Africa in particular, but in terms of the way that liberals should fight campaigns in general. Scott, a follower of Gandhi, argued that although he was a natural moderate, fighting for ordinary civilized values such as the equality of races, political freedom and freedom of expression one had to be immoderate in the means deployed against extreme opponents — such as Dr Malan. One had to be "extreme" against opposing "extremes"; and in South Africa the liberals had to be willing to fight as hard as the Communists against the Nationalists and face imprisonment or death. Astor's friendship was also very important to Scott. Mary Benson has written:

> ...no one was to be a more loyal friend and ally than David Astor. For all the glamour of Astor's family name, he was almost as shy as Scott, but over a series of lunches and meetings their friendship grew. What mattered to Scott was Astor's understanding and his readiness, as Editor of the *Observer*, for the newspaper to campaign on African issues — a lonely campaign which provoked sharp criticism, even ridi-cule. He also valued Astor's readiness to draw potentially influential people into his work.

Astor also occasionally provided Scott with much-needed funds, so he could continue his work in London and at the United

Nations in New York. On one occasion Scott fell ill in New York just before some important lobbying at the United Nations on behalf of South West Africa. Mary Benson found him in an "infernal bedlam" in a small public ward of a New York hospital.

> ...funds were low, [but] David Astor's sudden arrival on his way to Washington was a godsend. He arranged for Michael to move into the luxurious Carlton House Hotel, where delegates visited him.

Other members of the *Observer* also contributed to the African campaign, notably Bob Stephens and Martin Wight. Wight was an academic working in the field of international relations, an asthmatic who had spent the war at Oxford working on colonial constitutions. Wight accepted David's offer to go as the *Observer*'s correspondent to the United Nations in 1946−47, and David was so impressed by him that he offered Wight his own editorial chair as an inducement to tempt him away from returning to academe. The attempt was unsuccessful and Wight went on to become Professor of History at the University of Sussex.

Another key figure was W. Arthur Lewis, born in the West Indies of African descent in 1915, who from 1948 onwards was Professor of Political Economy at the University of Manchester. He wrote an article declaring that any further white settlement in Kenya would be "a crime", which caused a sensation. The *Observer* also provided a platform for Father Trevor Huddleston, who worked in the slums of Johannesburg in his capacity as Principal Superior of the Anglican Community of the Resurrection in South Africa. In August 1953 he wrote a celebrated piece in the *Observer* entitled, "For God's Sake, Wake Up!" in which he announced his own conversion to political resistance to the South African Government's policy. Huddleston's appeal for "the support of Christendom" against apartheid produced a large number of letters and a provocative correspondence on the letters page of the paper. Huddleston continued to write articles for, and letters to, the *Observer* throughout the 1950s.

To provide a focus for the activities of all these individuals working in the same field in England, David Astor was influential in setting up and financing the Africa Bureau. This was founded in March 1952 to give Scott, its director, and like-minded people a coherent organization. It was typical of David Astor's method of helping causes, as he provided the funds, contacts and institutional structure in which the campaigners could operate best. Until then there were two anti-colonial movements, the Fabian Colonial Bureau and Fenner Brockway's Movement for Colonial Freedom, but neither of these really represented African nationalistic views. The Africa Bureau was largely run by Scott and Mary Benson, but it was David who now gathered together a collection of reputable, well-known, all-party politicians who would make the bureau more mainstream, and therefore raise its profile and thus the profile of the cause for which they were all working. Astor's most important find was Lord Hemmingford, a Conservative peer who became chairman of the Africa Bureau from 1952 to 1962, thereafter becoming its vice-president. Also recruited to the executive council were Lady Longford (the wife of David's old friend Frank Pakenham, Lord Longford), Arthur Creech Jones (who had been colonial minister in Attlee's Government), and Dingle Foot. Isaac Foot, Dingle's father served as an honorary president. The principal aim of the Africa Bureau was that it should be "a well-informed and impartial mediary between Britain and Africa, providing a channel through which Africans, and other communities in Africa, Europe and Asia can convey their grievances to wide sections of the British public and to MPs; and also, where such representation is appropriate, to the United Nations. It can also give to these communities an objective appraisal of attitudes and policies in Britain that affect Africa." The Africa Bureau also became the umbrella organization for a number of other separate trusts to cater for more specific African needs. The Africa Protectorate Trust provided facilities for higher education and technical training for Africans from Southern Africa; the African Development Trust provided training for agricultural development; and in January 1958 the Africa Bureau Education Trust was founded to initiate and direct projects undertaken by the bureau. On the advice of Bishop Colin Winter, David Astor also made a more personal contribution to the problems of South West Africa by setting Winter up in a former rectory opposite his house in Sutton Courtenay to provide for Namibian exiles. This unlikely setting became the home for a community which later transferred to Oxford to become the Namibian Social Centre.

Out of this activity centring on the new Africa Bureau came the idea for a clear manifesto on the African question. This was David Astor's idea, and the book that later emerged as the manifesto, *Attitude to Africa*, was, in his words, "an attempt to draw up a general policy". To formulate such a general policy, David acted as host to a number of weekend meetings at his house at Sutton Courtenay where the Africanists gathered to compare ideas. This was typical of David Astor at work: acting as a host whose prime purpose was to bring people together and provide them with a convivial, stimulating atmosphere in which to work — which, after all, was no more than what the *Observer* became under his editorship. David chaired these meetings, ensuring that discussions remained focused closely on the objective at hand, which was to provide a coherent manifesto. As well as the four authors of *Attitude to Africa*, W. Arthur Lewis, Michael Scott, Martin Wight and Colin Legum, a number of others joined these weekend meetings to add their comments, including Margery Perham from Oxford. *Attitude to Africa*, published as a Penguin Special in 1951, became not only the manifesto of the liberal Africanist in England in general but also for the *Observer* in particular, for it was in Africa, as the authors of the book wrote, that Britain could "suffer our worst moral defeat or win our greatest moral victory".

While recognizing that the "tide of nationalism" was rising in Africa, which meant that Britain, like other colonial powers, would undoubtedly have to contemplate granting independence to her colonies, the authors of the book also stressed that Britain had a vital role in reducing the educational and economic gap between the Europeans and Africans so as to defuse the revolutionary potential of African nationalism:

> The major objective of British policy therefore must be to narrow the gap as rapidly as possible, not by lowering the European standards, but by raising the African. . . . the success of British policy in East and Central Africa must be tested by the rate at which it succeeds in reducing the educational and social gap between Europeans and Africans.

Only by doing this could the British retain the goodwill of Africans and therefore have an important part to play in guiding the transition to independent democratic status, which Britain should ultimately be striving for. As the authors continued, ". . . the freedom which Africa needs is not so much political freedom as self-government, which may easily prove to mean the tyranny of some little African Hitler, and freedom from poverty and disease, from soil erosion and economic underdevelopment". The latter had to be the British aim, if those, "little African Hitlers...were not to take over in the work of independence". The authors conceded Curzon's point that "men prefer to govern themselves badly rather than to be governed well by others", but hoped that Britain would live up to its historic opportunity of ensuring that the right economic and social circumstances would prevail which might make "little Hitlers" redundant. The Trust funds set up under the aegis of the Africa Bureau were designed to this end, as was the Intermediate Technology Development Group set up in 1965. This, the brainchild of "Fritz" Schumacher, was launched as a result of an article by him in the *Observer* in August 1965. Schumacher proposed that rather than flood the third world with expensive modern technology that the locals could not afford, developed countries should concentrate on reforming and improving indigenous tools and agricultural skills. His slogan was "Find out what the people are doing and help them to do it better" — a philosophy that would lead on to his celebrated thesis of "Small is Beautiful". David Astor became intimately involved with the setting up of the Intermediate Technology Group.

An issue which often divided the men and women who gathered at Sutton Courtenay, as it does Africanists to this day, was that of Communism. Under the guidance of David Astor, the *Observer* always took the line that Britain and the West *had* to recognize and come to terms with the rising tide of African nationalism, otherwise the Communists would fill the vaccuum left by the West. On April 19, 1964, an *Observer* leader by Legum and Astor, advocating sanctions against South Africa, made this quite explicit:

> If it is left to the Communist powers alone to assist the Africans to bring about the eventual dislodgement of the present regime, it is likely that the regime that follows this one would be Communist influenced. This would present the Russians...with the only industrialised African country. It would also prove to all the coloured peoples of the world that Western support for the rule of the majority ceases when the majority is not white-skinned....If we simply do nothing or the right thing too late, the West may lose enough political credit to become, itself, a minority influence in world affairs.

During the course of the 1950s and 1960s *the Observer* became involved in several African problems which helped to highlight the injustice of white minority rule. The first involved the plight of Seretse Khama, who found himself at the centre of a controversy that stirred deep passions in 1950. Seretse Khama was designate chief of the Bamangwato tribe in the Protectorate of Bechuanaland, an area between South Africa and what was then Rhodesia. Seretse Khama was being educated and prepared for chieftainship by his Uncle Tshekedi Khama, but Seretse's sudden marriage to an Englishwoman, Miss Ruth Williams, brought an abrupt end to his orderly progression to the chieftainship. Tshekedi objected to his nephew's action, largely because he had failed to consult the Chief's Tribal Council; but more importantly the neighbouring South African and Rhodesian governments, horrified at the prospects of such a high-profile mixed marriage occurring on their borders, put pressure on Whitehall to exile Seretse, still in London, from the Protectorate. Dr Malan of South Africa used this controversy to press for the incorporation of the three British protectorates of Bechuanaland, Basutoland and Swaziland into South Africa. The British Labour Government, bowing to South African susceptibilities on this subject, exiled not only Seretse but also Tshekedi, not from the entire Protectorate but from his tribal area.

In the *Observer* Legum condemned the action of the British Government as a "policy of expediency" and the Africa Bureau started a campaign to get the decisions reversed. Tshekedi came to London to lobby Parliament, and his plan of campaign was mapped out by Michael Scott and David Astor, amongst others, at Sutton Courtenay. David also took a more personal interest in the case by looking after Tshekedi's two sons, who were to be educated under the care of the Bielenbergs in Ireland. The Africa Bureau lobbied Parliament on Tshekedi's behalf, and the *Observer* scorned the Labour Government's apparent subservience to the apartheid regime of South Africa. Tshekedi eventually achieved his objective and returned to his tribe, but only after several years of tireless activity on his behalf. The most important result of this episode was that for the first time the policies of South Africa were brought to wider public attention.

The most serious and bitter campaign that the *Observer* fought on behalf of Africans during the 1950s was that against the Central

African Federation. This was an idea nurtured by the Attlee Government but put into practice by the Churchill administration in 1953, whereby the territories of British Central Africa, Nyasaland (now Malawi), Northern Rhodesia (now Zambia), Southern Rhodesia (now Zimbabwe) and Tanganyika (now Tanzania) were grouped together as the Central African Federation, in which the white minority would have an inbuilt majority role in government. There was solid political and economic reasoning behind this idea; the new federation, utilizing the great mineral wealth of Northern Rhodesia, the labour resources of Nyasaland and the agricultural wealth of Southern Rhodesia, would become a powerful economic, white-led unit able to resist the increasingly expansionist Union of South Africa to the south. But though the plan looked good in Whitehall, it was flawed from the start by opposition from the Africans in all the territories, who boycotted the preliminary conference setting up the federation. The *Observer* and the *New Statesman* were the only British papers to question federation, on the grounds that it obviously flew in the face of African wishes in these territories. The *Observer* was not against federation in itself, but was against a federation *imposed* on Africans by white minority rule.

As a consequence, the *Observer* gave much coverage to African leaders in opposition to federation, including Kenneth Kaunda in Northern Rhodesia, Joshua Nkomo in Southern Rhodesia and Dr Hastings Banda in Nyasaland. These, and other African leaders, relied on the *Observer* as a conduit to the outside world, even when in prison. In June 1967 Colin Legum sent the following internal memorandum to Astor:

> I've had a request from detainees in Rhodesia for a copy of the *Observer* to be sent to them. Do you think we could arrange this? It should go to:-
> Robert Mugabe,
> HM Remand Prison,
> PO Box 8035,
> Causeway,
> Rhodesia.

In an editorial of April 27, 1952 the *Observer* outlined its case against the impending start of federation:

We believe it would be foolish to impose a Federation on Central Africa if the Africans, who outnumber the Europeans by 400 to one in these areas, are actively opposed to it, as they are. The ultimate sufferers from such a rash course would be those who had to rule an unruly community.

Let the British maxim of Rule by Consent be applied in Central Africa, if a peaceful outcome is to be expected. The adoption of the less reliable maxim of Rule by Imposition may carry British policy in Central Africa along a disastrous course.

Violence and bitterness related to the federation increased throughout the 1950s, with white Rhodesians, such as the belligerent Roy Welensky, objecting to any alteration of plan. The *Observer*'s fears had been justified. On March 1, 1959, it looked back on "six years of failure of the Central African Federation", and argued that this period had seen a "formidable growth in the African nationalism which was but recently derided as negligible...." It urged that the federation should be scrapped:

> ...the only practicable hope of economic development is an honest partnership to which Europeans and Africans can contribute their special skills. But it must be based on the full and free consent of the Africans. Without that, the economic and social life of these territories will be built on a volcano.

As if on cue, this editorial was followed a few days later by riots in Nyasaland during the course of which fifty-two Africans were killed and a state of emergency was declared by the governor, Sir Robert Armitage.

The paper's attitude brought David Astor into collision with the British Government; but found him an ally in his old friend and fellow disciple of Cripps, Sir Walter Monckton. Lord Home, Secretary of State for Commonwealth Relations from 1955 to 1960, naturally objected to the *Observer*'s attitude, and Home and Astor entered into an earnest correspondence on the subject in 1957. Home alleged that the *Observer* policy was "harmful to the best interests of Britain and the Commonwealth", but Astor replied that he believed that on this issue they, "rather than the Government, are the upholders of British Imperial history — surprising and improbable though that may seem to you".[2] Monckton, a famed negotiator of great charm and character, was sent out by Prime Minister Macmillan in July 1959 to head a Royal Commission to try to improve the climate of opinion for the federation to work in. Astor was invited to call on Monckton at the Midland Bank, of which he was chairman, before he left for Africa, and Astor was surprised to learn that Monckton's private attitude to federation was almost as hostile as his own. Monckton declared that his personal aim on his mission to Africa, likely to be his last contribution to the politics of the Commonwealth, would be to try to modify the federation himself. It was not, however, a policy that he could advocate in public. If Monckton was looking for support from the *Observer* for his mission, Astor could only assure him that "I think you should expect this paper, and those who take its general view, to feel bound to support an African refusal to operate even the most liberal constitution for the federation...."[3]

The political temperature was heightened by the publication of the official British report on the March Nyasaland riots, which was certainly no help to the Government. The report found no evidence to support the Government's assertion that the Nyasaland Congress Party had been plotting murder and assassination — the motive for imposing a state of emergency — and further described Nyasaland as a "police state". Dr Banda and his lieutenant, Chipembere, were arrested in the wake of the riots. However, the report (known as the Devlin Report after the head of the team of investigating lawyers) cleared Chipembere of being involved in crimes against whites. The *Observer* judged this to be of such significance that, for the second and last time, its front page was cleared (John Pringle's decision, as Astor was on holiday) and it published the Devlin Report in full. This, like the treatment of Khrushchev's speech, was dangerously bold journalism; but as this report seemed to invalidate the Government's fears about black revolution in Nyasaland, a similar judgement was made that it was so important that it should receive the maximum publicity

2. Correspondence in Dept. Monckton 30, folio 125; Monckton Papers.

3. Astor to Monckton, December 23, 1959, Dept. Monckton 30, folio 124.

possible. (As a point of historical interest, however, Colin Legum was later to learn that Chipembere made a death-bed confession of the crimes of which the judicial report had cleared him.)

In December 1960 the Monckton Report was published, the result of his commission's year-long deliberations, and his controversial recommendation that the States be allowed to "secede" from federation at some future point amounted to an overall indictment of the whole concept of federation. The *Observer* naturally supported the Monckton Report, which proved to be the beginning of the end for the federation. It was eventually disbanded in 1964, paving the way for the creation of Zambia and Malawi, and the rather longer process that would eventually produce Zimbabwe in 1980. The *Observer* had undoubtedly played an important, and lonely, part in making British public opinion and the Government aware of the futility of what Macmillan liked to call "a noble experiment".

As well as guiding the paper's campaign against federation, David Astor was also more closely involved on the spot through his backing of the *Central African Mail*. The plight of this paper representing African opinion in Northern Rhodesia, in opposition to Roy Welensky's Government, was brought to his attention by Anthony Sampson. It had a circulation of only 30,000, but it was, none the less, the only paper of any importance that reflected African opposition to federation. David put money into the paper. Dick Hall was its editor when Astor came in:

> The *Mail* was the *Observer*'s echo on the spot, in that very part of the continent where the drive for independence was meeting the harshest resistance.

Dick Hall was immensely impressed by David Astor's devotion to the paper, despite the huge problems of producing it in such a hostile political and commercial environment:

> Astor stuck by us unswervingly, even though the paper did not turn the financial corner as soon as he expected. Despite having the largest sale of any "non-white" publication in central Africa, it could never pull in enough advertising: too many big firms boycotted us because of our political opinions. We also spent more than we should have done in distributing the paper to places that were politically important but

impossibly expensive to reach. Some of our selling agents turned out to be crooks; one of the most reliable was a leper.[4]

Kaunda was very enthusiastic about the paper and Hall relates how he told Jim Rose, of the International Press Institute, that "he didn't know what he would do without it". However, despite the enthusiasm it never made money, and by the end of the first half of 1964 was losing £3,751 a year. In divesting himself of the loss-making *Central African Mail* David Astor was to experience the realities of African independence. With the ending of federation and the creation of the new state of Zambia, he decided to sell the paper. The asking price was £100,000, which is what he had spent on it over the four years of his ownership; he was not seeking to make any profit out of the paper. The first approach was from a certain "Tiny" Rowland, the recently appointed chief executive of Lonrho, a company with large business interests throughout Africa. Lonrho had backed the Central African Federation and had given donations to Welensky's "build a nation" campaign. However, much as — according to Hall — Rowland wanted the paper, he apparently found himself strapped for cash and swerved off to buy the white-orientated *Northern News* instead. This was the first skirmish between two of the most dominant British-based figures in Africa. Before Astor could cast around for further offers, the new Zambian Government headed by Kaunda announced that they wanted it for "national guidance". David Astor objected to this and was further alarmed to find that Kaunda had had it valued in Lusaka by his own agents at only £40,000. There then followed a meeting at the Dorchester Hotel in London between Kaunda and his advisers and David Astor, who judged Kaunda to be "embarrassed" as he and his advisers poured praise on David for being "a true freedom fighter". But embarrassment did not prevent Kaunda from stating that he had been advised not to offer more than £40,000 for the paper, and if that was not accepted they would have to start a new paper which, alone, would receive government advertising. It was an ultimatum. David was "disgusted" at Kaunda's behaviour, but there was nothing he could do and the paper duly (if not altogether surprisingly) became merely

4. Richard Hall, *My Life with Tiny*.

a mouthpiece of the new regime. David lost something over £60,000, which was a lot to pay for such a generous and disinterested investment in Zambia's independence. He was also helpful in involving the Aga Khan in setting up a paper called the *Daily Nation* in Kenya during the late 1950s, to give a voice to the minority communities in the country; but in this case he acted as an adviser rather than an investor.

The *Observer*'s campaigns against Central African federation and on behalf of Seretse and Tshekedi Khama both proved to be effective; but South Africa, the most intractable of all colonial problems, was a different matter. The paper invested a great deal of journalistic effort in its opposition to apartheid, to very little avail. For many years the *Observer* all but had an "exclusive" on the country, as in those days few other papers took much notice of it. From the start the *Observer* devoted considerable space to reporting the gathering momentum of legislation which created the apartheid state during the late 1940s and early 1950s. In a lead article by Colin Legum on June 11, 1950, entitled "Races Set Apart", the setting up of the Group Areas Act was chronicled. In an editorial of March 4, 1951 the paper published what amounted to a rallying cry to Britain to stand up to her responsibilities in South Africa:

A whole continent is stirring into political life and we in Britain are as directly responsible for the political fate of whole African communities as the people of America are for what happens in their Southern States.

As early as 1952 the *Observer* advocated that sanctions or embargoes should be applied against South Africa to try to force a change of attitude on Dr Malan, and in February 1956 the paper was urging that South Africa should leave the Commonwealth. It was unequivocal about the evils of apartheid, and saw both Dr Verwoerd's South Africa and Roy Welensky's Rhodesia as:

relics of Africa's rapidly disappearing colonial past....The decolonisation of Africa must inevitably go forward and it must mean the ending of all forms of white supremacy. Disagreeable though this transformation must be for those who have made their homes in Africa, the facts of the situation give them little choice. Either they can try to fight it out with the prospect of ultimately losing, or they can readjust themselves perceptibly to the new circumstances.

South Africa had to wait until F. W. de Klerk to face up to the realities of this logic.

In the course of bringing the iniquities of South Africa's apartheid system to world attention the *Observer* inevitably came into contact with the African resistance in South Africa, led by the African National Congress. Oliver Tambo, later president of the ANC, became a close friend of David Astor's and in the mid-1950s the paper also began to take an interest in the very intelligent and articulate ANC campaigner Nelson Mandela. The *Observer* aroused considerable animosity by supporting the armed struggle which the ANC committed itself to, arguing that the struggle in South Africa was comparable to that of the French *maquis* against the Germans during the Second World War.

One evening towards the end of June 1962, David got a telephone call from Oliver Tambo who said that he was going to bring "someone interesting" around. A few hours later Tambo appeared with Nelson Mandela, who was then on the run from the South African police and had entered Britain on a false passport. Virtually Mandela's first words were: "I have come to see you to say thank you for what you are doing for my people."

During the course of a long conversation, Mandela repeated the message that he had carried through Africa on his journey to London, that the armed struggle was only *one* way of fighting, that everyone had a different way which they must follow, the Church through the pulpit, liberals through various international organizations, pacifists through the printed word. David Astor saw Mandela very much as an African Adam von Trott; like Trott, he was a man from a chieftain's family who had dedicated his life to freeing his people from what he regarded as an alien tyranny. Curiously enough, David soon found himself giving the same advice to Mandela as he had given to Trott twenty-two years before, arguing that he should not return to South Africa, as he could be of more use to the cause by campaigning in freedom in London or Washington. Death or imprisonment awaited him, eventually, in South Africa. Like Trott, Mandela appreciated the advice but did not take it. More immediately, David Astor arranged for him to meet the two leading Opposition politicians, Hugh Gaitskell of the Labour Party and Jo Grimond of the Liberal Party. As Mandela was a "fugitive", these meetings, which took place at the beginning of July, had to be conducted very discreetly — but clearly the discretion was overdone: on July 3, 1962 David Astor had to write identical letters to Gaitskell and Grimond informing them that the man they had met *was* Nelson Mandela:

> ...although it is important to keep his visit here dark, it is absurd you should not realise who he was, as the whole point of meeting him was that you should better be able to understand his future actions.

After only a few days in London, Mandela returned to South Africa, where he was soon caught by the police and brought to trial, together with several co-defendants, in 1964. This famous trial was given extensive coverage by the *Observer*, and Anthony Sampson covered the proceedings from the courtroom itself. It was now, more than ever, that many Africans came to regard the paper as "their link with the West". The *Observer* ran a Profile of Mandela, and kept the story in the front of the news throughout the trial. That Mandela received a life sentence instead of the death penalty was in no small measure due to the publicity that he received in the Western press, led by the *Observer*. On June 12, 1964, Mary Benson, who had been monitoring the situation very closely, wrote to David Astor:

> I wonder whether you realise how much you and the *Observer* must be largely responsible for Nelson's life? In the UN and Washington, people were tremendously inspired by the various articles — including the profile and the earlier quotations from Nelson's previous defence — and the fact that so great a newspaper was pointing to the stature of this man and the significance of the case hugely impressed people with influence. Not to mention what it's meant to all the "believers" to have such encouragement and support.

In 1964 Nelson Mandela started his prison sentence. The next time David Astor was to see him was in Sweden in 1990.

The years after Mandela's imprisonment were perhaps the hardest of all for the anti-apartheid movement because the temporary defeat of the ANC ushered in a period of apparent calm and the international spotlight slipped to other conflicts, such as Vietnam and the Congo. On a visit to South Africa for the all-white elections in 1970, Sampson was astonished at how the issue of the ANC had successfully been relegated to the political sidelines. None the less, the *Observer* and others did what they could to keep the "cause" alive and ensure that Mandela and his fellow inmates were not totally forgotten. Throughout these years the Swedes were hugely important in helping Mandela and his co-defendants through the International Defence and Aid Fund, which enabled them to employ some of the finest lawyers in South Africa. This contribution was important, and the ANC's closest European connections were subsequently always with Sweden.

David Astor acted on a more personal level when he learnt that the imprisoned Mandela wanted to study American law, so needed American law books. David asked the British ambassador in Pretoria to get the books to Mandela through official contacts. This unusual arrangement was allowed by the South African authorities, and continued until the South African police stopped Mandela's surreptitious education in 1970. The law books became quite famous on Robben Island, as he encouraged other prisoners to take up the study of law as well. When Mandela met Sampson in February 1990, he immediately referred to this supply of books, including Sampson's own *Anatomy of Britain*, which was among the first book that David Astor had managed to send him. During his imprisonment it was hard for any of Mandela's family to communicate his thanks, but on December 15, 1966 David received the following letter from Winnie Mandela:

You do not know me personally....I am Nelson Mandela's wife. I would like to thank you so much for assisting my husband with books for his studies. You have no idea just how much we appreciate your kind assistance at a time when it is so welcome. Just to say thank you does not seem to be enough at all. I do hope that one day I shall be able to thank you in person.

Nelson was looking fine when I saw him. Recently he has lost a lot of weight of course due to much labour and the poor diet. He sends you his fondest regards, and he says I should tell you that he is doing well with his studies.

David Astor was also active in supporting white liberal opposition to the regime in South Africa itself. The *Observer* chronicled the Government's attempts to intimidate the domestic liberal press, particularly the famous *Rand Daily Mail* edited by Laurence Gandar. The *Observer* ran a long piece highlighting the plight of the paper and it was David Astor who nominated the *Rand Daily Mail* for the prestigious American Newspaper Publishers Association World Press Achievement Award in 1966, which — as Gandar has written to the author — "helped me to fight off an attempt by the paper's board of directors to fire me outright and replace me with a very conservative-minded editor". In the late 1980s Astor continued this link with the *Rand Daily Mail* by investing in a paper called the *Weekly Mail*, edited by Anton Harber, run largely by journalists who had been on the *Rand Daily Mail*.

In an attempt to overcome some of the post-colonial problems that had beset other educationally backward African countries, David Astor also became the instigator of an interesting educational exercise called the South African Advanced Education Project (SAAEP), set up in 1987 in conjunction with Anthony Sampson and Oliver Tambo of the ANC, and funded by the Rockefeller Trust, Ford Foundation and Shell. The purpose of SAAEP was to try to remedy the lack of an educated, post-independence African middle class by funding South African blacks to come to England to attend business and economics courses, including some at the London Business School. The need for modern accounting and economics skills amongst black South Africans is obvious: of 13,000 chartered accountants in the Republic of South Africa, only twenty-nine are black. SAAEP is an attempt to learn from the often unhappy lessons of the rest of post-Imperial Africa.

The *Observer* thus served as the medium of communication between black Africa and the outside world. It had little influence within the white community in South Africa, but it had great influence amongst the African community and played a prominent role in bringing the plight of those living under colonial rule to the attention of the West as a whole. In Britain the *Observer* slowly and persistently won a reputation for itself as the premier authority on Africa, necessary reading for anyone who had to deal with that area of the world.

One such figure was Harold Macmillan, who, as prime minister from 1957 to 1963, had to oversee the process of decolonization which the *Observer* had been advocating. His heart might not have been in it, but his head ruled that, ultimately, the *Observer* was right. Tim Bligh, Macmillan's principal private secretary, confided to Anthony Sampson, with whom he lunched nearly every week, that Macmillan always read the *Observer* to keep abreast of events. Indeed, he took the paper very seriously, seeing it as the "thinking man's" constituency. During the course of writing a Profile of Macmillan, Sampson was granted an interview of two hours duration; Macmillan took great care over the *Observer*. The climax of Macmillan's Africa policy was, of course his tour of the British colonies in 1960, culminating in his speech in Capetown on February 3, 1960. Anthony Sampson covered the prime minister's whole tour and was in the gallery on that famous occasion to hear the prime minister tell the attentive audience of the South African Parliament that:

> ...the most striking of all the impressions I have formed since I left London a month ago is of the strength of this African national consciousness. In different places it takes different forms, but it is happening everywhere. The wind of change is blowing through this continent, and, whether we like it or not, this growth of national consciousness is a political fact. We must all accept it as a fact, and our national policies must take account of it.

It was a clever speech, couched in terms of flattering praise for the achievements of the white community, but making it equally clear that Britain and the Commonwealth could have nothing more to do with a country practising apartheid. But what was more striking to Sampson was that it seemed to bear out everything that the *Observer* had been saying for the previous thirteen years, since that initial leader attacking Malan in May 1948.

The authorship of Macmillan's famous speech has always been in dispute; it has variously been attributed to Sir John Maud, the British High Commissioner to South Africa, Lord Home, David Hunt of the Commonwealth Office and Norman Brook — amongst others. But it is evident that the *Observer* also played its part. Just before Macmillan left for Africa, he drew the attention of the various Whitehall departments involved in his speech to an "open" letter in the *Observer* of December 20, 1959 from representatives of anti-Government parties in South Africa, including Chief Albert

Luthuli, president-general of the ANC, Alan Paton, author of *Cry,
the Beloved Country*, and Jordan K. Ngubane, vice-president of the
Liberal Party. The signatories of this letter urged Macmillan in his
forthcoming speech in Cape Town "not to say one single word that
could be construed to be in praise of apartheid". Tim Bligh sent a
letter dated December 29, 1959 from Downing Street to the Colonial
Office and the Foreign Office asking for their views on the open letter
in the *Observer*:

> I expect you will have seen the "open letter" addressed to the
> Prime Minister on Sunday December 20. The Prime Minister's
> feeling is that on the whole the signatories of the letter would be
> satisfied with the current draft of the speech, but he would be
> glad to know what the Departments think.[5]

Sadly the departmental responses to this request do not survive; but
it is a good illustration of the way in which the paper came to
represent the views of Africa in Whitehall.

With the exception of South Africa, the process of decolonization
that the *Observer* had urged on Britain had come to pass by the time
that David Astor retired as editor in 1975. Although in retrospect,
such a process seems to have been inevitable, at the time the
Observer encountered more opposition to its views on Africa than to
any other campaign that the paper ran. When it began to attack the
Government of South Africa, it was way in advance of public
opinion, to say nothing of British politicians, even in the Liberal or
Labour Parties. It was out in front of the Labour Party, and David
Astor and Colin Legum spent a considerable amount of time talking
to Labour politicians and persuading them of this; it was, after all,
the Attlee Government which had originally planned the idea of
Central African Federation. In 1952, with Attlee in opposition again
and the federation just about to be imposed, Astor and Legum went
to see Attlee to alert him to the dangers of federation. He received
them in his room at the House of Commons and heard them in one of
his famous silences, at the end of which all Attlee said was: "I suggest
that you go and see David Stirling. Good day." (Stirling, the
celebrated special forces commander, was running the Capricorn

---

5. PRO CO 1027/143.

Society, an organization aimed at racial harmony.) Just as they got nowhere with Attlee, so the *Observer* took several years to persuade the Labour Party of the merits of the expulsion of South Africa from the Commonwealth and the imposition of sanctions against that country.

With the Conservative Party it was a different matter. Whereas the Labour Party might have been broadly sympathetic to the *Observer*'s policy, if not specifically helpful, the Conservative Party was openly hostile. The right-wing case against the *Observer* was much the same argument as that deployed against Macmillan's "Wind of Change" speech — that by bowing to those winds of nationalism, the prime minister merely encouraged a process of violent and premature African independence which resulted in the petty, undemocratic dictatorships which flourished in so many post-independence states. The case of the right rested on a fundamental perception that the Africans were not developed enough to rule themselves. As soon as the *Observer* declared itself an enemy of white colonial rule, David Astor had to fight a long and often acrimonious battle against not only his political opponents but his own family circle on this issue. "Uncle" Bob Brand represented the classic Tory view in a letter to David of May 18, 1951:

> The African races. . . are like children; they live for the day and are consequently always cheerful until evil hits them on that day, when they are inclined to collapse. It is difficult. . . to know whether they may not ultimately reach any standard that other races have reached. I have met some of the most experienced judges who think that at any rate it will take them a very long time. What is quite certain is that they cannot run a modern productive state.

Brand accused the *Observer* of being ". . . hopelessly impractical"; others accused the paper of naïveté and extremism. Pressure was certainly put on through the trustees to get the paper to change its attitude. White settler friends of Lord Portal, a trustee of the paper, quickly appealed to Portal when the *Observer* began to justify civil disobedience in Nyasaland against the imposed Central African Federation. Portal approached Dingle Foot, at that time chairman of the trustees, but Foot proved invaluable in defending David Astor from his fellow trustees. Foot was a natural political ally of Astor's. He was also the lawyer of Hastings Banda. At a meeting of the trustees Portal lodged a formal complaint against the *Observer* for preaching open rebellion against the federation, and demanded that the editor be replaced. Foot, however, exercised his authority as chairman and told Portal that the editor was entitled to run his own policy, and the trustees could interfere only if he breached the principles on which the Trust was founded. Portal accepted this, although reluctantly. Arthur Mann also complained about the paper's policy at the meeting, as well as tackling Legum personally on the subject. The *Observer* was also attacked in Parliament on more than one occasion. The resignations of Mann and Portal at the time of Suez were but the culmination of their growing disenchantment with much of the *Observer*'s politics.

More damaging to David personally was the oft-repeated opposition of Nancy Astor to the paper's policy. Nancy Astor had become increasingly disenchanted with its alleged "socialism" throughout the 1940s and this was in part the cause of the family rift. By the early 1950s, deprived of her public life and increasingly unable to control the irrascible and emotional side of her temperament, she lost no opportunity to attack the *Observer*, be it in public or in private. She frequently used the occasion of the annual Cliveden office party to bad-mouth the paper, often with David sitting at her side, attempting in vain to conceal a pained expression. It was on one such occasion, in 1950, that Nancy described the *Observer* as "written by Germans for Blacks". She would then mingle with the staff and single out those whom she held to be responsible; on one occasion she buttonholed Colin Legum and told him: "You're the one who's turning the *Observer* into the Coon gazette." It distressed her friends, and Brand wrote a note of sympathy to David, who naturally had to try to avoid her. The tragedy was neatly summarized by Brand:

> Your Ma yesterday begged me to urge you to see more of her. She longs to see you but I fear might relapse into criticism of the *Observer*. Nevertheless she must not.

But by this time of her life such restraint was unfortunately beyond her. Waldorf Astor, on the other hand, remained quietly supportive. Throughout the last years of his father's life, David used to stop by at Cliveden on Mondays on his way back to London from Sutton Courtenay for advice and consultation. As long as he was chairman of the trustees, Waldorf was a rock of

support. Virtually on his deathbed in 1952 Lord Astor telephoned
Legum out of the blue just to reassure him privately that he would
give all his backing to Legum and David if they ever needed it
over Africa. Lord Astor's quiet and dignified support during these
early controversial years of David's editorship was all important
and must have given David considerable moral courage in facing
Nancy. "A wonderful man", as Colin Legum recalls. Waldorf's
death in 1952 deprived David of a loyal friend as well as a father.

The *Observer* itself always stood by its Africa policy and argued
that the failure of some African states to be fully "democratic"
after independence was no reason to prevent them from charting
their own destinies. It reminded its readers that it was hardly
consistent for Europeans to lecture the Africans on the virtues of
democracy, when it was Europe which had produced some of the
most terrible tyrannies of modern history. As the newly liberated
Ghana seemed to slip into an ever more dictatorial regime, the
Observer warned in an editorial on October 8, 1961 that this was a
situation which would become more familiar in the newly liberated
states:

> Democracy has always been a rare phenomenon in the history
> of the world, and it would be absurd to expect the newly
> emerging nations of Asia and Africa to adopt easily and at
> once a method of government which it took us several centuries
> to develop and which many Europeans have never achieved
> at all. This does not mean that we should hold up our hands
> in horror at the first sign of deviation. The road to parlia-
> mentary government and the rule of law is long and hard;
> and nations such as Pakistan and Ghana must get there at
> their own pace and in their own way. But it would be
> dishonest if we did not apply to them the same standards that
> we apply in other countries, both black and white. Nothing
> could be more contemptuous than to suggest that Africans
> and Asians are not capable of democracy.

It would also be wrong to think that the *Observer* was always
on the side of Africans against white settlers, regardless of what
the Africans did. David Astor based his principles on political
freedom and freedom of expression, and was just as prepared to
criticize African leaders who ran oppressive dictatorships as he
was the whites who ran such regimes in the rest of Africa. From

an early stage, the *Observer* was as ready to criticize those African leaders who seemed bent on nothing better than a petty dictatorship to replace colonial rule, white and exclusive as that rule may have been. In a Profile of Kenyatta on November 2, 1952, the leader of the fearsome Mau Mau rebels in Kenya was characterized thus:

> He seems to have adopted an irrational attitude that the Kikuyu are always right. Henceforth he was to assert with powerful sub-Hitlerian oratorical effect that Kenya would be a paradise if the White man departed.
>
> This obvious nonsense marks the eclipse of the studious anthropologist by the demagogue appealing to the national pride of his followers....

David might have been angered over Kaunda's takeover of the *Central African Mail*, but he was not entirely surprised. The *Observer* always retained a rational, alert view of African affairs. It is ironic that the main argument deployed by *Observer* journalists against the Lonrho takeover in 1981 was that since Lonrho was so thick with many African leaders due to its pursuit of commercial goodwill and opportunities, a Lonrho-owned *Observer* would no longer be able to criticize undemocratic black African leaders as the paper had been able to do in the 1960s and 1970s.

A practical illustration of David Astor's impartiality was the formation of the Minority Rights Group in 1961, an organization formed largely by him and Michael Scott to publicize the cause of oppressed minorities in the post-colonial world. The first director was Laurence Gandar. Others involved were Roland Oliver, the Africa expert, and David Kessler, editor of the *Jewish Chronicle*. The Minority Rights Group produced studies of the plight of ethnic or national minority communities, whether they be Kurds, Palestinians or Eritreans. For highlighting the conditions of these minorities, the *Observer* was frequently as abused by the newly independent nations as it had been abused by their former colonial rulers. The most famous case concerning minority rights was that of the Nagas, a tribe near the Burma hills who were fighting to regain their independence from India. It was Scott who met President Phizo of the Nagas, lobbying the United Nations in New York on behalf of his people, and soon after David Astor invited Gavin Young to undertake a very dangerous journey into Nagaland, one of the remotest areas in the world, to make contact with the Nagas and report on their situation. This might have pleased the Nagas, but it caused a lot of bad blood in India, where the *Observer* had previously been greatly admired for its support of independence and its anti-Suez line. But as soon as it began pointing out the political rights of the Nagas on their own borders, the Indian Government let it be known that they were extremely dismayed. The same motivation led the *Observer* into taking an interest in the problems of the Tamils in Sri Lanka in the late 1960s.

The fight for the classic liberal causes of political rights and freedom of expression thus extended from white colonial rule to post-colonial African or Asian rule. It was a consistency that most of the paper's right-wing critics liked to ignore. Whether the *Observer*'s campaign for African independence was "premature" will always be a matter of debate, but in retrospect the least one can say is that David Astor was one of the first to sense the "Winds of Change" and to argue for a new policy to adapt to the changing circumstances of Imperial rule. His critics might have wanted to "reform to preserve" but it is difficult to see how this policy could have had any lasting success; the policies adopted by South Africa were perhaps the only alternative. The *Observer*'s African campaigns were perhaps the paper's most conspicuous success and became its most important mission.

Having waged the last liberal war against old-fashioned imperialism, the *Observer* was left to see the enemy fleeing from the field. But before that point was reached, the Suez crisis was to provide the most testing examination of the paper's anti-imperial credentials.

7

Suez

In retrospect it is clear that the year 1956 marks a turning point in the fortunes of David Astor's *Observer*. However, this is not how it seemed then. In September 1956 the paper edged ahead of the *Sunday Times* for the first time: the *Observer* sold barely a thousand copies more than its rival's 654,557, but this was enough to cause panic at Gray's Inn Road, where Lord Kemsley hastily convened a special Monday Conference — "Black Monday", it was later called. It took some time for anyone to pluck up the courage to inform Kemsley that the unthinkable had finally happened; as his paper's official historians put it:

> . . . it was perfectly understandable that he would feel personally disgraced if his paper had to take second place to the inspired amateurs of Tudor Street. There were stricken faces at the Conference.[1]

Few people at Tudor Street had time to notice, let alone savour, this triumph. The *Observer* was wholly preoccupied with its most famous campaign of all, that against Eden's handling of the Suez crisis which dominated British and international politics

---

1. Phillip Knightley *et al*, *Pearl of Days*, p. 288.

throughout the summer and autumn of 1956. The *Observer*'s crusade against British armed intervention in the canal zone culminated in its famous leader of November 4 during the course of which the paper accused the Government of "folly" and "crookedness" and invited the prime minister to step down. For the rest of the year, as the paper's accusations of collusion and political bungling began to seem increasingly realistic, its moral stature reached probably its highest peak. Yet beneath the surface of commercial and moral success, circumstances were combining rapidly to bring to an end the effortless growth of the previous fifteen years.

Contrary to the popular impression, its stance on Suez was only one of a number of factors that began to conspire against the *Observer* after 1956. Much more important were the commercial and financial innovations with which its rivals were taking advantage of the changing economic climate in the newspaper industry. That the Suez crisis coincided with the beginning of the end of the *Observer*'s golden age is, to a great extent, coincidental.

For both David Astor and his father, Anthony Eden had always represented the progressive ethos of modern conservatism and Eden had often been a guest at Cliveden before the war. Like many of their ilk, they had looked to Eden to succeed Churchill and to lead the Conservatives domestically and internationally in a new direction. The *Observer* had praised Eden's considerable diplomatic skills displayed during his spell as foreign secretary from 1951 to 1955 when he had, amongst other things, broken the deadlock on European defence arrangements by getting West Germany into NATO.

Eden succeeded Churchill as prime minister on April 6, 1955 and almost immediately set a date for a general election. This took place on May 26 and Eden won handsomely, the Conservative Party gaining an overall majority of 60 seats in Parliament. However, despite this impressive victory at the polls and Eden's own equally impressive performance on the new election medium of television, the new year opened with a flood of hostile criticism directed at the Government. This criticism was, as yet, unfocused, but amongst other things the prime minister was accused of being weak, indecisive and slow in addressing important domestic problems. As the historian of Eden's government has written:

...few Prime Ministers have encountered such a barrage of hostile press criticism as assailed him [Eden] in January 1956[2]

The Times of January 2 declared that the Government had already lost its grip and should show more "high purpose", while even more devastating criticism came from the normally ultra-loyal *Daily Telegraph* which on January 3 published a famous leader entitled "Waiting for the smack of firm government", written by the paper's deputy editor Donald McLachlan. In its most famous passage, this leader read:

There is a favourite gesture of the Prime Minister which is sometimes recalled to illustrate this sense of disappointment. To emphasise a point he will clench one fist to smack the open palm of the other — but this smack is seldom heard. Most Conservatives...are waiting to feel the smack of firm Government.

This was not merely a piece of inspired personal spite on the part of Lady Pamela Berry, the proprietor's wife, but a serious piece of journalism which seemed to reflect a wide body of opinion amongst Conservative ranks — to say nothing of the Opposition.

On January 8, the *Observer* declared on its front page:

EDEN MUST GO MOVE GROWS

Hugh Massingham went on to report that:

...underground — if persistent back bench rumours can be relied on — some vigorous tunnelling will be going on. And before the year is out — some even say by the summer — the submerged time-bomb is due to explode.

Sir Anthony would be lifted to the House of Lords — on grounds of ill-health. The question of who would succeed him is still not clear; some of the discontented seem to favour Mr Macmillan rather than Mr Butler.

All this would come to pass — Suez would only complicate the

---

2. Richard Lamb, The *Failure of the Eden Government* (Sidgwick and Jackson 1987), p. 13.

story. Six months before the Suez crisis began, Eden's stock was already very difficult to sell. He enjoyed a remarkably short honeymoon period with the press and electorate.

The effect of all this press criticism on Eden can only be guessed at. One likely reaction was that the prime minister would want to *appear* to act more decisively, to appease his critics. To a certain extent this is how it seemed to the *Observer*, as in March 1956 Eden took a strong line in the dispute with Greece and Turkey over Cyprus and dispatched the Greek-Cypriot leader Archbishop Makarios to the Seychelles. The *Observer* of March 11 criticized this action, employing much the same logic that it was later to deploy against Eden over Suez:

> The banishment of Archbishop Makarios and other Cypriot leaders will be represented as an act of firmness by the British Government. What matters is whether this action is likely to be effective. That is the test by which the Government's decision should be judged.

To add further spice to the story of the *Observer* and Suez, the man officially charged with controlling the press on Eden's behalf was William Clark, the paper's former diplomatic correspondent. The gregarious Clark had resigned in 1955 to take up the position of Eden's press secretary in Downing Street. Like many on the *Observer*, he had been an admirer of Eden's from afar. At first, like many press officers new to the job, he was agreeably surprised by the power at his disposal through his twice daily lobby briefings at Downing Street, recording in his diary that it was, ". . . amazing to see how much of one's lightest guidance over the 'phone appears in the papers next day from the Political Correspondents'".[3] But he soon began to experience the jumpy, stormy side of Eden's character that was to make his eighteen-month stay in Downing Street progressively more miserable. On October 24, Clark recorded that Eden had got into a "great state" about a mildly critical *Daily Telegraph* leader. The prime minister was "a bit incoherent but in general it appeared that this was worse than anything the Nazis had ever done and he intended to devote the

---

3. Clark Diary, October 3, 1955; Clark Papers, Bodleian Library.

rest of his time to hitting back at them".[4]

This was sensitivity to press criticism on a grand scale and there was very little that Clark could do about it. In January 1956, when press criticism was at its height, he persuaded Eden to hold a series of meetings with editors, but this seems to have done little good: by the beginning of April Clark was recording in his diary that "...the PM's press has been very bad". Eden's hostile press must have helped to undermine Clark's position at Downing Street but the situation was exacerbated by his connection with the *Observer*, as that paper quickly became the arch-critic of Eden and the Government, even before the Suez crisis erupted. Some in Downing Street suspected that Clark actually fed the *Observer* with hostile material; certainly, after less than a year of Eden's premiership, relations between the prime minister and his press secretary had — to say the least — cooled. By June 5, 1956, Clark was confessing to his diary that he was "feeling very low as a result of a general persecution complex arising out of a whispering campaign designed to make me appear disloyal to the PM. The difficulty is that I no longer do see enough of the PM to feel that I enjoy his full confidence. Perhaps I don't since the steady attacks on him by the *Observer* certainly must be a disappointment to him."

A typical exchange from this period illustrates the situation perfectly. Eden rang up to congratulate Clark on a good Saturday press, but then "...began to carp. 'I hear Massingham's never out of your room...he's my enemy so it's not much good seeing him, is it?'"[5] Clark's loyalties became further strained when the Suez crisis began and he found himself siding more and more with the *Observer* against the prime minister's belligerence. This was hardly surprising, as he had been one of the architects of the paper's whole anti-colonial post-war foreign policy. Clark liked to think that Eden *was* the kind of progressive Conservative who should "get some support from the liberal press (*Manchester Guardian*, *News Chronicle*, *Observer*, etc). He really is their man: if only they knew it".[6] But when it came to the crunch in November 1956

---

4. Clark Diary, October 29, 1955.

5. Clark Diary, June 5, 1956.

6. Clark Diary, July 16, 1956.

Clark was to resign in protest at Eden's policy. However, although he dissented from Eden's Suez policy, there is no evidence that he ever leaked anything to the *Observer* or conspired against his masters in Downing Street. He remained loyal to Eden and it was only at the crisis point at the beginning of November that Clark's reserve broke and he confided his doubts to David Astor — but by then he was merely expressing opinions that had been put far more forcefully in print by the *Observer* itself.

The Suez crisis began in earnest on July 26 when President Nasser of Egypt nationalized the Suez Canal and proclaimed martial law in the canal zone. Relations between Nasser and the West — Britain in particular — had been deteriorating for several years and the unilateral seizure of the canal was only the culmination of this unfortunate process. Immediately Nasser was denounced in the House of Commons by all sides, and the inevitable comparisons were made with Hitler and Mussolini. Whilst, at one level, the Government took Nasser's action to the UN and the rounds of international diplomatic conferences started, at another level an Egypt committee was formed within the Cabinet, charged with planning aggressive action against Egypt.

Although David Astor could understand the political reflexes of a generation that had fought for six years against totalitarianism, he was never impressed by the comparison between Nasser and the Fascists. Mussolini and Hitler were solidly expansionist leaders, unlike Nasser who was "a weak man in a weak country asserting his minimum rights". This analysis was shared by his Middle East editor, Bob Stephens. Furthermore, given the *Observer*'s coherent policy on Africa, the paper saw the Egyptian problem in the wider context of the African anti-colonial struggle, fearing that if Britain went to war with an Arab country with no legal or international support — as was the case — the greatest danger was that Britain would forfeit all its goodwill among the Arabs, built up over the previous century. Moreover (and this was probably the most bitter pill for English readers to swallow) the paper stated quite boldly that even if Britain *wanted* to occupy Egypt and topple Nasser, it was no longer strong enough to do so and to finance an occupying army. For a country in which many people still saw themselves as a "Great Power", this line of thought in 1956 was a rude awakening. Having always contended that withdrawal from Africa was inevitable, the *Observer* now argued that what Nasser had done *could not* be undone, so some sort of compromise had to be reached. From the very start it opposed force and suggested instead the internationalization of the canal under the jurisdiction of the United Nations. It was particularly attracted by the idea of the Suez Canal Users' Association (SCUA), floated by Dulles, US Secretary of State, in early September. A leader of August 12, entitled "What to Do?", put the paper's case admirably:

> In the past few weeks, many doubts and warnings have been expressed by critics of the British Government's policy. What has not been clearly shown is the fundamental reality of our position. It is, simply and bluntly, that we are no longer in a position to safeguard even our vital interests effectively by our own efforts.... No single State or combination of States can now effectively police the world. The choice in our time is between paying the price of world anarchy — disastrous for a trading nation such as ourselves — or creating effective organs of international control.
>
> That was, and is, the choice in the Suez Crisis. When the British Government did not take unilateral military action in the first flush of indignation, when it decided to call an international conference and to propose the creation of an international authority, it in fact made its choice — and the right one. But the Government has continued to act and talk as if the road to unilateral action was open to us, and it has therefore entirely failed, so far, to get the political benefits of that choice. We have appeared as people who hesitate to use force, not as pioneers of a new and broader concept of international law. Yet it is that latter role which offers us our only chance.

As the autumn wore on and the pace of international negotiations picked up, so did the pace of Britain's military preparations centred on an invasion fleet based at Malta. Throughout this period, the *Observer* argued its case in a quiet, deliberate manner, partly due to the risks of inciting too much hysteria on the subject and partly because no one on the paper, least of all David Astor, could imagine that Eden's Government would eventually ignore all the calls for restraint that were coming from Washington and the rest of the international community. In retrospect, if David Astor had known what Eden was contemplating, the *Observer* would have made much louder noises much earlier. On September 2, in a long leader entitled "The Crucial Debate", it once again tried to lift jaded political imaginations, obsessed by Nasser, to the broader horizons, arguing that the dispute in Egypt was but a small sideshow of the "main issue" of international politics, which remained "the co-existence in conflict of the Communist and Western power-blocs — and above all their competition for the friendship of the new, uncommitted ex-colonial nations of Asia".

The paper went on to argue that any intemperate action against Nasser would weaken the Western position in the long run by pushing the other Asian and African states into an anti-Western stance and perhaps into the clutches of the Kremlin. Many politicians were fond of comparing the impudence of Nasser to the impudence of Hitler's invasion of the Rhineland in 1936, but the *Observer* warned that such comparisons were misleading:

> Swift military action against Hitler in 1936 would have ended the menace — the only serious menace at that time. Swift military action against Nasser in 1956, even if successful, could end a minor menace only at the cost of incalculably increasing the major one. Only those whose sense of injured dignity has warped their sense of proportion can ignore the wider issue.

This was the view of the Americans and of the other Western powers — to say nothing of the United Nations. In Downing Street William Clark began to have his doubts about Eden's real intentions. Clark was becoming ever more a supporter of the *Observer*'s policy, especially as it was shared by the most important people that he had to deal with, President Eisenhower's administration in Washington. In September he recorded in his diary that he had seen a "...devastating telegram from Ike. It seems at first sight to be an absolute ban on our use of force, arguing very strongly along *Observer* lines. It is this that has brought the PM racing back almost in despair."[7]

In its early stand against force, the *Observer* was joined by the

---

7. Clark Diary, undated pp. 124–5.

Manchester Guardian and the *Daily Mirror*, although the latter paper was later to modify its attitude. Other papers (of the Sundays, the *People*, *Reynold's News* and the *Sunday Pictorial* and of the dailies, the *News Chronicle* and the *Scottish Daily Record*) were to oppose the use of force when it actually happened in November, but only the *Manchester Guardian* and the *Observer* argued consistently against it throughout the crisis (accompanied by the *Economist*, which came out against it in the plainest of terms on Friday, November 2 as the British assault on Egypt started). Ranged against these papers were the massed ranks of the Conservative press which all supported, in varying degrees, the Government's policy. There was a stark contrast between the *Observer* and the *Sunday Times*, as Lord Kemsley seemed to want to dispatch Nasser to the uttermost parts of hell. Never was there to be a clearer contest between what Roy Thomson described as the "question-asking" *Observer* and the "reassuring, establishment" *Sunday Times*. As the crisis worsened through October and November the differences between the "hawks" and the "doves" deepened and the tone of the press began to reflect the bitter divisions in society over an issue that excited passions in a way unseen since the Munich crisis of 1938.

By the middle of October a stalemate seemed to have been reached as negotiations ground to a halt. More importantly, the military ground now looked increasingly unlikely as the logistical, military and economic complexities of an invasion of Egypt were fully explored. It was also apparent that the unilateral use of force against Egypt, or indeed the bilateral use of force in conjunction with France, would have very little legitimacy in international law and would command no support at the United Nations. It was precisely at this moment, when Eden's policy of impotent belligerency seemed to have run into the sands, that the French came up with the plan for secret military collusion between Britain, France and Israel that would provide Eden with a pretext for his much cherished military invasion of Egypt.

On October 14, the French acting foreign minister, Albert Gazier, and General Maurice Challe, a deputy chief of staff of the French Air Force, called on Eden at Chequers to present him with the secret French–Israeli plan. Israel would be encouraged to attack Egypt across the Sinai desert; the British and French would give them enough time to defeat the Egyptians and then demand that both sides withdraw from the canal to allow the Anglo-French forces to occupy it, posing as a "peace-keeping" force separating the two warring contestants. The plan had nothing to commend it other than affording Eden a way out of the cul-de-sac he now found himself in. It involved deceit and disingenuousness, which is why so few people within the Government were let into it. On October 24, the secret plan was officially agreed upon and a treaty signed at a meeting of Israeli, French and British ministers and officials at Sèvres. As even Eden's official biographer is prepared to admit, the prime minister now found himself moving from what could be seen as "an absolutely legitimate position to what was perilously close to being an illegitimate one".[8]

The Government was now committed to aggressive military action whatever happened. To the outside world, unaware of the approaching date of the Israeli attack on Egypt, little seemed to have changed. However, the considerable disenchantment felt by many in the Government at Eden's general policy and the Sèvres agreement in particular — Sir Walter Monckton had resigned as minister of defence as early as September 24 — was bound to filter out, and the *Observer* began to pick up odd hints that something secret was going on which would dramatically alter the situation. R. A. Butler, Leader of the House of Commons and, as Lord Privy Seal, one of the few privy to the Sèvres plan, had a talk with Hugh Massingham towards the end of October. Butler, a journalistic "source" of some renown, told Massingham that "When I sit with some of my colleagues, I sometimes think that I am surrounded by madmen, talking about things I can't understand." In Downing Street, William Clark, by now operating very much on the fringe of things, was excluded from the circle of politicians and officials cognizant of the Sèvres plan. But working in Ten Downing Street during late October it was impossible not to notice the atmosphere of subterfuge and furtive activity that began to grip the building. Clark later told David Astor his grounds for suspicion. One of his stories concerned a general — a long-standing acquaintance — who came into Number Ten to attend a meeting, and assuming that

8. Robert Rhodes James, *Anthony Eden* (Weidenfeld & Nicolson 1986), p. 533.

Clark was in on the secret pressed his forefinger to his lips in a mocking gesture and went "Sssh!" before turning to march into the Cabinet room. It was not difficult for David to deduce what was really happening when the Israelis, as their part of the Sèvres agreement, attacked Egypt on October 30 and the Anglo-French forces immediately began to cross the Mediterranean to "separate" the two sides. In an attempt to confirm his suspicions, David wrote to Sir Walter Monckton, whom he knew to be out of sympathy with the Government's policy, on November 1. It was a plea for understanding as much as anything else:

> Dear Sir Walter,
> Surely something terrible is happening. I have the feeling that the nation is being disgraced. Please excuse this urgent cry.

Monckton refused to be drawn, and replied loyally on November 5 that he "understood" why David had written his note but felt that "in present circumstances" it was "extremely difficult for [him] to give a considered reply".[9]

When the British forces reached Egypt and bombers started attacking the Canal Zone, it became increasingly obvious to David that a pre-planned attack was now in full swing, aiming to destroy Nasser under the pretext of saving the peace in the area. Eden's biographer concedes that the plan was merely ". . . a pretext for achieving the destruction of Nasser; but it was so obvious a pretext that one still wonders why [Eden] believed it would not be seen as such."[10] The only paper let into the secret was *The Times*, whose diplomatic correspondent, Iverach MacDonald, was told of the Sèvres plan by Eden himself. If Eden thought he could automatically rely on the support of *The Times* he was very much mistaken: MacDonald and his editor, William Haley, were both appalled at the prospect of what Eden was planning. Clark, by now aware of what was up, levelled with MacDonald and found the normally urbane *Times* man in despair. "He thought the whole

---

9. Correspondence in Dept. Monckton, folios 22−23; Monckton Papers, Bodleian Library.

10. Rhodes James, p. 523.

project had been grotesquely mishandled, and above all it was collusive and dishonest. Clearly he had been shocked to the marrow by the revelation of duplicity which the PM had made to him in believing that *The Times* was an unshockable government supporter. Haley was very distressed too."[11] Their knowledge put *The Times* in a difficult position. Haley could not bring himself to support the plan and yet he did not want to betray Eden's confidence by attacking it with the benefit of his special knowledge. The result was that *The Times* played dumb; from being a vigorous supporter of Eden, the paper now became non-committal. The *Observer*, on the other hand, had independently worked out what Haley had been told and so was now free to criticize the plan without fear or favour.

In the first few days of November, British and French aircraft destroyed 260 Egyptian aircraft on the ground as the Israelis advanced deeper into Egypt. A full-scale Anglo-French landing was obviously no more than a day or two away. On the *Observer*, there was almost complete unanimity in condemning the British action. Only two members of staff are known to have dissented from the paper's opposition to the Government: O. M. Green, the Far Eastern correspondent, and one of the cartoonists. The *Observer* would clearly have to make its position known on the coming Sunday, November 4. On Thursday, November 1, Dingle Foot came into the office and offered to write a leader on the subject. Dingle Foot was a barrister specializing in Commonwealth affairs who had, until recently, been chairman of the trustees of the paper. He was an old personal friend of David's, with whom he had a natural political affinity. Indeed, Foot had been David's nominee to succeed his father as chairman of the Trust shortly before his father's death in 1952. Foot had always been an unusual chairman and had incurred the wrath of his fellow trustees by actually writing an article in the paper and by meddling in editorial matters. Just before Suez, Lord Portal and Keith Murray had combined to have Foot sacked — David Astor being summoned by Murray to be told the news personally. As has been seen, Foot had been very important in deflecting the wrath of Portal and

---

11. Clark Diary, November 1, 1956.

Murray during the early 1950s when they had made complaints about the paper's anti-colonial policy in Africa, so he had served Astor well at a difficult time. None the less, Foot's dismissal meant that at the time of Suez the Trust was in something of a limbo, which probably made it easier for Astor to act in the way that he then did.

On that Thursday the two men quickly found themselves in full agreement on the lunacy of the Government. Foot offered to produce a draft leader for Sunday, which he did overnight. Due to his controversial position *vis-à-vis* the paper, let alone the trustees, his involvement was kept secret. The draft leader that Foot then presented to Astor was a product of their dual thinking, although it was Foot personally who added the appeal to the Conservatives to rebel against Eden over Suez as their predecessors had done against Chamberlain in 1940. The leader as it stood was very good, but David felt that it was still a little on the legalistic side and "not passionate enough". It was he who added the decisive lines at the end of the first paragraph, hinting fairly openly at the suspicion of collusion and deceit surrounding the whole crisis: "We had not realised that our Government as capable of such folly and crookedness." This was David's only change to Dingle Foot's draft, but it was enough to transform the tone of the leader from that of reasoned protest to that of bitter dissent. He meant the leader to be "provocative and offensive" because he was dealing with a Government that was being provocative and offensive in its international behaviour. The *Observer* had always prided itself on its moderation and reasonableness, but now was the moment, he felt, when these moderate people must "get off their backsides and shout". The leader began thus:

EDEN

We wish to make an apology. Five weeks ago we remarked that, although we knew our Government would not make a military attack in defiance of its solemn international obligations, people abroad might think otherwise. The events of last week have proved us completely wrong: if we misled anyone, at home or abroad, we apologize unreservedly. We had not realised that our Government was capable of such folly and crookedness.

Whatever the Government now does, it cannot undo its

air attacks on Egypt, made after Egypt had been invaded by Israel. It cannot undo the deliberate employment of haste so that our nearest allies had no opportunity to express disagreement. It can never live down the dishonest nature of its ultimatum, so framed that it was certain to be rejected by Egypt.

Never since 1783 has Great Britain made herself so universally disliked. That was the year in which the Government of Lord North, faced with the antagonism of almost the whole civilized world, was compelled to recognize the independence of the American Colonies. Sir Anthony Eden has the unenviable distinction of leading the first Administration since the days of George III to reach such an isolated moral position. His eighteenth-century predecessors succeeded in losing us an empire. Sir Anthony and his colleagues have already succeeded in losing us incalculable political assets.

So long as his Government represents this country we cannot expect to have a good standing in the councils of the nations. It has attempted to prove those councils futile by rendering them futile. This it has done by, first, frustrating the Security Council of the United Nations through the use of the veto, and then by defying an overwhelming vote in the General Assembly. The Eden Government has become internationally discredited. . . .

The leader concluded:

Whether the Conservative Party can save itself from obliteration for a generation now depends on whether it produces an honest parliamentary rebellion that contributes to retrieving the national situation. But whatever the Conservative Party may do, it is essential that the world should know that the Eden Administration no longer has the nation's confidence. Unless we can find means of making that absolutely clear, we shall be individually guilty of an irresponsibility and a folly as great as that of our Government.

The Eden Administration has, throughout this summer, shown that it does not understand the sort of world we live in. It is no longer possible to bomb countries because you fear that your trading interests will be harmed. Nowadays, a drowning man on a raft is the occasion for all shipping to be diverted to try to save him: this new feeling for the sanctity of human life is the best element in the modern world. It is the true distinction of the West. Our other distinction is our right of personal independence and responsibility in politics — a right that must be exercised.

It is for every individual in this country who is against the Government's attack on Egypt to say so by writing to his Member of Parliament, lobbying him, demonstrating in every legitimate way. Nations are said to have the governments they deserve. Let us show that we deserve better.

Everyone on the paper who saw this leader before it went to press approved of it. Another man who would have approved of it was William Clark, who spent Saturday, November 3 drafting his letter of resignation, a little under forty-eight hours before Anglo-French paratroops dropped on Port Fuad and Port Said. To his diary, Clark confided his "terrible quandary" as he could no longer "defend a policy I candidly dislike".[12] That evening he wrote a letter from his office at Ten Downing Street to David Astor, confessing that "...the bottom has fallen out of my world". He went on:

> "Clearly I must go as soon as possible, yet I hesitate (fatal) to go at the moment that our forces and our whole country's future is in the balance. We cannot go back at this moment I know — the best is that we should carry out our raid successfully. Some good can still be done here (the von-Trott fallacy? a truth!) and perhaps not all will be lost. I doubt it.
>
> All I ask is your composure in overwhelming disorder. I dread/anticipate reading you tomorrow.
> William

By Monday, November 5, he was writing to David from his rooms in Albany to say that he had handed in his resignation, ending his letter "no compassion needed now".

---

12. Clark Diary, November 3, 1956.

The paper appeared on the morning of November 4, one day before the paratroop assault on targets in northern Egypt which was followed a day later by the main seaborne assault. The whole operation was called off under intense American pressure the next day. On reading the leader headed "Eden" in the early hours of Sunday morning, Clark wrote that the *Observer* "seemed hysterical and I was really too tired to read it so I took it home and fell to sleep reading that Eden must go!" At first glance, Clark's assessment of the leader page was not too far wrong: the whole page was given up to a comprehensive attack on the Government, with the attack on Eden on the left, two articles in the middle of the page setting out the "fallacies" behind the Government's policy and the use of force, and on the right a series of letters, headed by the Bishop of Chichester and Trevor Huddleston, denouncing the Government's attack on Egypt. The pugnacious and uncompromising language of the leader shook regular readers and non-readers alike. However, all the rest of the editorial pages were the usual well-argued, cogent re-statements of what the *Observer* had been saying since the beginning of the crisis — in this respect, the paper was being absolutely consistent. Even the official historians of the rival *Sunday Times* are moved to write that:

> The total attack was as well-marshalled as it was destructive. It was what old Barnes of *The Times* would have called firing ten-pounders.[13]

Just as damaging as the personal attack on Eden and the cry for the Tories to revolt against him was the charge of collusion and perfidy on the part of Israel, France and Britain. Attacking the Israeli assault on Egypt and all that followed from it, the *Observer* concluded:

> Despite the consistent rulings of the United Nations, which Britain and France have supported in the past, against such unilateral action even in retaliation, Britain and France have not merely vetoed resolutions censuring this action but have in effect joined actively in assisting it. This is surely the strangest police action in history.

13. Phillip Knightley *et al*, *Pearl of Days*, p. 296.

Considerable doubt was also cast on French motives. Bob Stephens saw French involvement as a way of strengthening their hand in their own colonial struggle in Algeria, a struggle in which the *Observer* had supported the indigenous Algerians against the French.

The *Observer* of November 4, 1956 caused a furore and opinion divided bitterly over it according to people's view of the Suez crisis itself. It was particularly controversial because British forces were in action at the time: such an attack on the Government was seen by many as little short of treasonable. (The same reaction greeted Hugh Gaitskell's famous anti-Government broadcast on November 3.) David Astor seems to have attracted abuse and admiration in equal measure. Amongst others who wrote to support his stand were C. P. Snow, who wrote a private letter explaining that due to his "official position" (in Whitehall) he could not declare his opinion openly, but that he wanted Astor to know that he had his "unqualified support, for what it is worth", and Violet Bonham-Carter who thanked David for his "great leadership — shining courage and such matchless integrity". On the other hand, less than flattering letters came from such old friends as Marcus Sieff and Robert Birley. The former wrote of his "distress at the *Observer*'s attitude, particularly as it reflected so badly on Israel". Most surprising, David's old mentor Robert Birley wrote a long letter on the Sunday declaring his adherence to principles of liberal internationalism which they both shared, yet arguing that Egypt had to be attacked, otherwise it would have destroyed Israel. Despite these complaints, David was fairly sheltered from the passions and anguish that now divided parties and friends on the Suez issue because he had the whole paper solidly behind him, as well as his family. One of the more remarkable aspects of the Suez affair was the fact that the Astor brothers, from the liberal David to the more conservative Jakie, Michael and Bill, all opposed Eden's use of force. The essential Atlanticism of all the Astors was at work, all four of them seeing the greatest peril of the Suez expedition to be the strains it imposed on the Anglo-US relationship and the possible unravelling of the Western Alliance. Jakie got up in the House of Commons to denounce the Suez expedition on November 8; he was one of only eight Conservative MPs to disagree openly with the Government's policy. As David Astor recognized, this took some courage amidst the serried ranks of angry and emotional Tory MPs around him, and he wrote to Jakie the next day:

> Bloody Good! Very brave indeed. I don't think I would have had the courage to do it. It must have been quite an ordeal to speak in the House against the Government at such a time... very much admire what you've done. Proud to be connected.

Bill also spoke against the Suez expedition in the House of Lords, where he would have been even more exposed to hostility. However, contrary to what many of the more conspiratorially minded Tories might have liked to think at the time, there was no collusion between the four brothers.

Other families were not so lucky. Alastair Buchan, who was sent out to Washington on behalf of the *Observer* in the middle of November to report the crisis from there, found that his elder brother refused to speak to him for over ten years afterwards as a result of his objection to British policy over Suez.

Closer to home, a storm erupted over the paper. The *Observer* was denounced in Parliament by Julian Amery, the leader of the Suez Group of right-wing Tory MPs, for showing "weakness". More importantly, during the course of the following week three of the trustees resigned. The first to go was Lord Portal who, as Chief of the Air Staff during the Second World War, obviously felt that he could no longer be associated with a newspaper which attacked the Government while the armed forces were engaged in action. None of these resignation letters survives, but on Sunday, November 11, the *Observer* announced on its front page that Portal had resigned because of "fundamental disagreement" with editorial policy. Portal's going was the end of an uneasy relationship with the paper. The paper also revealed that Arthur Mann had resigned from the Trust because he considered that "The style of our leading article was out of keeping with the kind of journalism that he himself has stood for and that the *Observer* had hitherto upheld". Mann's resignation was also very understandable, as he was a lifelong supporter and close friend of Eden; he had lost his job at the *Yorkshire Post* defending Eden's anti-appeasement stand in the late 1930s. What was more curious was the fact that Mann was no longer a trustee. He had, in fact, resigned earlier in the year, but David Astor refrained from pointing this out, out of deference to all that Mann had done for the *Observer* in the past.

Sir Keith Murray found the leading article "intemperate" and announced his intention to retire from the *Observer* Trust at the end of the year. As well as the resignations of these real or imagined trustees, one of the directors of the paper, a friend of Portal's, also resigned. The paper had thus lost half its trustees — resignations prompted by the prose of the former chairman of the Trust. Theoretically, they could have combined to rebuke the editor and possibly sack him, as they obviously felt that the paper's policy was a departure from the policy and principles laid down in the Trust deed. That they resigned instead, without ever attempting to administer a rebuke or exercise any effective control over David Astor, demonstrated not only a remarkable lack of mutual understanding amongst them, but also the fact that they commanded no effective control. That the trustees, supposedly the guardians of the paper's conscience, should resign over the Suez issue, rather than the editor, was one of the more bizarre but illuminating episodes of the Suez crisis as far as the *Observer* was concerned. The fact that these resignations made no discernible difference to the policy of the paper tells its own story.

As well as abuse in Parliament and resigning trustees, the paper also had to cope with an avalanche of correspondence. By the end of the week after the leader had appeared 474 readers had written in to indicate that they were giving up the paper; 866 letters against the paper's policy were received and 302 in support. On November 11, it published a selection of these letters, both "for" and "against", but what is probably more astonishing is that Charles Davy insisted on sticking to his routine and, assisted by Gritta Weil, replied to every one of them. All the members of the staff, although sure that the paper was right, quickly became aware of the hostility that they had aroused, especially in Government circles. However the *Observer* persisted in its course, and on November 11 published a long article on the possibilities of collusion. The case it made was, of course, strengthened by the immediate collapse of the invasion on November 6 and the simultaneous Russian invasion of Hungary, which seemed to bear out the *Observer*'s thesis that the assault on Egypt would only, in the wider perspective, play into the hands of the Communist world. (Almost inevitably, the inimitable Lajos Lederer was on hand in Hungary to report from Budapest, sending back dramatic descriptions of a bewildered and crushed Hungarian population, which appeared in the paper on November 18.)

It would be many years before the *Observer*'s charge of collusion was confirmed, but the immediate military, political and economic consequences of Eden's attack on Egypt were all just as disastrous — if not more so — as the paper had been predicting since July. Even if one disagreed with the *Observer*'s policy, there were many professional journalists who admired the paper's response to the Suez crisis, its independence of judgement and clarity of thought. One such was "Bill" Deedes, who went on to become a very distinguished editor of the *Daily Telegraph*, but in 1956 was a junior minister in Eden's Government. Although he could not bring himself to appreciate the paper's politics concerning Suez, he admired its journalistic flair. "Poor politics, but bloody good journalism", as he put it to the author.

At the same time as the *Observer*'s public campaign against the Government's handling of the Suez campaign, David Astor indulged in some supplementary private campaigning as well. Echoing the *Observer*'s challenge in its leader of November 4 to the younger Tories to repudiate Eden's leadership of the party and the Government, Astor wrote to Ian Macleod, the young and ambitious minister for labour, on November 14:

> I perfectly appreciate your unwillingness to let me call on you at this time...Meanwhile, as I believe time is short, I will try to put briefly the gist of what I would have said....
>
> I believe the "collusion" charge is going to be proved — that we knew of a French–Israeli military understanding which we either endorsed or connived at, but certainly did not seek to prevent. If the proving of this charge is left entirely to other countries, to the opposition and to serious newspapers (you realise that the *Economist* and King-Hall are both on to it, and that *The Times* is said to have ceased to support the Government because they knew of the collusion), the damage to the Conservative Party will be very great and of long duration.
>
> As I believe that the collusion was arranged by two Ministers and was made known only to a minimum of others, it is in fact unfair that this fate should befall your Party. Certainly the back benchers had no knowledge of it. Presumably most Ministers did not know.

Whether the whole Tory Party is to be disgraced by this story depends on whether the uncovering of the knowledge and the necesary action to clear our national reputation is carried out by a substantial element in the Tory Party or not. If that does not happen, the Party will be tarnished until it is led by people who are today too young to have been in responsible positions.

You may wonder what all this has to do with me and why I am approaching you. The fortune of your Party is certainly not my responsibility, but I believe it would be a national calamity if one of our two great parties were to be discredited for a generation. I also believe that it would be a great injustice to the back benchers and rank and file supporters. The reason I approach you is that you have a reputation for honour and for courage, you are also of an age which makes the future of the Tory Party even more particularly your concern than its present.

I hope you will excuse my intervention and that you will not read any meaning into it other than exactly what I have said. I assure you that I am trying to convey a simple and sincere message to you as plainly as possible and only hope that you will not misunderstand this as impertinence. I assure you that I feel, as do most of us, awed and humbled by the size of the mistake that we seem to be involved in.

Yours sincerely,
David Astor

David had misjudged Macleod who, unimpressed by this call to arms, promptly took this letter round to Ten Downing Street. Unable to see the prime minister, he saw Bishop, Eden's private secretary, and Sir Norman Brook, the Cabinet secretary. Bishop wrote a note on their deliberations for Eden:

Prime Minister
Mr Macleod brought this to me this evening. Sir Norman Brook happened to be with me at the time. Mr Macleod has no intention of replying, but wanted you to see it as soon as possible, as Astor may have made similar approaches to others.

That Astor is using these tactics makes us feel quite sick, but it shows that he, and others, are pressing this point very hard.

We wonder whether this state of affairs affects your plans for a rest. Might it not be wiser to ask three or four of your senior colleagues to meet you on Saturday afternoon, to discuss all this? (Bobbity [Salisbury] is the only other who has seen this).[14]

Eden did not think that any meeting of ministers was necessary on this occasion, but he was clearly concerned enough about Astor's charge of collusion for the issue to be discussed at Cabinet on November 20. The matter was probably raised by Macleod himself, as a result of Astor's letter. The minutes concluded:

> Attention was drawn to the continuing speculation in certain sectors of the press about the extent of the knowledge which the United Kingdom and French Governments had had of Israel's intention to attack Egypt. While there would be no question of acceding to requests for an independent enquiry on the past, the Government might well be pressed to make some further statement. It was the general view of the Cabinet that the best course would be to repeat the assurances given by the Foreign Secretary in the House of Commons on 31st October....[15]

The last sentence is a reference to Selwyn Lloyd's flat denial of collusion as Israeli forces started invading Egypt.

The Eden Government stuck to its story of "no collusion", but the mounting evidence of such collusion acted like a slow fuse, and rather than waiting for detonation the Conservative Party did indeed pick a new leader, Harold Macmillan, in January 1957. Although Astor's approach to Macleod might have done little good, the *Observer*'s continued airing of the collusion issue did help to undermine Eden's political credibility in the eyes of a disillusioned party and public. David Astor also spoke on the subject to another dissenting Tory minister, Edward Boyle, who refused to take any action against Eden. Less wisely, Astor also

---

14. Letter and Correspondence in PRO PREM 11 1127.

15. Quoted by Richard Lamb, p. 302.

wrote a letter to a leading trade unionist asking him to call a strike of transport workers to demonstrate disagreement with the Government. To suggest such a "political" strike was both reckless and, as the author of this plan quickly recognized, "silly". Luckily, the trade unionist concerned did not reply.

If there were any remaining doubts as to the full ramifications of the Suez Crisis as it affected Britain's position in the world, these were dispelled by the *Observer*'s leader entitled "GREAT-NESS" on December 9. It was a scenario which demanded a complete revaluation of Britain's world role:

> The Suez crisis has shown that Britain has not got the resources to act as a Great Power in her own right, even in a traditional sphere of British interest. The complaints that we were frustrated by the Americans only prove the point that, where Great Power politics are concerned, we are dependent on America. . . .
>
> This relegation of Britain to the ranks of the secondary powers has been evident for a long time — at least since the end of the World War II. Nevertheless, many people, both inside and outside Britain, have not fully realised the change. The reason is that the fact of reduced British power was partly disguised by the extraordinary phenomenon that Britain's influence continued to operate despite her reduced military and economic strength. The true greatness of post-war Britain has lain in this intangible asset.

Many readers might not have wanted to see this laid out in black and white, but it was true none the less.

The *Observer*'s outspoken denunciation of Eden's Suez policy may well be considered the paper's finest hour, but it is legitimate to ask whether it, and others like it who opposed the invasion, had any influence on events. Due to the great speed and secrecy of the invasion, there was virtually no time to get up a head of indignant public steam against the combined Israeli—French—British operation: the public could not resent what it did not expect. However, in the wake of Suez, the *Observer*'s constant references to the question of "collusion" and other unresolved aspects of the crisis must have made it more difficult for the Tories to retain as leader a man who was always going to be under a cloud of such suspicion. The *Observer* did help to raise the political temperature at a vital moment and thus made it much more difficult for Eden to carry on with the invasion of Egypt.

In the long run, it mattered much more that certain newspapers had voiced the doubts of a large section of the British public, because as the entire Suez operation became increasingly discredited, so those who had spoken up became more valuable in restoring relations with the outside world. One such person was Alastair Hetherington, editor of the *Manchester Guardian*, who later wrote:

> In my view it mattered a great deal that the opposition was heard and seen, not only in Britain but abroad, and from the earliest moment. It mattered that Eden and his colleagues were known not to be speaking for the whole British people. When the time came to restore relations afterwards — with the Americans and Canadians, as with others in Europe and Africa — it was more readily possible because within the United Kingdom there had been a vigorous and vocal resistance to the Government's aggressive action. The following year I was in India for three weeks and was told plainly by the Prime Minister, Pandit Nehru, and by others in Delhi, that they had believed the *Manchester Guardian*'s outspoken words.[16]

David Astor had a similar experience several years later when he was invited by Mountbatten to lunch at Broadlands. The only other guest was Nehru. Mountbatten had also opposed the Suez invasion, but, as head of the Navy, had had to keep his doubts to himself. However, to show Nehru that there were *other* Englishmen who had felt as he and Nehru had done, he invited David Astor, who after lunch was left alone for a chat with the Indian prime minister. David has written of this potentially enthralling encounter: "But he [Mountbatten] could not have known how tired the editors of Sunday newspapers can feel on Sundays. Fortunately, Nehru also seemed tired, so we just managed to talk enough to keep each other from actually going to sleep: but it was a close run thing."

16. Alastair Hetherington, *Guardian Years*, p. 16.

A similar occasion was a dinner held at Ten Downing Street several months after Suez to re-establish friendly British relations with Dag Hammerskjöld, the great secretary general of the United Nations, who had always opposed the Suez operation. Hammerskjöld was a friend of Astor's and an admirer of the *Observer* for the paper's keen and often isolated support of the UN. Macmillan had invited all the chief opponents and chief proponents of the Suez adventure — thus showing off the opponents to Hammerskjöld and yet not apologizing for what he and the others had done. David Astor was the first guest to arrive and found himself alone in a large drawingroom with Macmillan for a few moments. After a formal greeting, Macmillan just stood looking in front of him and saying not a word — as near to a formal rebuke as the Edwardian Macmillan could probably manage in such circumstances. Astor was obviously not forgiven.

If the *Observer* had little immediate effect on the politics of the Suez crisis, its trenchant views on Suez certainly had an almost immediate impact on the paper, although not necessarily in the way that has passed into popular mythology.

It is often alleged that the paper immediately lost readers because of its stand on the Suez issue. This is not true. The Audit Bureau's chart of six-monthly averages for the *Observer*'s circulation during this period, which gives the best long-term guide to a paper's circulation, is as follows:

January — June	1955	:	564,307
June — December	1955	:	573,632
January — June	1956	:	601,401
June — December	1956	:	633,064
January — June	1957	:	641,417
June — December	1957	:	633,537
January — December	1958	:	638,074

So the Suez crisis of June—December 1956 does not seem to have affected the paper's rise in circulation, which started to level off only in the winter of 1957—58, by which time Suez was yesterday's news.

The monthly figures for the period of Suez are as follows:

1956

July	622,711
August	611,035
September	625,080
October	640,761
November	659,613
December	641,628

1957

January	629,630
February	643,174
March	643,854

There *was* a dip in circulation from November to December; but little larger than the dip between July and August of the same year. Both downturns can be attributed to seasonal factors affecting all newspapers, not just the *Observer*. Many readers did undoubtedly give up the *Observer* over Suez; indeed, as we have seen, 474 wrote in to say that they were doing just that. They were doubtless people who had not quite realized how far the paper had changed since the Garvin days of Imperial Conservatism. But, for every reader who ceased to buy it there was a new reader who was attracted to a clearly progressive and liberal paper. What *did* matter, however, was the type of reader that it lost, for the more conservative who deserted it tended to be those who had larger disposable incomes and were thus an attractive target from the advertisers' point of view. From that angle the students and Labour supporters that the paper gained might have kept the circulation figures up, but they could not compensate for the loss of the more affluent readers. The slowdown in circulation did come; but some time after Suez and for reasons which had nothing to do with Suez, and which are discussed in the next chapter.

What mattered more from the paper's long-term point of view was the effect that its stance over Suez had on its advertising revenue; the Suez episode provided an object lesson in the power of the advertiser over the Western capitalist press. There were two groups of advertisers who were bound to be affected by the *Observer*'s stand: Jewish-owned companies and ultra-patriotic British companies. As David Astor has written to one writer on the subject:

Another factor that was seldom publicly mentioned but meant

everything to one section of the public was the fate of Israel. Many British Jewish supporters of Israel felt that defeating Nasser was vital to Israel's survival. They also felt that to criticise the French-British attack was by implication to criticise Israel's part in the operations. This caused the strongest possible agitation among Israel's supporters. As the *Observer* had always taken a special interest in Israel and probably had a higher percentage of Jewish readers than most papers, it suffered a sharp rebuff. I have met many Jewish individuals who have never read the paper since...and the loss of Jewish advertisers was very marked.

Just as Jewish advertising fell off, so did the advertising from various British firms with chairmen of a patriotic or militaristic bent. English Electric, for instance, a major industrial and defence company, was chaired by Lord Nelson; English Electric immediately withdrew all its advertising. Ten years later the *Observer* wrote asking them to reconsider their advertising ban, but the company still refused to come back. Unfortunately, no records of the *Observer*'s advertising revenue survive from this period, but Bill Smart, who was brought on to the paper in 1958 to try to restore the advertising situation, remembers that "There were so many [companies cancelling orders], it becomes impossible to remember them." A lot of "patriotic" City companies also cancelled their company meeting advertisements, which constituted a major part of the paper's revenue. Bill Smart learnt of at least one advertising agency, Masius and Fergusson, which on political grounds advised all its clients not to place advertisements in the *Observer*.

The loss of regular advertisers was the most serious and painful immediate consequence of the paper's stand on Suez. There was also a long-term effect. Advertisers now saw the paper as "younger" and more "left-wing", so it became a struggle to attract the more lucrative advertisements, which would tend to go to the *Sunday Times* and, after 1960, to the *Sunday Telegraph*. None of this would have mattered so much if the Suez crisis had not occurred just when the old cosy world of minimum competition and newsprint rationing, in which the *Observer* had flourished during the 1940s and early 1950s, was being swept aside. In 1955 commercial television had started, which immediately attracted advertisers who had formerly been drawn to newspapers; the *Observer* could no longer pick and choose, but had to fight for any advertising it could get. Then, at the beginning of 1957, newsprint rationing, imposed in 1940, was finally ended. The *Sunday Times* had planned very carefully for this, and at once increased its number of pages, carrying more advertising and therefore making it a better advertising medium. Finally, on February 5, 1961, the *Sunday Telegraph* was born, which put on sales of 650,000, catering for a more conservative readership than the *Observer*'s. This was followed by the arrival of that purest of advertising media masquerading as journalism, the Sunday colour magazine.

The *Observer* was thus hit at its weakest point at a time when the competition suddenly stiffened. For reasons discussed in the next chapter, it would have been squeezed anyway by the new competition for advertising, but the Suez crisis exacerbated this problem at a most delicate moment. As a result of Suez, the paper had to put most of its energy into making up lost ground in the coming years as far as its advertising revenue was concerned, while its rivals just forged ahead. This made its financial position increasingly precarious and would eventually force a gradual and reluctant change in its character.

All this became apparent only later. At the time, 1956 seemed to be the *annus mirabilis* of David Astor's *Observer*; the year when the paper exercised its cherished independence and attacked a government on moral and ethical grounds, and had these attacks vindicated by events. David Astor's stubbornness was shown to its best advantage when he stuck to the charges of collusion and military adventurism, as was his Astoresque disdain for those bullying, hectoring politicians who might have swayed him from his chosen path. Yet his ship was holed below the water-line just as she had to negotiate the heavy seas of the new commercial atmosphere: an expensive leak which came at the worst possible moment. The Suez crisis was indeed a turning-point, even if it was more a matter of coincidence than of cause and effect.

8

Decline and Fall

On November 7, 1959 David Astor wrote to Sir William Haley, editor of *The Times*, that the *Observer* was faced with "...fairly formidable problems". The remaining years of David Astor's editorship of the *Observer*, until his retirement in 1975, were to be spent grappling with these ever more formidable problems. During the 1960s the paper had to change its character or face extinction, and as the efforts of the staff became increasingly focused on keeping it going from week to week, so it undoubtedly lost some of the intellectual distinction that had marked it out from the competition in the 1940s and 1950s. In the end, it was perhaps inevitable that in the era of increased competition prevailing in the 1960s the *Observer* was doomed in its attempt to continue publishing on its own, separate from any of the increasingly large newspaper groups that often relied on other industrial activities for their cash flow. It was much to Astor's credit that he did change the character of the paper in order to survive, whilst newspaper proprietors like the Berrys of the *Daily Telegraph* buried their heads in the sand, but in the end the Astor *Observer* was beaten, not only by the inexorable logic of the market-place but by internal industrial and labour-relations problems.

These problems the *Observer* shared with the rest of Fleet Street, and indeed with the rest of British industry. In this respect, it was perhaps more than mere coincidence that in the same year,

1976, that the *Observer* was sold to an American oil company, Great Britain Plc itself was mortgaged to the International Monetary Fund by Prime Minister James Callaghan in an attempt to restore the nation's finances. The newspaper industry, and the *Observer* in particular, was only one example, albeit *in extremis*, of Britain's outdated, under-funded, over-manned and badly managed industrial base that finally ploughed into the sand in 1976 — ushering in the age of Thatcherism.

To these heavy pressures on the *Observer* must be added the amateurism of its own management, which had not anticipated the new commercial environment and did not seem capable of exploiting new opportunities when they arose. Tristan Jones, in particular, was unsuited to the task of planning a business strategy to take account of the new operating environment. He controlled the costs of the paper very well, but he was not a strategic business thinker; indeed, he was simply not a businessman. Moreover, he was in a false position, because he never had the final authority to conduct an aggressive commercial policy even if he formulated one. John Biggs, who resigned as secretary and assistant manager of the *Observer* in December 1960, wrote to David Astor:

> I would say that I am convinced that the existing management set up is a bad one with which I am no longer happy to be associated. The *Observer* needs either a strong Board or a strong manager (better still both). Then a commercial policy will be developed and then the right decisions may be taken for the right reasons. I feel it is unfair to the individual [Tristan Jones] trying to do a responsible job when responsibility at the higher level is neither defined nor taken, when he just does not know who is the boss.

David Astor stuck by Tristan Jones out of loyalty, but by the time that the necessary financial restructuring of the paper took place in the mid-1960s, the damage had been done and the competition had raced ahead.

In contrast to the *Observer*, the paper's direct competitor, the *Sunday Times*, had prepared for the end of newsprint rationing and took full advantage of it. After the shock of seeing the *Observer* snapping at its heels during 1956, the *Sunday Times* poured money into enlarging the paper — mainly to attract new advertising — and introducing new features. George Papas, an advertising expert, was brought over from Canada to create a vigorous classified advertising department which was to become one of the hallmarks of the *Sunday Times*. However, the most important weapon in its armament was the "Big Read". This was started by Denis Hamilton, the editorial director of Kemsley's newspapers. Soon after the war, Hamilton had started serializing books in the *Sunday Times* — on a modest scale, due to the lack of newsprint. In 1957, he struck a very rich seam of war memoirs, beginning with the two volumes of Lord Alanbrooke's memoirs, *The Turn of the Tide* and *Triumph in the West*. A wartime brigadier on Montgomery's staff, Hamilton realized that in the wake of the disappointments of the Suez crisis, the patriotic public wanted war memoirs that would remind them of the more successful days of the Second World War. The response was dramatic, and serialization of *The Turn of the Tide* in 1957 added tens of thousands of readers. However, Hamilton's greatest coup came in 1958 when he secured the serialization of his old chief's autobiography. "Monty's Memoirs" were frank, pugnacious and made riveting reading. Serialization of the memoirs of Britain's most famous war hero over the course of several weeks added one hundred thousand extra readers to the *Sunday Times* almost over-night. Such was Kemsley's gratitude to Hamilton for having rescued the paper that he gave him a £5,000 bonus for Christmas. It was certainly well deserved.

Worse was to come for the *Observer*, as in 1959 the staid and unadventurous Kemsley sold the *Sunday Times* and the rest of his newspaper empire to the ebullient Canadian businessman Roy Thomson, who had entered the British newspaper scene in 1953 with the purchase of *The Scotsman*. What proved to be the turning point in his fortunes in Britain was his success in winning the Scottish ITV contract in 1956, which proved, as he himself boasted rather indiscreetly, "a licence to print money". Thomson was totally unlike David Astor: he lived for competitive success in business. As the new owner of the *Sunday Times* he cared little for the policy of the paper, but his avowed aim, as he announced to a somewhat surprised audience at an *Observer* Wednesday lunch, was "to bury the *Observer*". He pursued this end with good natured pertinacity throughout the 1960s. His master-stroke was to endorse Denis Hamilton's appointment of the young Harold Evans as the editor of the *Sunday Times* in 1967. Evans cared little for serious politics, but he believed in a more aggressive, intrusive style of journalism that proved a very successful formula with the public. By appointing Evans Thomson cut much of the ground from under the *Observer*'s feet. It was an astute commercial move. Moreover, while the *Sunday Times* enjoyed a revival in its fortunes under Denis Hamilton and Roy Thomson, Lord Hartwell of the *Daily Telegraph* took the opportunity of the end of newsprint rationing to start the *Sunday Telegraph* in 1961. After a chaotic start, the *Sunday Telegraph*'s circulation rose to about 800,000, more than the *Observer*'s. This was achieved partly by good writing and partly, once again, by serialization. One of the most successful serializations was of "Chips" Channon's diaries in 1963, which added several thousand to the circulation. The *Sunday Telegraph* never competed with the *Observer* to the extent that the *Sunday Times* did, because it appealed to a very different kind of reader, but it did draw a lot of valuable advertising away, attracting, as it did, a more affluent, consumer-orientated readership.

A further innovation that Roy Thomson introduced was the colour magazine. This was launched in 1961, initially to much derision. However, under the youthful guidance of Mark Boxer the magazine soon established itself as an indispensable part of the Sunday paper, and, more importantly, proved to be the most attractive advertising medium that journalism had to offer. The *Telegraph* followed suit in September 1964, publishing their colour magazine on a Friday to accompany the *Daily Telegraph*, which gained some 85,000 readers as a result, and removed a considerable amount of advertising from the competition.

Whether innovations such as colour magazines, serializations and classified advertising had anything to do with "journalism" was a moot point; the fact remained that the reading public responded to them with enthusiasm and the *Sunday Times* and *Sunday Telegraph* drew both readers and advertisers away from the *Observer*. It was a cruel irony; David Astor might be said to have invented the formula of modern Sunday journalism, treating issues with a reflective, in-depth, almost magazine-like approach that proved to be both good journalism and popular with the readers. He had, in many ways, created the public appetite for Sunday journalism which his rivals were now exploiting. In the scramble for higher circulation after 1957 no paper *lost* readers. The *Observer*, the revitalized *Sunday Times* and the new *Sunday*

Telegraph were all catering for a public taste for quality Sunday journalism. By 1960, 900,000 more copies of quality Sunday newspapers were being sold than in 1950. It was a tragedy that, in many ways, the explosion of popular demand after 1957 should have failed to benefit the *Observer*.

The *Observer* was not slow to realize that the years of effortless success had come to an end. In 1956 its circulation was almost level with that of the *Sunday Times*, but by May 1957 it was selling 639,000 to the *Sunday Times*'s 725,000. At the trustees' meeting of May 28, 1957 the first note of concern was sounded on this increasing lead:

> This situation might be dangerous for the *Observer* owing to the recent increase in the advertisement rate to within £1 of the Sunday Times charge. It was therefore vital for the *Observer* to undertake an extensive advertising campaign.

At the same meeting David Astor told the trustees that the paper would have to follow the *Sunday Times* into the market for books for serialization, although "these books would be selected with care and the paper would not be swamped with serials...Mrs Dylan Thomas's autobiography was now being serialized as a 'holding operation'."

Thus, only six months after Suez, David Astor made the tacit admission that the *Observer* would have to follow the lead of the *Sunday Times* in a chase for circulation; it was the end of the self-confident *Observer* of the golden age.

The main and most difficult task was to attract back the advertisers. In a typically amateurish move, the diplomatic and defence correspondent, Alastair Buchan, was appointed to the post of "business manager" with the specific brief of increasing advertising revenue. Buchan knew a great deal about nuclear and strategic thinking, but precious little about advertising. It was a job that he neither enjoyed nor made a great success of. Michael Davie watched his efforts with a mixture of amusement and despair, writing to William Clark on October 20, 1957:

> By contrast to all the sackings and semi-sackings Alastair has been translated to the business side. One part of his job...will be to take the Lord Chandos out to lunch at Brooks's and explain that the *Observer* is not just a left wing vehicle for

nigger lovers and central European Jewish intellectuals and that it is in fact rather smart and public school. Immediately after lunch, the idea runs, the Lord Chandos will give orders for thousands of pounds worth of advertising to be placed in our columns. The paper was, in making this appointment, animated by three ideas: to strengthen the business side (which it has naturally done by appointing someone who knows little about business); to change the image of the paper prevalent particularly in the city and...since the Suez crisis; and to back up the advertising.[1]

Buchan himself was not convinced of the efficacy of the paper's policy of book serialization, complaining to Clark in June 1957 that "We are madly trying to beat the ST at the dreadful game of big name serials and I am stalking J. Wheeler-Bennet at the moment."[2]

Buchan's attitude towards book serialization was indicative of a wider reluctance on the part of the *Observer* staff to contemplate chasing the *Sunday Times* by changing the character of the paper, and in some quarters this reluctance would harden into outright hostility. Nevertheless, after the *Sunday Times* had regained the initiative at the end of 1957, the *Observer* continued to do just that. The *Observer* might have kept the intellectual high ground, but the journalistic pace was now being firmly set by the *Sunday Times*.

While Alastair Buchan focused his mind on the distasteful business of chasing books for serialization, David had to re-evaluate the paper as an advertising medium. The *Observer* could no longer afford to ignore the power of the advertiser in the capitalist press. Strokes of journalistic boldness, such as removing most of the advertising from the paper to accommodate Khrushchev's "Secret Speech", became a thing of the past.

In 1958, Bill Smart arrived from the *Daily Telegraph* to try to win back the advertising lost at Suez and seek out new customers. He found that the paper was handicapped by its politics, which

1. Davie — Clark: October 20, 1957; Clark Papers, 118, Fls. 144—148.

2. Buchan — Clark: June 21, 1957; Clark Papers, 117, Fl. 155.

were considered to be too radical, and its readership, which was considered to be too young and impecunious. Politically, for instance, the *Observer* forfeited all South African advertising to the *Sunday Times* and *Sunday Telegraph* because of its outspoken opposition to apartheid. As Smart has commented, with considerable understatement, "There was no queue of advertisers at the door of the *Observer*." To rectify matters, there was a deliberate effort to become a more attractive medium, and David Astor had to concede more space to bold advertising copy than he had previously liked to do. Buchan and Smart toured the leading advertising agencies with a half-hour presentation on the *Observer*, to drum up business. Old shibboleths were cast aside in the hunt for advertisers. One of these was liquor advertising, which had been banned ever since the teetotal Waldorf and Nancy Astor had taken over the paper in 1911. Even during the depths of the 1930s depression this self-denying ordinance had been religiously maintained. However, in 1958 Tristan Jones asked Smart why the *Sunday Times* was able to run a 32-page paper, whilst the *Observer* was only producing a 28-page paper. The answer was that the *Sunday Times* ran about twenty-nine columns of drink advertising. So Tristan Jones put it to the trustees that the *Observer* should embrace drink advertising: twenty-nine columns of advertising represented a considerable amount of revenue. In the autumn of 1958, the ban was lifted and that December the *Observer* carried its first drink advertisement — for dry sherry, "a quality product" pointed out the advertising department to soften the blow. However, it took at least another three years to break down the distillers' residual resistance to advertising in the *Observer*.

The advertising department also had to try to curb the anti-advertising instinct of the editor. David Astor had always felt that the tie-in between the coverage of consumer products, such as cars, and the advertising industry was corrupt, and had occasionally tried to illustrate the point by thorough journalistic investigation of certain products. He had decided that motor-car journalism was the most corrupt of all, because any criticism of a particular product meant that the company concerned might withdraw advertising from the newspaper. On the occasion of the annual Earl's Court Motor Show in 1961 he therefore decided to import an unknown Swiss journalist, unexposed to the lavish hospitality of the British motor-car manufacturers, to report the show. The journalist gave a balanced report and put the British car firmly in its place as a product sliding complacently down the ladder of world excellence and competitiveness. As David has described it, this report "caused hell". Dozens of British car manufacturers announced that they would never advertise again in the *Observer* if the paper criticized them in this manner. The advertising department, struggling against the odds as it was, was distraught. In an attempt to save the situation, David was prevailed upon to attend a car manufacturers' dinner held at the Lancaster Gate Hotel in London as a penance; he had to sit next to the chairman and discuss the finer points of wing mirrors and hubcaps over several courses of humble pie. For a man with no interest in cars whatsoever this was an embarrassing experience. He jokingly remarked that it was "most humiliating" experience of his editorial career; but this was the sort of thing that he now had to do to save the paper.

However, such tinkering with the image was merely staving off a larger question that would have to be faced sooner or later. If the *Observer* was to compete with its new rivals successfully, it would have to shed some of its exclusive, intellectual integrity. Those who recoiled from this prospect advocated an alternative course of action: that the paper should ignore the headlong rush for circulation and operate solely as a "Top People's" paper with a circulation of perhaps 300,000—400,000, thus preserving its essential character. Another idea along these lines was to contract significantly and become a new kind of political weekly. However, as the advertising department pointed out, a "Top People's" newspaper with a comparatively small circulation could not survive unless these "Top People" were also "Rich People", which in the *Observer*'s case was not necessarily so. The readership profile was not affluent enough to support such a venture; Jaguar cars would not be drawn to advertise in a paper catering for a relatively small number of students, intellectuals and Africanists. The logic was ruthless, but persuasive.

The "Top People's" paper idea was supported in the office by John Pringle and Terry Kilmartin (the latter was always critical of the alternative course that was eventually adopted). It did not, however, convince the management. David Astor, the directors and the trustees decided in late 1960 to work for a bigger circulation and catch up with the *Sunday Times*. Although advertising revenue had increased by sixty per cent during the financial year 1959—60, it still lagged some way behind that of the *Sunday Times* and barely offset a range of new costs incurred by the paper during the same period. Circulation had risen by very little — the *Sunday Times* was still steaming ahead. Furthermore, the *Observer* would soon have to meet the new competition of the *Sunday Telegraph*. A decision was taken to identify groups of potential readers, and for the first time a market research company was invited in to analyse the *Observer*'s readership more precisely. David Astor was very reluctant thus to concede the point that they were now "interested in fighting for readers just to please the advertising and marketing men", but the alternatives were as bleak, including, possibly, the closure of the paper. The *Observer* could no longer afford the luxury of being simply a very good newspaper; like its rivals, it now had to become an attractive advertising medium, an entertainment sheet and a "life-style" magazine as well. The moment when David Astor had to chase readers with journalistic material he was not really interested in was the moment when the *Observer* lost its intellectual momentum. This moment, perhaps, came later but from 1960 the *Observer* was involved in an often desperate search for new readers which changed the character of the paper significantly.

At the sixty-first meeting of the trustees on January 24, 1961 David Astor presented his report on

> the journalistic policy of the paper which, he said, was in the process of change. This was not due to simple editorial decisions but to major economic and social factors. It had been decided that the *Observer* must move with the tide of events rather than ignore it...the *Observer* would attempt first to hold and then expand its circulation within the given character of the paper.
>
> Discussing the changes made in the *Observer*'s contents, the Editor said that the women's pages had been expanded and a different aspect given to them in direct response to the fact that the *Sunday Times* was stronger in this field than the *Observer*. A strong accent was being put on the consumer angle and the *Observer* had associated itself with two consumer bodies. Certain other features were included in the paper

only with circulation in mind, i.e. the conversations which Kenneth Harris had with certain notabilities. . . .

The market research carried out by the paper suggested that the *Observer*'s most successful job advertisements were for scientists; this was apparently the only group of readers which the advertisers were attracted to, so as an advertising-led exercise the *Observer* took a conscious decision to become more science-orientated. Equally, the market research exposed the fact that

> our gains in male readership (7 per cent) have been more than offset by a loss of 15 per cent of our women readers, giving us a net loss of about 9 per cent. Until we can arrest and reverse this decline of women readers, we shall be building on sand. . . . If we could attract the middle-class woman reader of between twenty-five and forty-five, I think we should see a more rapid increase in circulation than from any other single cause.

As a result of this research more space was given to women's issues, and in 1963 the paper — with its usual quixotic flair — appointed a man, George Seddon, to become women's editor. He also became features editor, and it was Seddon who recruited writers such as Katherine Whitehorn. David told Seddon that his task was to "humanize" the paper, which, in other words, was an attempt to create a readership for the *Observer* outside its normal strengths of politics and foreign affairs. The husband of the education correspondent, Caspar Brooke, set up the Consumers' Association in 1957—58, based on an American model, and the *Observer* was the first paper to print surveys by the Consumers' Association, and was later involved in setting up the consumers' magazine *Which ?* George Seddon was an excellent women's editor, although he often clashed with David. In a further attempt to attract readers, a conscious decision was made to "lighten" the paper, introducing new features and light entertainment articles on the women's pages. "The Week", started by William Clark, was one such feature, as were Kenneth Harris's set-piece interviews with the great and the good. The journalistic side of the paper was strengthened by the introduction of the "Daylight" column in 1963. "Daylight" was started by Anthony Sampson, together with Thomas Pakenham and Kathleen Tynan, as an attempt at more committed "investigative" journalism, which the *Observer* had hitherto eschewed in favour of "think-pieces". It was a modest success, but one of the journalists who worked on "Daylight", Clive Irving, defected to the *Sunday Times*, taking the idea with him. "Daylight" was thus turned into "Insight" (a title discussed and then rejected by the *Observer* team), and became probably the single most famous feature of Harold Evans's new-look *Sunday Times*. The success of "Insight" was achieved by throwing journalists and money at the idea — money that the *Observer* did not have. David Astor also had to accept more entertaining writers, such as A. J. P. Taylor and Anthony Howard, whom he thought were important for the circulation of the paper.

These changes dismayed many on the paper, and were pushed by Astor only reluctantly. All the innovations of the 1960s were too late and too little to make any real difference to the competitive situation with the *Sunday Times* and *Sunday Telegraph*. Some on the *Observer* refused to change. Terry Kilmartin, the literary editor, resisted any change on the book pages, and refused to allow David Astor's request that notes on the book reviewers be printed at the end of the book reviews. As a result of Kilmartin's reluctance to adapt, a new arts editor was appointed in 1962, Richard Findlater, to oversee the changes that circumstances demanded. In fact, Findlater made no discernible difference, other than to antagonize Kilmartin. On June 23, 1965 the disgruntled literary editor wrote to Alan Pryce-Jones to turn down a piece on "living in America" and, by way of explanation, added that:

> As you may have noticed, the *Observer* has changed a lot in the last couple of years, and articles no longer seem to be judged by their intrinsic merits as much as by their ability to rope in another few thousand readers. One has a constant struggle to try and keep some sort of standard, but the ghastly circulation chase goes on and the advertising and promotion men rule the roost.

John Pringle later wrote sympathetically of the economic problems piling up in the early 1960s:

> I felt deeply sympathetic with David Astor during this crisis, or rather crises, for one succeeded another. He was forced to devote more and more of his time to financial and management

affairs. Moreover, as the *Observer* grew bigger and more popular it inevitably lost some of the individual distinction which it had before...David Astor often used to look weary in those days. We moved from our crazy patchwork of Victorian offices in Tudor Street to the hygienic modernity of the new Printing House Square. In many ways the *Observer* became more organised, more disciplined, a more efficient newspaper. On the other hand, it was then, I think, that it developed its besetting sin of "Trendiness", of trying to be first with every fashionable name, every new artist or writer, every lunatic folly in that lunatic period. David Astor fought against this but to some extent was forced, by commercial reasons, to imitate our rivals.[3]

David's policy was to try to preserve the integrity of the most important part of the paper, the political and foreign affairs coverage, whilst "popularizing" the rest. In the 1960s even some of the more stalwart readers wrote to protest. One was Hugh Casson, an old friend of David's, who wrote in 1962 to complain of the trivial and seemingly frivolous selection of articles that seemed to dominate much of the paper. David could do little but agree, replying to Casson on November 26, 1962:

> I am sure you are right, but we have to make strenuous efforts to hold our advertisers as well as our readers. Hence the occasional bit of spirited confusion. Will try to limit this to the bare essentials.

There were many who felt that "spirited confusion" was an appropriate "leit-motif" of the new, "popular" *Observer*.

The ultimate concession to the *Observer*'s rivals was the birth of the *Observer* Colour Magazine in the autumn of 1964. Just as Astor had initially resisted the serialization of books, so he initially resisted the idea of a colour magazine, arguing that it was not the *Observer*'s style, and would add little to its journalistic content. It was Sir William Haley, editor of *The Times*, who persuaded him that the paper had to have a colour magazine to raise circulation and attract new advertisers — for the colour magazine was, and

---

3. John Pringle, p. 152.

still is, essentially a marketing and advertising exercise. There was much resistance to the idea in the office, but David Astor determined to overcome it, and also his own reluctance. The launching of the colour magazine raised the question of cost, for it quickly became obvious that with this sort of expansion and the further costs incurred by the need to "popularize" the paper the old "Trust" system of self-finance would no longer do. The Trust set up in 1945 had been an editorial asset, but now proved to be a cruel financial burden, as it did not allow for the raising of new cash to finance such expansion as was now needed, and which had not been envisaged in 1945. David Astor himself was hardly sanguine about raising the kind of money needed to launch a colour magazine, writing to John Pringle on September 20, 1961:

> the chance of raising a loan of this sort of size for a non-Tory paper owned by a Charitable Trust is obviously not unduly good, although we have not yet proved it to be impossible. It would mean finding individuals willing to underwrite our gamble out of love for what we do and stand for.

To raise the necessary finance, David Astor and Sir Mark Turner, a director of the paper and himself a merchant banker, went round the 'liberal' tycoons cap in hand but, as Astor had predicted, they found the prospect of investing in the faltering *Observer* somewhat less than alluring. There was only one alternative: David Astor himself had to raise the money from his own Family Trust. To get the magazine off the floor, the trustees for David Astor's Family Trust put in a loan stock to the Observer Ltd of £500,000, with a further £200,000 to follow. This injection of cash marked another turning-point in the *Observer*'s fortunes, for David Astor now took on the role of *de facto* proprietor of the paper as well as editor, and the paper's survival increasingly depended on the extent to which he was prepared to dip into the Family Trust to keep it, and its expansion plans, afloat.

The colour magazine was launched in October 1964, edited by Michael Davie. The cost was kept down by a fortunate agreement with the printers, Purnells, who agreed to print the magazine on their spare colour-printing press, and who also agreed to inject some working capital into the new publishing venture, without demanding any editorial control. John Littlejohns, the financial director of the paper, pulled off this deal with Purnells, which helped to keep the cost of printing within bounds. The magazine was launched with the help of Lord Mountbatten, David Astor's old chief at Combined Operations, who, as a special favour to his former press officer, agreed, while still serving as Chief of the Defence Staff, to give a full length interview about his war career to the new magazine.

After initial teething problems, the magazine began to make money quite quickly, and within a few years the paper had become financially dependent on it. It was a very profitable venture, and fully justified David Astor's at first reluctant faith in the project. The magazine continued to be the object of some snide editorial comments, but nobody could dispute its financial contribution.

Circulation during 1962 and 1963 had dropped in consecutive years for the first time since David had assumed command of the paper in 1942, and despite a rise from 1964 to 1967, in the wake of the launch of the magazine, in 1968 it dropped again, and would do so every year until 1977 (except for a small gain in 1974). From a peak of 905,248 in 1967, sales declined to 667,010 in 1977. This loss of circulation coincided with the start of a long financial depression in the British economy, fuelled by high, and later soaring, inflation which hit the *Observer* very hard. From 1966 onwards the paper had to raise its cover price every year, and during the 1970s sometimes twice a year, to cover escalating costs. In a frantic search for economies, hallowed *Observer* traditions were axed; the last Christmas dinner-dance was held at the Café Royal in November 1965. This, perhaps more than anything else, marked the end of the old "paternalist" office organization favoured by David during the 1940s and 1950s. As the numbers employed by the paper grew, and each journalist was forced to do his or her job with fewer resources, the old system of endless discussion and perpetual conferences came to an end. Attention turned more and more to the requirements of news-gathering, to compete with the *Sunday Times* and *Sunday Telegraph*. With this lack of daily discussion and contact with the staff, David Astor became a more remote figure in the office and the *Observer* lost its former collegiate sense of purpose. For the younger journalist joining the staff in the 1960s there was little in the way of high pay or open-ended expense accounts to compensate for this communal loss of purpose and morale, for in January 1967 David Astor had told the trustees that "...in view of the present economic difficulties, the *Observer* felt it necessary to impose cuts in almost all the departments including the editorial".

In 1967, some restructuring of the Observer Trust took place to acknowledge the change in its financial structure since the launch of the colour magazine in 1964. A new company was formed, Observer (Holdings) Limited, constituted of newly subscribed shares contributed by the Astor Family Trust. Observer (Holdings) Limited now owned a majority of shares — the "A" Shares — in the Observer Limited, the company which published the paper, whilst the Observer Editorial Trust now held only a minority holding of shares — "B" Shares — in the Observer Limited. However, the Editorial Trust retained the right, through its "B" Shares, to appoint and dismiss the editor and manager of the *Observer*. This restructuring would better reflect David Astor's financial contribution to the paper, although the Editorial Trust — the original trustees — still retained their theoretical right to hire and fire the editor. Sir Ifor Evans stayed as chairman of the trustees until December 1968, when he was followed by Arnold Goodman (later Lord Goodman), a lawyer of liberal political inclinations who quickly earned a great reputation as an *éminence grise* to the Wilson governments of 1964—70, in his capacity as a close friend of the prime minister and chairman of the Arts Council and a member of other public bodies. Goodman, whom Astor admired tremendously, was an excellent choice as chairman and was to deploy all his legendary powers of persuasion and conciliation during the paper's negotiations with the print unions during the 1970s. His sense of confidence and his humour did much to buoy up the management during the tough years that lay ahead.

Together with this company restructuring, David Astor and his managers also began to turn their minds to the wider issue of whether the *Observer* could survive *alone* against competition which could call on the resources, in the case of the *Sunday Times*, of the rest of the Thomson newspaper empire, and in the case of the *Sunday Telegraph*, of the highly profitable *Daily Telegraph*. One option was to broaden the base of the *Observer's* operations. The creation of Observer Magazine Limited to publish the magazine was the first step away from straight newspaper publishing, but in 1967 the *Observer* took a more significant step by buying a 10 per cent voting stock in London Weekend Television for £420,000. Although this should have proved a profitable venture in an age when independent television licences were a "licence to print money", LWT was, in fact, a shambles. In Roger Harrison's words, "the company was a disaster" — until Rupert Murdoch took control of it. Another, more long-term solution to the paper's problems was to combine with another newspaper — or newspapers — to create a publishing venture with more resources. The obvious bed-mate of the *Observer* was the equally liberal and independent-minded *Guardian* newspaper. This was an attractive idea for both papers, as since the *Guardian* had moved from Manchester to London in 1960, it began losing up to £500,000 a year. During the mid-1960s exploratory talks between the two papers came up with two alternatives: the first option was to create a consortium of the *Guardian*, the *Observer* and *The Times* which would publish a "Times-Guardian" daily and the *Observer*, as well as the *Manchester Evening News*, the *Guardian's* sister paper in Manchester. This was turned down by all sides in October 1966. *The Guardian* was supported by the profits of the *Manchester Evening News*, which made about £1 million a year (it was this paper, ironically, not any of the three "greats", that was integral to the success of such a deal). A second option, proposed by David Astor, was for the *Guardian* to take over the *Observer*, and, if necessary, close the *Guardian* in order to use the resources of the *Manchester Evening News* to sustain the *Observer*. As Alastair Hetherington, the editor of the *Guardian* wrote later: "David was looking both for a means to inject new money into the *Observer* and to let the *Guardian* keep something of itself alive. He was willing to sacrifice his own editorial and managerial control." However, negotiations foundered on the objections of Hetherington himself and Lawrence Scott, chairman of the Scott Trust that owned the *Guardian*, to any such deals with *The Times* or the *Observer*. Scott put the matter like this:

> We would find ourselves surrendering the profits of the *Evening News* to subsidise *The Times* and the *Observer* while the *Guardian* died. Indeed, the new edifice which the consortium is now planning seems to me to be assuming more and more the character of a mausoleum in which the relics of the *Guardian* might be preserved with decorum and without

loss of face to nourish and sustain a more thriving *Times* (and *Observer*).[4]

These were the only negotiations that offered any chance of bearing fruit, and with the collapse of these *Times-Guardian-Observer* talks the *Observer* had to struggle along alone. *The Times*, owned by David's cousin Gavin, was sold to Roy Thomson on September 30, 1966 while the *Guardian* limped along on the back of the *Manchester Evening News*. Without the support of such a prosperous partner the writing was on the wall for the *Observer*.

Despite David Astor's increasing preoccupation with the commercial predicament of the paper, the *Observer* did manage to maintain its tradition of intellectual originality, and to attract a new generation of young writers to its pages. In the political arena, David became involved in the question of world peace, and Britain's contribution to such a peace. The radical proposal put forward by the *Observer* in a series of articles entitled "The Central Question" in April 1958 was that Britain, and the smaller nuclear powers, should disarm, leaving America and the Soviet Union with a biopoly of nuclear power which it would be in their interest to preserve. The argument for a super-power biopoly was based on the premise that

> the two Super-Powers — so long as a balance of mutual deterrence is maintained between them — have, in fact, a greater real self-interest in preventing small wars from leading to large ones than they have in extending their political systems.

The *Observer*'s proposal that the smaller nuclear powers should disarm led it to support the Labour Party openly during the 1959 election for its avowed policy of unilateral nuclear disarmament. This was the sole occasion on which the Trust-owned *Observer* supported a particular political party at a general election. David Astor's interest in the possibilities of a world government resting on a communality of interest between the Soviet Union and America led him to help set up the World Security Trust in 1962, in co-operation with the Labour MP and former minister John Strachey

---

4. Hetherington: *Guardian Years*, pp. 162–3.

and the Conservative MP, Duncan Sandys, former defence minister and son-in-law of Winston Churchill. It was largely on behalf of the World Security Trust that David visited the new Kennedy administration in July 1962, presenting their ideas to a receptive John F. Kennedy, Robert Kennedy and Robert MacNamara. On his return, the World Security Trust, encouraged by the favourable American response, continued to meet and debate these issues. The council was joined later by George Thompson, now Lord Thompson, and Dr David Owen, the future Labour foreign secretary from 1977 to 1979. The *Observer* also debated the issue of world peace based on such a formula of super-power nuclear biopoly in its own columns, demonstrating that despite the onerous commercial pressures it had lost none of its appetite to tackle the big intellectual issue of the day in a challenging and novel way. In retrospect, the idea of the World Security Trust for a world government based on the communality of interest of the two super-powers was premature; as with Africa, the *Observer* was perhaps too right too soon. In the post-cold-war era, however, the two super-powers do seem to be edging towards acknowledging such a communality of interest and thus demonstrating a willingness to oppose regional acts of aggression (such as the aggression of Iraq against Kuwait in August 1990) that would previously have divided them.

Another intractable area of world affairs which the *Observer* tackled fearlessly during the 1960s was the Middle East. It was never a Zionist newspaper, but had wholeheartedly backed the creation of a Jewish state of Israel in 1948, and had gone on to support the defence of Israel against Arab hostility during the course of the following decades of struggle. During the Six-day War of 1967, it supported Israel again, and it was from the battle-front of the Six-day War that Patrick O'Donovan wrote some of his most memorable, and emotional, dispatches. The question of Israel was always an emotional one, and David Astor's own interest in the subject, dated back to a family visit to Palestine during the 1920s when he and his mother had been threatened in a field by Arabs wielding their farm instruments who had mistaken them for Zionist land prospectors. The *Observer*'s support for Israel had earned it the admiration of the Jewish community in England as well as the gratitude of the Israeli Government and the friendship of successive Israeli ambassadors to London. However, its policy towards Israel was a result of principled, deliberate support for an oppressed and displaced people; the Israelis attracted the paper's support for much the same reasons as the black Africans in South Africa did. The *Observer* thus found it hard to justify the territorial expansion of Israel that occurred after the 1967 War, and in particular the annexation of the Palestinian West Bank. This provoked the paper into publishing a leader entitled "The Two Rights", which argued that the Palestinians also had rights and that in their occupation of the West Bank the Israelis were behaving increasingly as oppressors and imperialists. "The Two Rights" argued that a liberal had to acknowledge the legitimate rights of all states, and went on to give more publicity to the plight of the Palestinians than anyone else had done. As a way out of the impasse, the *Observer* suggested that Israel should choose her moment of strength in the wake of the Six-day War to hand back the lands that they had grabbed. This raised the ire of the Jewish community, and the *Observer* now found itself attacked for betraying the cause — Gerald Kaufmann wrote angrily in the *Jewish Chronicle* that its suggestions were impractical and un-realistic. As the *Observer*'s opinion of Israel's increasingly mili-taristic and Likud Party influenced Governments declined, so the previously friendly relationship between the paper and the Israeli Embassy in London deteriorated. In the early 1970s relations reached a new low when on one occasion Colin Legum and David Astor were invited by the Israeli ambassador to have the benefit of his views on the *Observer*'s Middle East policy. The ambassador was "so rude" to the *Observer* pair that Colin Legum walked out of the interview, while David stayed and absorbed the punishment which, as editor, he felt he had to. The *Observer*'s stand on the Palestinian issue during the late 1960s showed that the paper had lost none of its intellectual robustness or independence of mind despite the gathering commercial gloom. After his retirement in 1975, David Astor continued to work on the Middle East problem, writing his own book on the subject, *Peace in the Middle East*, with Valerie York, published in 1977, and becoming involved in the International Centre for Peace in the Middle East in Tel Aviv.

As well as continuing to raise a challenging and influential voice on foreign affairs, the *Observer* continued to attract a high calibre of writer. Rudolf Klein joined it from the *Evening Standard* in

1961 as a leader writer on home affairs, and stayed with the paper until 1971. Neal Ascherson joined as a correspondent in 1960, and reported from Paris and Bonn. In 1962 Michael Frayn came from the *Guardian* to write feature articles, and stayed on the *Observer* until 1968. He left to pursue a very successful career as a playwright and translator. John Heilpern came straight from Oxford at the age of twenty-two in 1965. Heilpern regarded the *Observer* as "the house of writers", and was delighted to find himself writing Profiles within two years of joining it. As the *Observer*'s small contribution to the pop culture of the 1960s, it was John Heilpern who interviewed a new group called "The Who" for the colour magazine in 1965 — the front cover photograph for the magazine showed The Who draped in a large Union Jack, an image that became one of the icons of the 1960s. Despite such manifestations of contemporary cultural awareness, however, Heilpern was aware that the paper was in an uncomfortable state of flux, a "small village trying to become a city", with many of the older hands looking nostalgically back to the days when it was untroubled by commercial and financial difficulties. Polly Toynbee, the daughter of Philip Toynbee, also joined the paper at this time. However, during the mid-1960s, as another concession to the opposition, the *Observer* was forced to abandon its policy of taking on writers who could be turned into journalists; under the pressure of the ferocious journalistic competition for scoops, exclusives and stories (as well as pressure from the National Union of Journalists), it started to recruit professional journalists rather than writers of potential.

Of this new breed, none was to be more important to the future of the *Observer* than Donald Trelford. Trelford submitted an application letter for a job as an assistant to news editor John Thompson, and, as one senior *Observer* journalist commented at the time, "his letter wiped out all other applications". Twenty-eight years old when he joined the paper in 1966, Trelford had won an Open Exhibition to Cambridge, served as a National Service pilot in the RAF and had been editing the Thomson organization's *Nyasaland Times* in Malawi for two years. He had also been writing reports on rugby matches for the *Observer* since 1958. It was his obvious professionalism and versatility that attracted David Astor. So quickly did Trelford impress with his talents that when a vacancy occurred for the deputy editorship in 1968, when Michael Davie remained absent from the office for several weeks after the breakdown of his marriage, David Astor appointed Trelford as his new deputy. He found the young man a reassuring presence because he had all the administrative and professional journalistic skills that David himself, and many of his generation, lacked and which would be increasingly in demand as the *Observer* expanded and began to be more like an "ordinary" newspaper. Representing, as he did, the spirit of the new *Observer*, Trelford was the natural successor to David when he retired in 1975.

Meanwhile the management team had been strengthened by the arrival of John Littlejohns as finance director in 1965 and the appointment of first, Peter Gibbing, then in 1967, Roger Harrison, as deputy manager to Tristan Jones. Gone were the days when David Astor ignored the paper's financial position in an attempt to keep its editorial side free from commercial considerations, and left the latter in the hands of Tristan Jones who did not have the training, the inclination or the authority to deal with them. When in 1976 IPC, owners of the *Daily Mirror* publishing company, prepared a report on the possible acquisition of the *Observer*, it concluded "that [the *Observer*'s] 'house-keeping' is as efficient as any in Fleet Street and better than most".[5]

Despite these responses to commercial pressures, however, the financial position remained precarious throughout the late 1960s and the 1970s. Circulation fell both in absolute terms and relative to the competition. After peaking at 905,248 in 1967 it fell to 775,007 in 1973, then recovered slightly before falling again in 1976 to 664,937. Meanwhile, like all newspapers, the *Observer* was hit by the financial squeeze introduced by Harold Wilson's Government in 1966, which diminished advertising throughout the print industry. Furthermore inflation, always the sleeping partner of the Keynesian economic consensus, began to rise in the late 1960s and became rampant in the early and mid-1970s. Costs rose every year, particularly of newsprint. As a result of these factors the *Observer* began to lose large amounts of money: £467,000 in the financial year 1973−74. It was not unique in this

---

5. Confidential IPC Report, September 1976; Astor Papers.

respect, but was unique in its isolated position, standing apart
from the newspaper combines which could support loss-making
papers such as *The Times* or *Guardian* with revenue from other
publications or, in some cases, from non-printing activities such as
oil production. More than any other national newspaper, the
Observer was exposed to the harsh winds of the new economic
climate in the late 1960s and early 1970s. The worst crisis came in
1973 with the oil-price rise which induced the first world-wide
recession since the beginning of the post-war economic boom. In
the newspaper industry energy costs soared and classified advertising
collapsed. And these were also the years of runaway inflation,
which rose to 25 per cent in 1975, so that the cost of newsprint
escalated to an alarming degree. It was these adverse trading
conditions that prepared the way for the collapse of David Astor's
Observer in 1976.

However, like the rest of Britain, the *Observer* was most severely
affected at this time by another factor: one that the rest of Western
Europe, and America, did not have to endure to the same extent,
which explains their relative prosperity even during the 1973–75
recession, while Britain went to the wall in 1976. This factor was
the power of the trade unions – and nowhere were the unions
more powerful than on Fleet Street. David Astor was to fight his
last great campaign as editor of the *Observer* against them.

David saw their power, both the journalists' unions and the
print unions, as no less illiberal than any of the foreign regimes
that his paper had fought in the past. For him the newspaper
industry faced a dual threat: from the journalists' union, the NUJ,
which from 1965 tried to force a closed shop on Fleet Street,
thereby restricting the right of editors to choose staff as they
wished, and from the print unions, who used every opportunity to
enforce their own closed shop in order to protect the extraordinary
levels of over-manning in Fleet Street. He responded to the union
challenge because he saw that more was involved than just the
survival of the *Observer*, important as that was. At the heart of the
matter were the very principles of a free society that the *Observer*
had always stood for. For what irked David most was the fact that
just as the NUJ's restrictive practices limited his right to choose
his staff, and ultimately acted to the detriment of British journalism
by judging new journalists on their union credentials rather than

their journalistic potential or ability, so the power of the print unions meant that the whole union issue — so important to the notion of a "free" society — could not even be discussed in print, because the unions always threatened to stop any paper that dared to print anything antagonistic towards them. To David Astor, the two most basic principles of a liberal society, the freedom of choice and the freedom of expression, were involved in this issue; the fact that the print unions' policy of enforcing over-manning also helped to destroy the *Observer* served to highlight the threat in his own mind, but was not central to it. David Astor and the *Observer* were sometimes accused of "moving to the right" in the early 1970s; David merely saw himself as defending basic liberal rights against the encroachments of selfish, self-perpetuating interest groups. If he did not fight, he wrote in 1977, union power would reduce "Fleet Street to perhaps three or four omnibus papers, produced by feather-bedded printers and written by men of a self-perpetuating guild".[6]

Since the technological revolution in the newspaper industry in the mid-1980s that saw all the titles on Fleet Street gradually decamp to new premises around London, free of the print unions, the malpractices of the print unions have become a matter of record. During the 1960s, however, the attitude of the unions on Fleet Street was unknown outside the newspaper industry for newspapers exercised a rigorous policy of self-censorship on the subject for fear of antagonizing the unions and having the presses stopped. None the less, the problem had existed for many years, at least since the 1930s when, in the chase after circulation and competitive advantage over rival newspapers, the Fleet Street proprietors had allowed the unions to start operating closed shops and had fuelled pay expectations by paying whatever was demanded, in return for uninterrupted working. This had resulted in severe over-manning throughout the industry. The newspaper industry began to be aware of the unduly high costs of maintaining such arcane and needlessly expensive work practices during the 1940s — but, interestingly, hardly a word about the problem appeared in the first Royal Commission on the Press, which reported in 1949.

---

6. *Index on Censorship*: January 1977, p. 8.

Arthur Mann, as editor of the *Yorkshire Post* during the 1930s, was well aware of these problems, and had written to Lord Astor in 1947 seeking to include an examination of the union problem in the *Observer*'s written evidence to the Royal Commission. Mann sought to tell the Commission of

> the great cost of starting new papers in modern conditions and what steps might be taken to lessen it. Berridge [the manager] for instance, stressed the number of needless men that Trade Union rules compelled newspaper owners to employ in machine, stereo and packing departments.[7]

In 1961, as the turn of the next Royal Commission on the Press came around, John Pringle once again took up the question in his suggestions as to what the *Observer* should include in its evidence. In a memo to David Astor on April 11, 1961 he argued that

> Personally, I should like to tell of our experience of restrictive practices when we first tried to divide the *Observer* into two parts. If I remember rightly, in order to get this done, which involved no extra work for anyone, we had to agree to pay the whole machine room staff more money including the men who sweep the floor.

Once again the Royal Commission neatly side-stepped this potentially explosive issue in its report. Meanwhile, a generation of titles went out of business due to the excessive cost of maintaining and paying a printing work-force that was not really needed. The most famous casualty was the Liberal *News Chronicle*, but even mass circulation papers such as the *Daily Herald* collapsed during the 1960s, as well as two of Lord Kemsley's papers, the *Daily Sketch* and the *Daily Graphic*. All of these had their own individual union problems, but the problems of over-manning and sharp union practices were common to the whole of Fleet Street — it is generally agreed that the *Daily Mirror* harboured the worst working practices of all. The following, however, is a description of working practices on the shop floor at the *Observer* by a member of the NGA (National Graphical Association) chapel (as

---

7. A. Mann — Lord Astor, November 27, 1947; D. Astor Papers.

the individual print unions were known): a description that could have applied equally well to any paper on Fleet Street:

The Machine Room chapel consists of 25 men....
1. These men average between £55 and £60 for a 12 hour Saturday night, but they are so over-staffed they work a 2 shift system. Part of the shift start work on the first half of the night for 6 hours then they go home and the other half start work on the second half of the night, which means the first shift is from 6—12 midnight (Saturday) and the second shift from 12 midnight — 5 a.m. (Sunday).
2. The other fiddle they work is known as "bingo-boys". A system is worked out where the 25 members' names go in a hat and if your number is drawn out (probably two a week) you don't appear for work at all the following Saturday night but you still pick up your £60 for nothing.

Looking at it logically, none of these men work a full night, at the most they work half a night and about every 12th Saturday night they take a night off, without permission, with full pay, apart from the fact they get 6 Saturday nights off a year for holidays.

All these Saturday night casual men are employed elsewhere on other newspapers during the week, so if they stop the *Observer* they just take another extra day's casual job elsewhere to make up for the money they will lose when they disrupt the *Observer*. This means they can stop the printing of the *Observer* but do not lose financially because they pick up cash elsewhere (they call themselves trade unionists?)....

As the above writer pointed out, a Sunday paper such as the *Observer* was peculiarly vulnerable to stoppages caused by the print unions because the printers could down tools with virtual impunity, safe in the knowledge that they could pick up the lost wages by working elsewhere during the week. As the financial situation of the *Observer* deteriorated during the 1960s, management became increasingly concerned with over-manning — not to mention its concern over its own ability to run the paper at all, since industrial relations had reached the point at which Tristan Jones, general manager, was not allowed into the printing works by the unions. At every turn, as John Pringle had reported on the introduction of the Review Section of the *Observer*, the unions used new working practices — whether the new development involved the need for extra staff or not — to press claims for an increase in staffing levels. These demands were usually made late on a Saturday night, and if they were refused, the paper would face the threat of sabotage. Over-manning reached such a degree that Roger Harrison, after visiting the American *Miami Herald*, estimated that the American paper was produced, per page printed, with one-eighth of the printing staff that the *Observer* employed.

This was bad enough: but what made it far worse in David Astor's eyes was the fact that none of these union practices could be reported in the press because of the certainty of its causing industrial disruption. To him this was a clear case of blackmail. His last great campaign was to ventilate this issue, and alert the public to the dangers of this kind of censorship. As with many other campaigns, the *Observer* was "too right too soon" — with almost fatal consequences for the paper.

The first run-in with the unions occurred in May 1970. For what may have been the first time in British newspaper history, David Astor, as editor of the *Observer*, commissioned an article by two members of the paper's editorial staff on the condition of the printing industry in Fleet Street. The two journalists themselves were very surprised at what they found: the article appeared prominently in the business section of the paper. After the appearance of the first edition of the paper at 6 p.m. on the evening of Saturday, May 2, the grandly named Imperial Father of the Chapel (FOC) of the NGA phoned Donald Trelford to point to an inaccuracy in the article, and, after consultation with the two authors, this "inaccuracy" was corrected for the next edition. At 11.20 p.m. a joint protest delegation from the machine assistants and the warehouse men (members of SOGAT) complained to the night-production manager about the article. The SOGAT officials, according to the official report on the incident, "were strongly critical of a number of points in the article and that there was a serious risk of the production run being disrupted and possibly abandoned unless alterations were made". Under this pressure, alterations were reluctantly made to the article, including the following two:

> Others earn from £20 to £30 for one evening's work packing newspapers in publishing departments, and often the job is so over-manned that even then they work only half a shift.

became:

> Others earn over £20 for a Saturday night's work packing newspapers in publishing departments; even then, some don't work the whole shift.

The second alteration concerned the printing presses:

> So delicate is the entire mechanical operation that a piece of chewing gum spat at the paper, whirling by at high speed through the presses, can rupture the whole process.

became:

> So delicate is the entire mechanical operation that the taut paper, whirling by at high speed through the presses, can be ruptured at the slightest touch.

As David Astor himself commented later, the result of these alterations was "an article of diminished intelligibility". The article was published in later editions as altered, and the NGA and SOGAT FOCs expressed their disagreement with it in a letter to the editor which was published in full on May 24, 1970. This letter, however, drew an angry response from a "Newspaper Worker" on the *Observer* who, understandably, wished to remain anonymous. His letter to the paper attacking SOGAT and the NGA went to press as usual with the rest of the paper at 5.20 p.m. on Saturday, May 31. However, at 8.20 p.m. the FOC of the Machine Assistants Chapel protested about the letter. After lengthy debates the night editor refused to alter or delete the letter and as a result of this the presses were stopped at 1.30 a.m. – thus threatening the loss of the whole *Observer* print run. David Astor was phoned at home, and, faced with the threat of losing the whole print run and hundreds of thousands of pounds, ordered the letter to be taken out – it was replaced by one on nursing problems. Asked next day by the BBC whether the *Observer*'s attitude had been weak-kneed, David Astor admitted that that was a "perfectly justified criticism". Amongst the points made in the original letter by the anonymous "newspaper worker" was that productivity deals on Fleet Street were "a euphemism for obtaining enormous pay increases while evading the structures of income policy". He confirmed that entry to SOGAT or NGA jobs was confined wherever possible to printing families and concluded that he himself was "a not very proud member of the silent majority who seem to be content to watch papers bleed and die". This was certainly true of the *Observer*.

After this incident the paper had to tread very carefully in its reporting of the Fleet Street unions. However, in October the problem blew up again when a journalist, David Howarth, attempted to write a story on internal union wrangling within SOGAT. On telephoning the SOGAT union leader to confirm the story, Howarth was told that if a word of it was printed "you will have no paper tomorrow morning". He accused Howarth of "shit stirring", poking his nose into the union's internal affairs and going beyond the bounds of normal journalistic curiosity. The SOGAT official got in touch immediately with the *Observer* machine-room officials to prime them to be ready to carry his threats into action. It was thus decided by the *Observer* not to publish the story at once, but a watered-down version of the original article did appear two weeks later. A further telling example of union power was provided by the publication of David Astor's *magnum opus* on the subject, which he could write only after he had retired in 1977. In the January issue of *Index on Censorship* Astor wrote an article entitled "How the British Press censors itself", in which he developed more fully the argument that society had been diverted by its concern over such issues as the Official Secrets Act from the real problem of censorship in Britain — which lay with "the operations of trade unions". In this article he gave a far-reaching account of the problems of the print unions, which is worth quoting at some length:

> The print unions have increased the burdens on so-called national newspapers by insisting on much higher manning levels in Fleet Street than those required on the same machines outside London. Rates of pay in Fleet Street are also much higher than elsewhere. There is, of course, no question of these wages being needed to tempt men into Fleet Street, in the way that high wages are needed to tempt men into coal-mining, for instance. On the contrary, entry into the print unions and especially into their Fleet Street "chapels" is a much-sought-after privilege, guarded as jealously as entry into the old-time guilds.
>
> How have the print unions managed to impose these heavy burdens of over-paid and over-manned staffs on the London

papers, so that most of them are running at a loss? The rather surprising answer is that it has been done by the threat and use of sabotage. Printing staffs are divided into many union groups or "chapels": engineers, engineers' assistants, electricians, compositors, linotype operators, foundry staff, machine minders, machine assistants and several more. Any one of these groups can hamper or prevent production at any time. It is most usually done simply by holding chapel meetings during production time or by "withdrawing cooperation", a term which means refusal to do some part of the normal duties.

It is extremely easy to interrupt publication, either by such delaying methods or by direct acts of physical sabotage, like breaking the paper as it passes through the presses at high speed. This is easily done by squirting it with an oil can or sticking chewing gum on the side of the reel, so that the paper tears when it reaches that point. Once broken, the reel has to be laboriously re-threaded through the machines. Interruptions caused by any of these means ensure that thousands of copies will miss their train.

The effect of missing trains on newspaper economics is graver than it may sound. If a car factory is stopped by strike action for a month, extra cars can be produced in subsequent months with overtime, and the same total number of cars sold (although with some financial loss) at the end of the year as if there had been no stoppage: but, of course, a newspaper cannot sell its commodity even one day late. Moreover, if copies of a newspaper don't reach readers, the company has to refund the advertisers the cost of all advertisements that have not been seen. So all a newspaper's high costs (apart from its consumption of paper) remain unchanged when it is stopped, but it loses all its revenue. As working delays are legitimate and acts of physical sabotage can never be proved, these tactics involve no risks to those using them.

David Astor added that "word of these practices seldom appears in any Fleet Street paper — for no more subtle reason than that it is almost impossible to get it printed". He then alluded to the *Observer*'s own faltering attempts to publish articles about the print unions and continued with a sideways glance at his own colleagues on Fleet Street:

The way newspaper publishers justify to themselves their own silence about this black mailing is curious. They assert (privately) that never will they allow the printers to censor one word of editorial copy, but make this bold attitude easier to maintain by not asking the printers to handle copy that they might want to censor. They would consider it folly to do so; and the sad fact is that they may be right. A newspaper might easily commit suicide by challenging the censorship of the print unions.

In 1977, this forthright and challenging article caused a storm. As if to bear out everything that David Astor had alleged, *The Times* lost a day's printing-run for trying to report it. The editor of *The Times*, William Rees-Mogg, asked a journalist to prepare a report on Astor's *Index on Censorship* article and this report was objected to by the NGA. *The Times* management refused to alter or delete the report, and as a result of unofficial action by the machine-minders' chapel of the NGA the presses were stopped and the paper lost all its editions on Thursday, January 14. This became a celebrated piece of union "political censorship", and the matter was taken up in Parliament during the course of the next few days. *The Times* itself published a leader entitled "The Conditions of Freedom" on January 15, in which it defended this principled stand not to bow to union pressure. The leader ended with a definition of the claims on editorial freedom with which David Astor would have wholly agreed:

Anybody, a citizen, a reader, a member of the editorial staff, a member of the printing staff, a trade union official, an ambassador, a private soldier, a public figure, can come to *The Times* and by way of letter or by word of mouth put his views or information to us, but he must not come on a claim of power. The editorial process entirely welcomes outside opinion and totally rejects outside pressure.

David Astor, through his efforts to raise this issue, certainly helped to bring the problems of Fleet Street to a wider audience, although such revelations proved to be of little help to the *Observer* in the early 1970s. Neither was the loss of the entire *Times* print-run unusual in Fleet Street. Official and, more often, unofficial union action, as happened in this case on *The Times*, accounted for an escalating loss of newspapers as the 1970s progressed. A survey conducted in 1978 found that in the first six months of that year Fleet Street lost 105 million copies to industrial action. The *Observer* lost 1,378,000 copies; but this was nothing compared to The *Sunday Times*, which lost 5,126,000 copies as a result of labour troubles on sixteen separate occasions. Mindful of the plight of the *Observer*, as well as the rest of the newspaper industry, David Astor lobbied the Heath government of 1970–74 about the problem, and in a series of meetings with Heath himself, and other members of the Government, Astor and Goodman, chairman of the *Observer*, tried to alert the Government to the dangers facing the newspaper industry.

As if the dangers from print unions were not enough, David Astor also fought a running campaign within the *Observer* against the encroachment of the journalists' union, the NUJ, on his editorial freedom to appoint his own staff. In 1965, the Newspaper Proprietors' Association (NPA) signed an agreement with the NUJ, accepting the NUJ's stipulations about the recruitment of journalists on to Fleet Street newspapers. The agreement meant that all journalists would have to have served for three years on the provincial press as a prerequisite for working on Fleet Street; this was a clear case of restrictive practice. The *Observer* went along with the agreement in 1965 because at that time the paper did not have many union members on the staff, but this position rapidly changed. The 1965 agreement, of course, totally undermined David Astor's power to recruit as and how he wished and since most of his brightest recruits had never even trained as journalists let alone trained in the provinces, this agreement threatened to remove at a stroke the very reason why the *Observer* under David Astor had become so successful. In fact, if the 1965 agreement had operated from 1942 onwards, David Astor's *Observer*, the greatest British liberal newspaper of the post-war era, could scarcely have existed.

The late 1960s and early 1970s therefore found him locked in a situation of guerrilla warfare with the NUJ about appointments on the paper, using as a weapon a clause which allowed in certain cases, "specialist correspondents" without the three-year provincial press requirement. The *Observer* clashed frequently with the NUJ over the paper's employment of professional sportsmen to write on their particular sport. It championed the work of Len Hutton, the English batsman, and defended his right, as a cricketer

rather than a professional journalist, to write in the paper —
something that David Astor had to defend to the NUJ. The
crunch came in 1973 over the appointment of a journalist called
Andrew Stephen who was only twenty-three, a recent graduate of
Essex University. Astor circulated the correspondence about this
appointment that he had to have with the NUJ FOC because he
wanted "...every individual member of the editorial staff to know
the issues involved. I regard the principle at stake here as important
for the future of our kind of journalism." Eventually a compromise
was reached over Stephen whereby he first worked for the *Observer*
in Belfast, which the NUJ accepted as his "provincial" training.
However, like the print unions, the NUJ proved very reluctant to
have the spotlight of publicity focused on them. At one point,
Astor commissioned a well-known journalist to write on their
practices, but he was turned away from reporting the NUJ's
annual conference by being told that it was not open to the press!
The *Observer* also campaigned against the attempt by Michael
Foot, as secretary of state for employment, to drive a bill through
Parliament in the Labour 1974—79 administration to give the
NUJ a closed shop on Fleet Street — which meant that journalists
would be recruited for their membership of the NUJ, rather than
for any journalistic ability. David Astor and Lord Goodman were
prominent in the campaign against this bill, which they perceived
as a serious threat to editorial freedom. Another strong opponent
of it was Nora Beloff, the *Observer*'s political correspondent, who
wrote a detailed account of their opposition to the bill entitled
Freedom Under Foot, published in 1976 by Maurice Temple
Smith. The bill was passed by Parliament into law in March 1976,
and it had to wait until the election of the next Conservative
Government under Mrs Thatcher to be repealed.

Given David Astor's own battle with the unions for what he saw
as not only the survival of his paper but the principles of freedom
of expression and freedom of choice, it was not surprising that he
should have supported Prime Minister Edward Heath during the
Government's bitter confrontation with the miners' union in
1973—74. This drew much criticism from the Labour Party and
the left: the paper had "deserted the fold", and was "drifting to
the right". Some members of the staff shared this dissatisfaction,
which meant that the cohesive intellectual atmosphere that had

been such a stimulating feature of the *Observer* during the golden age gradually began to disintegrate.

Such intellectual disagreement between David Astor and, particularly, the younger members of the staff had already been in evidence over the paper's attitude to the Vietnam war. The *Observer*, loyal to its tradition of Atlanticism, supported the American intervention in Vietnam, and argued that the USA was not being imperialistic. It did advocate a strategic withdrawal when it became obvious that the war was not winnable, but the paper's initial show of support for the Vietnam adventure was enough to disappoint many of the paper's younger journalists and readers. The struggle against commercial decline and the battle with the print unions were demoralizing enough; but perhaps even worse for David Astor were the divisions which opened up amongst the *Observer*'s staff — divisions exaggerated by the editor's increasing remoteness from the evergrowing number of journalists on the paper — given that he had always relied on the intellectual support of his staff for strength and the sheer enjoyment of editing the newspaper.

Matters came to a head within the *Observer* office in January and February 1974 as Edward Heath's battle with the miners' union reached its climax with the three-day week, "flying picketing" by Arthur Scargill and the final electoral gamble on February 28 that resulted in Heath's narrow defeat. The *Observer* gave consistent support to Heath during his dispute with the miners; indeed Heath occasionally telephoned David for reassurance. In reply, Astor sent the following note of support to the beleaguered prime minister on January 24, 1974:

> This paper has been supporting you in the miners' dispute with a consistency that has annoyed some of our readers. We are reaching the conclusion that, in the case of those Trade Unions able to paralyse the country, a bigger stick will be needed to deter them and that it can only be a financial stick. But a bigger stick will mean a bigger carrot also. That seems to mean offering greater social justice and a greater share in the management of a national incomes policy....
>
> Good luck in the strenuous and brave course you are pursuing.

The *Observer*'s political stance did not only "annoy" some

readers, it also angered some members of the staff. Tempers boiled over when the *Observer* published a leader on February 12, 1974 by Ivan Yates entitled "The arrival of the militants", which analysed the threat to a "free society" posed by the few "fashionable Marxists" and "predominantly left-wing leaders" in the miners' union. As this leader appeared only some two weeks before the election was due, about twenty members of staff submitted an angry letter of protest to the editor alleging that it did "not represent our views", adding that ". . . the article's hardly-concealed invitation to the readers to vote Conservative seems to us inappropriate". The letter alleged that most of the blame for the militancy of the miners' action could be laid at the door of the Government. Signatories to the letter included Neal Ascherson, Polly Toynbee, and — probably most wounding of all — Philip Toynbee "(by telephone)". Ivan Yates defended his leader sharply, denying that it had recommended the Conservatives in the forthcoming election, whilst David Astor was drawn into a lengthy correspondence with the signatories of the letter, stating that the paper had always been in opposition to the anti-democratic "left" or "right" wherever it was found; in Nazi Germany, Soviet Russia, South Africa or Britain. As Astor explained:

> As you know, the *Observer* has for some thirty years been a specifically non-party paper of the political centre. It has criticised the policies of both major parties when it has considered them illiberal. It has also been consistently anti-Marxist for the libertarian reasons that its former contributor, George Orwell, was anti-Marxist. If anyone is now surprised to find it near the political centre, nearer to the Tavernites than to the Tony Benn wing of Labour, this can only mean a failure on my part to make the paper's basic attitude to politics (which gives us different adversaries at different times) sufficiently clear.

Symptomatic of the rather furtive and conspirational atmosphere that now gripped the office was the leaking of a distorted version of this dispute, as well as previous disputes, to *Private Eye* and the *New Statesman*. The old loyalties of the paternalist regime of the golden age had all but broken down. Astor tried to end his letter to the twenty signatories of the letter of protest on a hopeful note:

I realise that everyone feels they are always acting from the highest motives. And I often remember that this paper has enjoyed a degree of loyalty from many of its staff that is quite unusual. This letter does not in the least mean that I think the open and comradely relationships that used to characterise the office are dead for ever.

In truth, such optimism now had a somewhat hollow ring to it.

However, David Astor was not deterred and friction with the office rose to the surface again with the publication in the paper of Arthur Scargill's celebrated interview with *New Left Review* magazine in which, for the first and only time, he made it quite explicit that the miners' disputes were "political battles", not just wage disputes. Nora Beloff spotted the article in *New Left Review*, and the *Observer* ran the whole interview over two consecutive issues of the paper in September 1975. It was an important piece of journalism and, perhaps, supported the *Observer*'s case that in fighting the illiberal, Marxist left which was trying to take over the Labour Party — and Britain — the *Observer* was doing no more than standing by its historic principles of fighting against illiberalism wherever it was to be found — in its own machine room or on the picket line at Saltley Coking depot.

By 1974, however, such political and ideological debates were once again overshadowed by the paper's deepening commercial problems. On December 11, 1974, at the trustees' meeting, Lord Goodman reported on an "alarming" situation: the paper's average circulation, hampered by a fresh price increase, had fallen to 761,000, and Tristan Jones announced a loss of £467,000 in the 1973–74 financial year. At the trustees' meeting of June 18, 1975, the finance director, John Littlejohns, reported that the paper had lost £342,000 in the months January to May of that year alone. The Astor Family Trust could not finance such deficits even if David Astor had wanted to; as it was, the trustees for the children's money refused to sanction further expenditure from the Family Trust for the very good reason that the use of money in such a risky manner clearly contravened their duties to safeguard the capital.

The paper was thus at the end of its financial tether, and Mr Littlejohns also reported that the banks refused to fund further operating losses. The *Observer*'s problems were exacerbated by its position as owner of New Printing House Square, the former home of *The Times* newspaper, at St Andrew's Hill. During the 1960s, the *Observer* was printed by *The Times*, under Roy Thomson, on *The Times* presses at New Printing House Square. Under this agreement, Thomson had to give five years' notice to the *Observer* if *The Times* no longer wanted to carry on the arrangement. In 1969, Denis Hamilton, the editor-in-chief of Thomson's papers, called on Lord Goodman in his capacity as chairman of the *Observer*'s trustees to inform him that *The Times* was moving to new premises in Gray's Inn Road, and he was giving the required five years' notice. Much to Hamilton's surprise, Goodman's immediate response was "What would you want for the building?" Hamilton mentioned the sum of £5 million off the top of his head, probably expecting that the ailing *Observer* could never afford such a price. However, at £5 million, the *Observer* stood to gain not only its own printing press, but a valuable piece of real estate at what seemed like a reasonable price. The building itself, a very ordinary sixties concoction of concrete and plate glass, had, at that time, only "limited use" planning permission, as it was stipulated that the site could only be used for publishing enterprises, but it was hoped that this could be changed. The *Observer* thus bought the building in a deal financed by Lazards bank, which was going to lease the larger part back from the *Observer*. The *Observer* offices occupied a small wing of the whole building; the rest of it was leased out, although Lazards themselves never took up their option to move into the building. The offices were vested in Observer Holding Ltd, the Astor Family Trust. The move into the new building seemed to be the best solution at the time to the problem of combining premises and printing site; furthermore, alternative locations for printing the *Observer* in London were explored, but with no success, so it had to be at *The Times* building. In the end, the purchase of *The Times* building was a shrewd investment, both for the Family Trust and the newspaper itself, and at the trustees' meeting of December 11, 1974 Goodman observed that

> . . . it seemed that all that kept the *Observer* solvent were the property investments; Mr Littlejohns agreed, and said they had a major task ahead in trying to restore the publishing account to a break-even account . . .

However, the major flaw in the new deal was that the *Observer*, in taking on the old *Times* presses, also had to take on the whole union staff that had formerly worked six days a week for *The Times*, to print a paper only once a week. The unions forced a full-time maintenance staff on the *Observer* for six days a week; this was topped up on Saturday evenings. The *Observer* management had to negotiate with no less than twenty-nine chapels that *The Times* had left behind. The result was now over-manning which was impressive even by Fleet Street's standards. Attempts to share the presses with *The Guardian* fell through, so the *Observer* was left with a complete printing staff and presses which were only in use once a week. It was a dangerously expensive situation, which was seen in some quarters as being management's fault. The paper's commercial position was further weakened by the 1973 recession, sparked off by the oil-price rise, which decimated the appointments advertising whilst paper and energy costs rocketed. It was a blow that the *Observer*, in its precarious state, could not survive. Something had to give.

As high labour costs were the major problem, in 1973–74 the management evolved a bold strategy which could have removed this problem at a single stroke. A plan was conceived whereby the *Observer*'s printing would be partly moved out of London; half the paper would be printed on the presses of the *Yorkshire Post* in Leeds and half at the *Financial Times*. It was the first time that a Fleet Street management faced up to the fact that national papers could no longer prosper in company with the unions on Fleet Street, predating the "Wapping" solution by more than a decade. Roger Harrison and John Littlejohns were prepared to take the risk of trying out the plan and taking on the inevitable union fury, but Tristan Jones was against it, as – less implacably – was Lord Goodman. As Roger Harrison commented to the author, the plan was "several years ahead of Wapping, but the *Observer* had none of the resources to do it". In December 1973, when news broke of the contractual negotiations being conducted for the move to the *Yorkshire Post* and *Financial Times*, all hell broke loose. There was an outcry from the printing unions who saw well over half their jobs with the *Observer* going if the plan were carried through. Lengthy negotiations followed with the seven printing unions involved, but no consent to the new arrangements was agreed. The alternative, strike action and prolonged confrontation, would have ruined the paper completely.

As the crisis deepened during 1974 and the first half of 1975, there was thus only one alternative left if the paper was not going to go out of business by the end of the year: to reduce costs at the existing publishing plant in New Printing House Square. To bring down operating costs, the paper had to seek redundancies in the machine 'room and the *Observer* thus became the first British newspaper to resort to negotiated cuts in manning levels to reduce overall costs — a course of action that had to be pursued by every other Fleet Street paper during the course of the following decade. At the trustees' meeting of June 18, 1975, the minutes record that

> Mr Littlejohns went on to say that the total wages and salaries budget was about £3.6m and a reduction in operating costs of about one-third of that sum, i.e. £1m, was looked for...against a publishing loss of £750,000 for the year 1975...Mr Littlejohns had told the unions he could not go back to the bank for finance for further operating losses, but he was hopeful a request for credit for redundancy payments to restore the publishing business to viability, would be met sympathetically.

David Astor added that

> ...it had been recognised that although the need for saving manpower on the journalistic side was different from the printing side, it nevertheless had to be carried out, if only to make the facts more palatable to the latter. He had been going through names trying to think who really was dispensable and had reached the conclusion he would have to be arbitrary, but on this basis it would be difficult to make such redundancies appear voluntary.

In July the management called the union leaders in to inspect the books, appealing for a 33 per cent reduction in manning levels. The unions were, as might be expected, unenthusiastic, but the serious plight of the paper, which could have closed altogether by the end of the year, produced an incentive for negotiation. There ensued seven weeks of intense negotiations. Individually, the union leaders were pleasant and co-operative, collectively they were, to use Goodman's phrase, a "horror". The most aggressive union negotiator was the fabled Bill Keys; on his first meeting with Roger Harrison he harangued Harrison with great passion for thirty minutes, and then turned round and sat with his back to him, staring out of the window, while he replied. Tristan Jones was not confrontational and did not relish taking on the unions, which meant that a large share of the responsibility for negotiating fell on the shoulders of Arnold Goodman. Astor paid this tribute to him in a letter to Robert Birley of August 20, 1975:

> The real hero of our struggle is Arnold Goodman. Although he is only a Trustee with a token remuneration, he devoted most of a week — throughout the worst of the heatwave — to sitting through lengthy meetings, sometimes going on into the evenings. During half the time in these meetings, he had to listen to rival trade union spokesmen showing each other how tough they could be on such an occasion. There are also intervals of up to one hour when the unionists withdraw to consult among themselves and our team is just left sitting. Although a very nimble-witted man, he apparently never blinked throughout the whole performance and only said one cross word, that to one of our team...and he puts in this terrific effort not because he is a special fan of anything in the paper, but just because he thinks it ought to exist.

The atmosphere of these long and painful negotiations was not helped by the introduction of television cameras. It was David Astor's belief that since the press was afraid to report the activities of the print unions, the BBC was the only branch of the media likely to expose the scandal of union work practices. He had therefore, on one or two occasions, lobbied the BBC about the importance of doing this. When the *Observer* crisis became known, a BBC producer took David at his word and asked permission to bring his cameras into the office. By then David felt doubtful, but he found it difficult to refuse a course which he himself had recommended. The programme "Crisis at the *Observer*", which was made over the course of several weeks, was shown just after the dispute had been settled. The decision to allow the cameras in proved to be naïve, to say the least. Their presence did not, as was hoped, "embarrass" the unions into behaving any better, and the programme had little propaganda value because the cameras were not allowed by the unions into the machine rooms. And in addition, the film proved, in Roger Harrison's words, "catastrophic" for the paper's commercial reputation: all the advertisers perceived was a newspaper in danger of going out of business. Their confidence in it collapsed, and advertising revenue nosedived. Whatever the result of the union negotiations, any chances of the paper recovering from the dispute were fatally weakened by the free publicity given to the "Crisis at the *Observer*".

After weeks of negotiation, the loss of occasional print runs as the negotiations hit a sticky point and the exercise of brinkmanship on both sides, an agreement was closed whereby a reduction in manning of eighty-eight full-time jobs and one hundred and sixty part-time jobs was achieved. This represented a 25 per cent reduction rather than the 33 per cent the management had been seeking, but, as Tristan Jones told the trustees in September, these cuts were still "far more than had been achieved in Fleet Street for a very long time". None the less, as John Littlejohns reported at the same trustees' meeting, the fact that not everything hoped for had been achieved in the way of staff reductions, together with the dramatic fall in advertising revenue, the cost of redundancy payments, 25 per cent inflation and a further fall in circulation meant that the *Observer* still stood to lose £570,000 in the next financial year.

In fact, this proved to be a conservative estimate. Within a year of the end of the 1975 union negotiations the situation had worsened to the extent that the *Observer* could not survive, and management started looking for a buyer. On August 24, 1975, David Astor wrote "A Letter to the Reader" tracing the outlines of the situation and reporting on the outcome of the cost-reduction negotiations. Looking to the future, he wrote that:

> The best long-term hope of independent papers surviving (and of new ones being launched, under new ownership — public, private or corporate) is that the costs of producing them should be drastically reduced. Eventually, this means a technological revolution.

At the bottom of the page, underneath this "Letter to the Reader", was the "Sayings of the Week" column, headed by this quote from Vernon Royster, former editor of the *Wall Street Journal*: "Britain offers a model study in how to ruin a once-vigorous nation." The fate of Fleet Street offered as good an example as any of the justice of Mr Royster's remarks.

David Astor's "Letter to the Reader" proved to be one of his last written contributions to the paper; on September 30, he resigned as editor and became a trustee. Tristan Jones resigned during the same week. During the course of the previous five difficult years, there had been moments when David Astor had been near resigning, but ultimately he wanted to see the paper through the last pangs of its restructuring. The senior journalists gave a dinner for him at the Gay Hussar in December 1975, and David wrote to Terry Kilmartin, who had organized the dinner, looking back on his career. In this letter he commented on what might have been:

> I mean that if I were to have gone on editing the paper, giving full rein to whatever were my strongest feelings, as I tended to do in our early days, and if the paper had consequently appealed to fewer and fewer readers, and had by now died, you would have given me no dinner.
>
> Had I not sabotaged my own inclinations, you would have had more warnings on the coming fuel and ecology crisis; a lot more investigations into war-prevention techniques; much more discouragement about what not to expect from the EEC; frequent reports on the major misdeeds of uninteresting countries, like India or Indonesia; unwelcome argument about the NUJ already reducing the flow of talent into journalism; lots more about what the mechanical unions do to blackmail not only newspapers but also broadcasting (which would have got those issues of the paper stopped altogether, at vast cost!); and there are other unpopular subjects I find of special interest. What I mean is that if the paper has lacked fiery causes in recent years, it might have fared even worse if I had allowed my convictions more play.

Despite all the vicissitudes of the previous fifteen years, David's proudest, and surely justifiable, boast was that "...given the deadly competition mounted by the *Sunday Times* and *Sunday Telegraph*, the paper has both survived and remained vaguely recognizable as the same publication it was twenty years ago".

Among the letters of tribute which David received on his

retirement there was one from Henry Kissinger, who wrote from the White House to say that he was "distressed" to hear the news, because "you know how highly I have always valued your thoughts, and I find the idea of your lapsing into silence unsettling". Roy Jenkins, who was then home secretary, also wrote to congratulate him on his "remarkable and distinguished" editorship, commenting that "no doubt there were problems, particularly towards the end, but I think it was one of the most outstanding feats of British journalism in this generation". Peregrine Worsthorne of the *Sunday Telegraph*, often a scourge of the *Observer*'s politics, none the less described David to the author, in 1990, as simply, "the greatest British editor of the post-war era".

But now the Astor editorial era was over, and the Astor proprietorial era was to come to an end in 1976. The new editor was Donald Trelford. Trelford's candidacy for the job was pushed strongly by David Astor, who recognized that the new era of newspaper publishing demanded, above all, an "organizing" rather than a "writing" editor. David explained his reasoning in a memo to the trustees:

> I have argued my belief that we need an organising editor, with talent on the commercial side of the business; rather than a writing editor, with his interests mainly in politics. The first type of editor will, of course, be interested in the paper's politics; but he will be equally interested in the many aspects of the paper that build its circulation, i.e. being speedy in reaction to news; enterprising in making its own investigations; always aware of the manysidedness of readers' interests (sport, gardening, fashion, motoring, etc); in other words, constant awareness of the paper and magazine as media of diversion and of practical helpfulness, as well as being vehicles of political discussion.
>
> In the first four or five decades of this century, the *Observer* flourished as a larger version of the *New Statesman* or *Spectator*, i.e. a paper for political and cultural discourse with an élite of society; a writing editor then was appropriate. But if you appointed a writing editor today, the paper would, I fear, die in a few years.

Formerly David would have preferred Anthony Sampson to succeed him as a "writing" editor. But now he was fully aware of how much Fleet Street had changed since he had come into it in 1942, when the *Observer* was an eight-page paper. A new breed of professional editor was needed to cope with it, and Donald Trelford was a representative of that breed whom he was glad to accept. It was indeed the end of an era, but when David Astor reached it he was looking ahead into the next one.

9

A Tale of Two Takeovers

Although David Astor's time as editor of the *Observer* came to an end in 1975, he remained a trustee until the termination of the Trust in October 1976, and after that was on the new board (representing Observer Holdings Limited), so he was involved, at first intimately, then somewhat less so, in the events of the next five years.

Despite the restructuring of the *Observer* and the cost reductions of 1975, by the summer of 1976 the paper was in deeper trouble than ever. It was still heading for a loss of £500,000 on the year; and the final nail in the coffin was the yearly increase in newsprint prices, which looked like adding a further £400,000 in costs: a burden that the paper could not carry. Advertising revenue dropped by a full 10 per cent, and circulation fell to a new low of 664,937. Once again, the paper was facing imminent extinction, but this time it was impossible to envisage the possibility of further cuts in costs. The immediate concern was how to save the 450 full-time and 400 part-time jobs on the newspaper under threat. The Astor Family Trust could no longer help as the trustees could not be readily convinced that substantial advances to the *Observer* publishing operation were in the best interests of their beneficiaries. The only option was to sell the paper.

In fact, the trustees and management had been secretly looking round for a potential partner since the autumn of 1975, when it was already obvious that the blood-letting of that summer was not enough to save it. The prime minister, Harold Wilson, had expressed an interest in the paper's plight. In two conversations with Lord Goodman, Wilson proposed an approach to IPC, the owners of the *Daily Mirror* group of newspapers. However, that proposal foundered on IPC's reluctance to add a further Sunday newspaper to their existing Sunday titles. A further option was for the Government to put up the substantial sums of money required to buy out over-manning and to introduce cost-saving new technology. While this idea was being actively considered, however, Wilson resigned and was replaced as prime minister by Jim Callaghan. Callaghan's new Government, faced by a mountain of economic difficulties of their own, took a very different attitude to hand-outs to ailing industries, and the new Secretary of State for Industry, Edmund Dell, turned cold on the whole idea. In August 1976, Callaghan asked the TUC whether they might be interested in buying the paper − a proposal containing an element of high farce considering the reasons for the *Observer*'s plight − before approaching IPC once again. But the TUC and IPC both rejected any involvement in the *Observer*. By mid-September 1976, therefore, the paper was back at square one, facing the need of an urgent injection of cash − or closure before the end of the year.

It was at this point that Roger Harrison suggested Rupert Murdoch as a possible buyer. Murdoch, the Australian newspaper tycoon, already owned *The Sun* and the *News of the World* in Britain and it was widely known that he was eager to purchase a "quality" newspaper as well. Harrison was impressed by Murdoch's managerial skills at his publishing group News International, while Astor had formed a favourable personal impression of Murdoch while serving on the board with him at London Weekend Television. Goodman was at first less enthusiastic, but warmed to the idea. The attractions of Murdoch were obvious, for he could instantly secure the *Observer*'s financial position and ensure its survival as part of a wider publishing group for many years to come. At that point in his career Murdoch had not yet acquired the odious reputation that has pursued him since the early 1980s. In 1975 it was known that he would try and shift the paper to the right politically, and possibly make it slightly less of a "quality" organ, but the *Observer* management had no fears that the essential character of the paper would be completely altered. The priority was to save jobs at the *Observer* — and as far as the immediate future was concerned, Murdoch seemed to be the best man for that purpose. David Astor summed the position up pithily when he remarked that an "efficient Visigoth" was better than no buyer at all.

So the approach to Murdoch was made, and he responded by flying to London from New York within three days to start negotiations. He was willing to buy the paper as soon as the *Observer* could sell, but stressed that he wanted editorial changes which would affect the position of Donald Trelford. Murdoch wanted Bruce Rothwell, former editor of the *Sunday Australian* to become editor-in-chief and the right-wing Tory Andrew Shrimsley, a political writer on the *Sun*, to become editor, with Trelford sandwiched between these two as editorial director. The implications for the paper, and for Trelford, were obvious and raised some alarm. It was at this point that news of the talks between the *Observer* and Murdoch broke in the *Daily Mail* on October 21. Who leaked the story is still a matter of some mystery, but the consequences were probably as intended, for a storm broke over the heads of Goodman, Astor and Trelford. Questions were asked in the House of Commons; a union delegation met the trustees and the editorial staff expressed great anger at the prospect of being delivered into the hands of Mr Murdoch. That evening, Murdoch issued a statement from across the Atlantic, that "In view of the breach of confidence that has taken place, together with the deliberate and orchestrated attempt to build this into a controversy, News International is no longer interested." However, Murdoch's withdrawal was purely tactical; the "efficient Visigoth" still remained the most likely buyer.

The leak brought the imminent demise of the *Observer* to a wider audience, and the publicity generated by the *Daily Mail* story mobilized a worldwide contingent of interested bidders. The offers that now came in were testimony to the worldwide reputation of the paper. Interested bidders included, from Britain, Vere Harmsworth of Associated Newspapers (owners of the *Daily Mail*), Sir James Goldsmith, the ebullient takeover specialist, Robert Maxwell, proprietor of the *Scottish Daily News*, and Tiny Rowland of Lonrho. From abroad there were several offers of Arab oil money, which the trustees felt that they had to reject because such money could "in certain circumstances put the paper in an embarrassing political position" in its coverage of the Middle East. One bid came from Olga Deterding, the forty-seven-year-old millionairess daughter of the founder of Royal Dutch Shell, who expressed a desire to make the *Observer* "more whimsical". Another bid came from Sally Aw Sian, a Hong Kong business woman, whose Sing Tao group was based on the profits of a patent medicine called Tiger Balm. David Astor asked a nephew, also called David Astor, to travel to Hong Kong to talk to Miss Aw Sian — he even travelled under a false surname so as to avoid publicity. There were no political objections to the deal, but Miss Aw's financial consultant advised against the investment. By the beginning of November, the various rival bidders had all been discounted as unsatisfactory for one reason or another, and opinion on the paper began to swing back to Murdoch. Spurred on by a considerable sense of urgency arising from the perilous week-by-week position of the paper, the trustees met in Lord Goodman's flat in Portland Place on Friday, November 12, to recommend that the paper be sold to Murdoch. They agreed to meet again on Monday to devise a way of putting this unpalatable decision to the staff. David Astor remarked that it was like attending a funeral; certainly, it seemed that the paper was now bound for Rupert Murdoch.

However, at this point Robert Anderson entered the fray. On the same Friday, November 12, Kenneth Harris, by then one of the *Observer*'s most experienced journalists, dined at Rule's restaurant with two old friends, Douglass Cater and his wife Libby. Lady Melchett, widow of the late chairman of the British Steel Corporation, was the fourth in the party. Cater, whom Harris had met in Washington during his time as the *Observer*'s correspondent there in the 1950s, was a former Washington editor of *Reporter Magazine* and a director of the Aspen Institute. The Aspen Institute was a liberal research institute founded in 1950, initially to celebrate and facilitate the re-absorption of Germany into mainstream western culture after the war. A few years after its foundation, Robert Anderson became chairman of Aspen, overseeing a considerable expansion of its work. Over dinner Harris explained at length the *Observer*'s commercial problems. Cater was impressed by the gravity of the situation, and that evening rang up Joe Slater, director of the Aspen Institute, in America to ask whether he thought Anderson might be interested in buying the *Observer*.

That night Anderson phoned Goodman to tell the astonished chairman of the trustees that, yes, he would indeed be very interested. Goodman agreed to keep Murdoch and Harmsworth of Associated Newspapers in play, while on Monday David Astor and Roger Harrison flew out to Los Angeles for a day of talks with Anderson.

What they found in Los Angeles was a dazzling suite of offices on the fifty-first floor of a state-of-the-art tower block, decorated with a considerable collection of modern art, and presided over by Robert O. Anderson. He was the fifty-nine-year-old-chairman of Atlantic Richfield, also called ARCO, which he had built up from nothing to become the second largest corporation in California and the eleventh largest oil company in the world, with a company revenue in 1975 of $7.8 billion. Although given to wearing a regulation Texan stetson even in London, Anderson was definitely not an average Texan oil developer: he was already noted for his many contributions to charitable foundations, his support for the arts, and his hard work for the Aspen Institute, which he had developed into one of America's premier think-tank-*cum*-conference institutes. He was popularly known in America as an "oil man with a conscience". As a white knight for the *Observer* he was almost too good to be true. David Astor was impressed by Anderson himself and by the Aspen Institute. Anderson promised to run the paper for the same ideals and in the same manner as David had run it, and it appeared that out of the blue all the *Observer*'s problems were solved. Anderson agreed to take over on Thursday, November 18, less than a week after Cater's initial enquiry.

Under the terms of the deal, ARCO bought a 90 per cent share of the newspaper and the plant on which it was printed. The buildings in which the newspaper was printed were retained by Observer Holdings Ltd for the Astor Family Trust, which then leased the *Observer* offices back to Anderson at a very competitive rate. Anderson acquired his 90 per cent stake for the nominal sum of £1 — but he had to provide an immediate cash injection of £1 million on top of that just to keep the paper afloat. As part of the agreement, Anderson pledged to spend a sum of money to guarantee the paper's survival. The last trustees' meeting met on October 6, 1976; the new board of the *Observer* met under the chairmanship of Lord Barnetson on behalf of Anderson. Lord Barnetson was a respected Fleet Street figure who was nominated by Trelford and

Harrison to restore some credibility to the paper after the weeks of damaging speculation about its future. The three Atlantic Richfield board nominees were Thornton Bradshaw (President of Atlantic Richfield), Frank Stanton and Douglass Cater. Both Lord Goodman and David Astor stayed on the board as representatives of Observer Holdings Ltd.

It was a remarkable coup; the *Observer* was saved well past the eleventh hour. Trelford was quoted as saying "This is an absolute godsend editorially", and had good reason to feel like that. In an opening "Pledge to Our Readers" in the *Observer* of November 28, Anderson promised "to preserve the paper's British character and perspective...I have spent many years working with institutions engaged in the development and exchange of ideas. It is in the spirit of renewing and building a vital institution for communications that I welcome this opportunity to become a member of the 'Observer' partnership."

Anderson's intervention was motivated by more than mere philanthropy. It was also a profile-raising exercise for ARCO, which at that time was virtually unknown in Britain. Neither David Astor nor Arnold Goodman had ever heard of Anderson before he made his approach. To promote ARCO, an annual "Astor-Goodman dinner" was proposed by Anderson, to commemorate the Anderson-*Observer* connection. His interest was both idealistic and business-minded; in many ways the perfect combination of motives. In Roger Harrison's words, he proved to be a "very good" owner of the *Observer*. He was a hands-off proprietor, who left editorial matters to Trelford, the editor, and to Conor Cruise O'Brien, who became the editor-in-chief. Under Anderson, ARCO pumped about £8 million into the *Observer* during the five years that Anderson owned the paper, without demanding any editorial input at all. During the trials and tribulations of the 1970s, David Astor had never dared hope for a knight in quite such radiantly white armour. As Astor wrote to Anderson on November 26, 1976:

> Everyone, great or small, connected with the paper seems to be fired by new hope and new confidence since you took over. For myself, I don't think I have ever experienced such a thrill as the three packed days beginning with our journey to Los Angeles and climaxing in the news that you were indeed ready to come in and do so on the most generous

terms.... We all look forward to welcoming you here. It will be a great pleasure to have you among us on an occasion that is for us nothing less than a renaissance.

In the back of some people's minds lay the suspicion that such luck could not last. A man who could take such a swift decision to buy the *Observer* was surely capable of selling it just as quickly? From 1976 to 1981, David Astor sat on the board of the *Observer*, together with Arnold Goodman and the Atlantic Richfield representatives. Lord Barnetson resigned his chairmanship of the paper on account of ill-health in September 1980, and was succeeded briefly by Thornton Bradshaw, before Anderson himself took over as chairman on February 20, 1981. Despite the injection of £8 million of Atlantic Richfield cash, the *Observer* still showed no signs of being able to exist without the oil company's large annual subsidy. Moreover, it was still plagued by the guerrilla warfare between print unions and the management. Even with the closure of the *Sunday Times* for a year from 1978 to 1979, the *Observer*, despite increasing in circulation to an average weekly sale of just under one million, failed to keep its new advertisers at the end of the closure. The deficit seemed to grow yearly. In 1980, Anderson was faced with the prospect of a deficit that year of about £6 million. By the summer of 1980 relations with the unions had worsened to a point at which the management threatened to close the paper down altogether. Although agreement was finally reached, after several weeks of intense negotiation, the resulting stoppages and lost print runs due to unofficial union action contributed substantially to the deficit. The Americans made it quite clear in July of that year that they had bought the paper on the clear expectation that it would make a profit within a few years. Such a prospect now looked extremely unlikely, and from the summer of 1980 onwards there was constant speculation in the press that Anderson would pull out within two years. *Now!* magazine, owned by Sir James Goldsmith, even predicted the identity of the man whom Anderson would sell to − "Tiny" Rowland. There is no doubt that Anderson endured much to try his patience: his initial commitment to the *Observer* in 1976 was a promise to subsidize operations up to £3 million over three years, but by 1980 he had spent twice as much over four years with no realistic prospect of gaining any return on his money. Kenneth Harris, Anderson's biographer, has suggested that Anderson realized that if the *Observer* was ever going to be profitable, a full confrontation with the unions was unavoidable. As an unknown Texan oil millionaire, directing operations from Los Angeles, he could have expected little sympathy from the British public if he was held responsible for the closure of one of the country's great national institutions. Anderson, a fan of Mrs Thatcher, was also disappointed that the *Observer* supported Labour at the 1979 general election. Furthermore, by 1981, the original ARCO executives who had sparked Anderson's initial enthusiasm for the deal in 1976 had retired. Thornton Bradshaw left ARCO to become chairman of RCA, and Douglass Cater had long since returned permanently to the Aspen Institute. Reluctantly, Bob Anderson thus took on the chairmanship himself, but it soon became obvious to him that this was no way to run a "sensible business operation", as he had declared he was setting out to do in 1976. The final straw for Anderson seems to have been a board meeting on Friday, February 20, 1981, when the board felt obliged to reject his own candidate for the vice-chairmanship, Kenneth Harris, because of his lack of managerial experience. Anderson, not accustomed to being crossed, now moved swiftly to divest himself of the *Observer*.

The man to whom he decided to sell was "Tiny" Rowland, Astor's old adversary from Africa days and the *Central African Mail*. It is unclear exactly when Anderson decided to sell the paper, or whether the Anderson-Rowland deal was part of a wider agreement that the two men fixed at their leisure. As early as January 14, 1980, Anderson had improved his grip on the paper considerably by acquiring the remaining 10 per cent Astor family stake for £250,000, with the result that Astor and Goodman became merely "courtesy directors". This move certainly made it easier to sell to an unpopular buyer. Anderson had known Rowland for some time. They had met through Daniel K Ludwig, one of the richest men in the world, who had sold Lonrho a string of luxury hotels in Mexico, an area of the world in which Atlantic Richfield was also interested. Whatever the truth of the Anderson-Rowland connection, on Wednesday, February 25, Anderson phoned Goodman at Oxford, where he was Master of University College, to inform him, out of the blue, that he had sold 60 per cent of his interest in the *Observer* to Outram's, the newspaper subsidiary of Rowland's Lonrho. As Goodman later told the

Monopolies and Mergers Commission charged with investigating the sale,

> I really was almost speechless — you will be astonished to hear that I could be reduced to that state! I said virtually nothing and telephoned the news around. That was how we heard it.

Astor heard the news from Goodman in his London house at Cavendish Avenue on that Wednesday morning. To both of them — and indeed, everybody else — it came as a complete shock. Harris writes of Anderson's secrecy:

> Bob [Anderson] did not consult his fellow directors on the *Observer* board beforehand, or let them know what he had decided to do. He did not take the editor into his confidence. He remembered how hard Lord Goodman and David Astor had tried to keep secret their original negotiations with Rupert Murdoch in 1976. Recalling the various kinds of damage done to the paper between the first Murdoch offer and its acquisition by ARCO, he feared that if he communicated his thoughts to the board, anything he said would become public and inevitably cause damaging speculation about the paper's future.[8]

Astor and Goodman, for their part, felt betrayed by Anderson's secrecy and angry at his furtive dealings with Rowland, while the *Observer* staff felt completely frozen out. Only a few days before the sale Anderson had assured both Lord Goodman and David Astor on separate occasions that all was well and that he had no intention of selling the paper. He had told Goodman: "You do not need to worry. I do not intend to sell the paper to Associated [Newspapers]. Vere [Harmsworth] has been chasing me but I am not prepared to sell it to Associated, do not worry." As Goodman told the Monopolies Commission of this conversation:

> Of course, as a simple soul I arrived at the conclusion that

---

8. Kenneth Harris, *The Wildcatter* (Weidenfeld & Nicholson 1987), p. 151.

this was an assertion that he was not going to sell it to anybody. If I may say so, I think almost anyone on earth would have taken that view.

David Astor breakfasted with Anderson a few days after the conversation with Goodman, when Anderson again talked reassuringly of the future. There was good reason to be disconcerted and angry at such secrecy; but what shook David even more was the identity of the purchaser.

It is hard to imagine two people more different than David Astor and "Tiny" Rowland, chief executive of Lonrho plc. Roland Walter Fuhrhop, who changed his name to Rowland in 1939, had been born in India of Anglo-German parentage in 1917, and had dedicated his life to making money. His Lonrho, which had grown since the 1960s into one of the world's major corporations, was subject in 1976 to a DTI investigation and had been accused of serious criminal offences including sanctions busting, fraud, theft and bribery. It had also been branded by prime minister Edward Heath, in 1974, as "the unacceptable face of capitalism". To Astor and Goodman, therefore, Lonrho seemed a highly unsuitable proprietor for the *Observer*. To David, more important than any of this was Rowland's involvement in Africa, where Lonrho's interests were bound to conflict with the *Observer*'s cherished record of independent and objective reporting. Lonrho had begun life as a Central African mining company, and it was Rowland who had masterminded the expansion of the company until it had mining, business and infrastructure interests all over the continent; in 1981, Lonrho had business in over sixty countries, eighteen of them in Africa. The vast bulk of Lonrho's profits came from Africa, which made the company particularly vulnerable to changes of government or shifts of opinion on that continent. Rowland's business interests were – and still are – heavily dependent on his own personal relationships with the leaders of the liberated African states. He needed the goodwill of these African leaders, and he was famous for going to great lengths to maintain it. His was, of course, a very different way of looking at Africa from David Astor's. Under Lonrho, David felt, the *Observer* risked becoming little more than a business weapon in the hands of "Tiny" Rowland – a corporate publicity magazine. Rowland wanted the *Observer* for the goodwill that it would buy him in Africa, and he admitted as much to journalists. A leader in *The Times* on February 27, 1981 set out the central problem of Lonrho ownership of the *Observer*:

> A deeper source of anxiety is the possibility of conflict between Lonrho's business interests and the *Observer*'s journalistic activity and editorial judgement. Lonrho is an international conglomerate of a structure difficult to bring into focus, extensive trading interests, and an appetite for takeovers. Proprietor and newspaper both have long-standing interests in Africa, but their interests do not necessarily coincide. Lonrho's is commercial penetration, the *Observer*'s is to open to public inspection the condition and affairs of that continent and to pass political judgement related to a characteristic moral position. Nor is it only in Africa that the now to be joined commercial and editorial courses may collide.

Indeed, there was such an outcry over the proposed sale to Lonrho that the Government prudently referred the bid to the Monopolies and Mergers Commission, which regulates corporate takeovers in Britain. The secretary of state for industry, John Biffen, might have been motivated to do this by the sharp criticism he had had to endure over his "nod" to Rupert Murdoch to buy his third national newspaper, *The Times*, only a few weeks before. Lonrho, through the holding company Outrams, also owned the *Glasgow Herald*, so there was a danger of a concentration of ownership in Rowland's case, as there had not been in Anderson's. Between March 17, when the bid was referred to the Monopolies Commission and the end of July, when the report was finally published recommending that the bid should go through, the two sides, Astor on the one hand and Rowland on the other, conducted an often bitter public battle over the *Observer*. The campaign against a Lonrho ownership was organized at Astor's home at 9 Cavendish Avenue; a campaign fully supported by Goodman and most members of the *Observer* staff. Astor and Goodman felt that they had a moral right to block the sale, if no longer a financial or legal right, because, as Goodman told the Monopolies Commission:

> We *gave* this paper to Atlantic Richfield (for £1) because we thought they were highly suitable owners, in circumstances where we thought we were led to believe that we could have acquired a substantial price for it. The Trust owned it and

we thought it rather better to put it in safe hands than to collect some more money for the Trust. So we were in circumstances where we had chosen a purchaser and were perfectly prepared to make the financial sacrifice involved.

Astor and Goodman were thus fighting to save the character of the *Observer*, which they felt that they had secured by the sale to ARCO. Leading the fight in public were David Astor and Colin Legum, the paper's African specialist and the most vociferous opponent of Rowland. Legum in particular presented a catalogue of *Observer* investigations into the nefarious wrongdoings of various African governments, investigations that would, perhaps, have been stifled under Lonrho because they would have forfeited the goodwill of the particular government under inspection, thus hurting Lonrho's business interests. Donald Trelford also objected to the sale to Lonrho. One of the strongest allegations against Rowland was that he had a track record of interfering with his existing papers in Africa and their political coverage. This charge, as it turned out, was the least impressive and the Monopolies Commission eventually reported on this subject that:

> On the available evidence to us we cannot conclude that Lonrho has interfered with the accurate presentation of news or the free expression of opinion in its African newspapers. The evidence rather suggests that as a newspaper proprietor Lonrho respected editorial independence.

While Legum, Astor and Goodman led the battle in front of the Monopolies Commission, David Astor tried to find an alternative buyer for the paper. The most attractive offer was from a consortium of the Aga Khan and the Melbourne *Age* newspaper group; the *Age* itself was edited by Astor's former deputy editor, Michael Davie. It was a compelling combination, as the Aga Khan could provide the resources, and the *Age* could provide the journalistic expertise. David Astor also gave public vent to his objections to Lonrho in a series of letters to *The Times*, and after the Monopolies Commission reported in favour of Rowland, Astor made it clear in a further letter to *The Times* that this decision was certainly not for want of an alternative. As Astor wrote, the Aga Khan-Melbourne *Age* combination "would have the expertise and the liberal outlook that Lonrho lacks, and just as many resources".

However, the anti-Lonrho lobbying fell on deaf ears. On June 28, 1981, the Monopolies and Mergers Commission reported in favour of the Rowland bid, ruling that the takeover "may be expected not to operate against the public interest". It was not a unanimous report, however, as Dr J. S. Marshall dissented from the majority report and argued that the proposed sale "should not be allowed to proceed". The Commission recommended that the sale should go ahead as long as certain "safeguards" were followed, the most obvious of which was the appointment of "not less than six independent" directors to sit on the board of the paper. This was condemned as unworkable and ineffective by both *The Times* and the *Observer*. Indeed, the arrangements were attacked on all sides. *The Times* also attacked Mr Anderson himself in a leader of July 9 entitled "Mr Anderson's Honour". The paper applauded Anderson's "public-spirited" gesture in saving the paper in 1976:

> ...But Mr Anderson made arrangements to sell the *Observer* to Lonrho without any prior consultation with its board or its editor or staff; both David Astor and Lord Goodman felt that he deliberately misled them. This is strange behaviour for the Chairman of the Aspen Institute for Humanistic Studies with a reputation for public service. Mr Anderson has insisted that his sole objective in entering into the transaction is for the good of the *Observer*...but he should weigh very carefully whether he has the right to over-ride the *Observer*'s creators and proceed with the sale. He, rather than Mr Biffen, is the man who should be on the spot today.

However, it was Mr Biffen's responsibility as secretary of state to act on the Monopolies Commission's report and in the middle of July he duly gave it his blessing. In a complex deal, the *Observer* became a part of Lonrho's newspaper subsidiary, George Outram and Company. ARCO acquired a 20 per cent share of Outram and $4.5 million in cash, whilst Anderson continued as chairman of the *Observer* for three years, before stepping down in favour of Rowland. It was Rowland's greatest coup. Astor and Goodman resigned from the board, and Astor has had nothing to do with the paper since.

The sale of the *Observer* to Lonrho in 1981 effectively ended the Astor era, which had lasted since the first Lord Astor bought the paper in 1911. It was particularly galling that it should pass to

Rowland, who seemed to stand for everything that the Astor *Observer* had fought against. The freedom and independence the paper had enjoyed under the Astors, it was feared, would come to an end. Whether this is so, is for the reader to judge.

10

Epilogue

Since his resignation as a director of the paper in 1981, David Astor has continued his personal interest in many of the issues in which the *Observer* was involved during his time in the editorial chair. He has sustained his commitment to prison reform through chairing Arthur Koestler's awards for prisoners' art, and later through his part in creating the Butler Trust for merit awards for prison staff. He has also campaigned on behalf of Britain's longest-serving woman prisoner, Myra Hindley. He was for nine years the chairman of the British-Irish Association, which holds weekend conferences on the political relations between Britain, the Republic of Ireland and Northern Ireland. In South Africa, he has been a backer of the *Weekly Mail*, a radical paper created by journalists from the old *Rand Daily Mail*. Apart from his relationship with Schumacher's organization, the Intermediate Technology Group, he has for some ten years backed an experimental farm near Newbury for the scientific development of organic farming techniques. Finally, he is involved in a centre for research into the causes of adolescent suicide and is a trustee of the Anna Freud Centre in Hampstead.

Since the sale of the *Observer* to Lonhro in 1981, David Astor has had nothing to do with the paper and considerable bitterness remains on both sides as to how the sale was conducted. Donald Trelford, Astor's choice as editor to succeed him in 1975, remains in the editorial chair at the time of writing (1991) and it is largely due to him that the *Observer* now is still recognizably related to the *Observer* of its Astor heyday. A Lonhro proprietorship often means editorial concessions — such as the farcical publication of a "mid-week *Observer*" in 1989 at the height of Rowland's uncompromising campaign against the Al Fayed brothers over their ownership of the House of Fraser stores group — but it is none the less true to say that the *Observer* remains the only "quality" liberal paper among the Sunday press. Virtually all the old Astor writers have left the paper, some as a direct result of Lonhro's takeover, but Trelford remains as an important link between the Astor past and the Lonhro present; it is not for nothing that he has often been called "the great survivor".

Even after the introduction of new technology and the massive cash injection by the Lonhro group, the *Observer* still loses money — as does much of the rest of the Sunday press. Indeed, it is one of the richer ironies of David Astor's career that for all the criticisms of commercial "amateurism" levelled against him and his paper during its golden age, much of which was undoubtedly justified, nobody since has actually managed to do any better, on the *Observer* or elsewhere: Astor has spent much of his retirement watching all those supposedly more professional newspapermen succumb to the same combination of commercial and human factors that forced the *Observer* to the wall in 1975. Few of Astor's rivals managed to outlast his own regime in Fleet Street by many years. Max Aitken, Beaverbrook's son, was forced to sell Express Newspapers in 1977 and, most famously of all, Astor's great rival Roy Thomson was forced to sell *The Times* and the *Sunday Times* to Rupert Murdoch in 1981 after a series of crippling strikes at both titles. Even the colossus of 1960s' newspaper publishing, the *Mirror* group, was finally humbled in 1984 and sold to Robert Maxwell. In 1986, Lord Hartwell had to sell the Telegraph group to the Canadian businessman, Conrad Black. The crisis of Astor's *Observer* was by no means unique; his sale to ARCO in 1975 merely anticipated a decade during which all of Fleet Street's ruling dynasties forfeited their inheritances.

It was the next generation of newspaper proprietors, notably Rupert Murdoch, who forced through the "new technology" revolution in the teeth of ferocious trade union opposition during the mid-1980s. New technology and Rupert Murdoch's intransigence in the face of union opposition during the year-long lock-out of print workers at his new newspaper plant at Wapping in the East End of London virtually saved the British newspaper industry, allowing some papers to publish in profit for the first time in a generation, and the intervening years have seen a proliferation of new national newspapers, all benefiting from the new conditions. And yet, at the same time, the type of serious journalism that David Astor pioneered in the 1940s and 1950s has all but disappeared, as the Sunday press competes for a declining readership with ever bulkier papers and ever more unreflective and uninteresting journalism. The recent proliferation of Sunday titles has met with a studied indifference from the reading public, since the aggregate number of their readers has progressively fallen. Maybe there is still a market for David Astor's brand of journalism. With the new printing technology that might have saved the *Observer* in the early 1970s, it is curious that the contemporary press ignores the journalistic techniques and standards set by the paper during its golden age.

Astor himself foreshadowed the *Observer*'s career in a letter that he wrote to Jim Rose in 1948 on appointing him literary editor of the paper. The letter conveys the spirit of what the *Observer* was trying to do better than any editorial or "statement of aims":

No doubt one will end by doing everything in the conventional way as being the result of previous trial and error. But before accepting conventions I think one ought to question their validity strenuously, consider experimental ideas and convince oneself that one is acting from sound reasoning.

So let's have some free, abstruse, irresponsible, speculative, wide-ranging discussions before settling down to doing things very much as they've been done before us, as I've no doubt we'll have to do in the end.

See you Tues,
David

Index

THE OB

Established ·1791: No. 8,627

London, Sunday, N

Middle East Peace Move by U.S.

Assembly Proposal for Working Out Canal Plan

Eden's Conditions for Halting Attack

Mr. Anthony Nutting

THE United States last night announced it was placing two resolutions before the United Nations General Assembly proposing a " new approach " to an Arab-Israel peace settlement and the working-out of permanent arrangements for the functioning of the Suez Canal.

It also called on " all parties to this conflict " to be " guided " by the General Assembly's cease-fire resolution, which was " conclusive evidence of world opinion."

This move towards a settlement of the Middle East crisis followed within a few hours a declaration by the British and French Governments that they would continue their military action against Egypt unless a United Nations force was sent to keep the peace until the Suez Canal and the Palestine disputes had been settled; and unless Egypt and Israel agreed to accept such a United Nations force and meanwhile agreed to accept limited Anglo-French forces " to be stationed between the combatants."

Ministers' Night Meeting

This Anglo-French decision, taken in the face of mounting opposition in Britain and abroad, was announced to the House of Commons yesterday by Sir Anthony Eden. The Prime Minister rejected the Opposition demand for immediate compliance with the United Nations call for a cease-fire. There is no question, it is understood, of delaying the Anglo-French landings in the hope that the conditions laid down by the two Governments can be fulfilled in time. Mr. Anthony Nutting, Minister of State for Foreign Affairs, resigned from the Government yesterday.

After a broadcast last night in .which he vigorously defended the Government's intervention in Egypt, Sir Anthony Eden immediately called a meeting of Senior Ministers at 10, Downing-street.

In the Middle East itself, British and French aircraft continued to attack Egyptian targets, and Allied Air Headquarters in Cyprus claimed the " virtual destruction of the Egyptian Air Force as a fight-

ing force." Cairo Radio claimed the repulse of an attempted Anglo-French naval landing in the Suez area, but according to Anglo-French official sources no landings had yet been made, though they were regarded as imminent.

An Allied communiqué last night said that the Egyptians had made a further attempt to block the Suez Canal by demolishing the supports of a bridge south of Port Said.

Following the occupation of Gaza, Israeli forces claimed to have captured two other towns, one at the southern tip of the Sinai Peninsula, and in Tel-Aviv the Sinai campaign was regarded as having been virtually completed.

Iraq Oil Flow Stops

Elsewhere in the Middle East the military and political repercussions of the conflict have begun to increase. Iraqi and Syrian troops have entered Jordan, raising fears of a spread of the fighting along the Arab-Israeli borders.

Reports that Egyptian blockships had been sunk to close the Suez Canal were followed by the stopping of the flow of Iraq oil across Syria and Lebanon to the Mediterranean. According to the Iraq Petroleum Company, this was due to interruption of communications between pumping stations, but unconfirmed reports stated that three pumping stations in Syria were on fire.

In the Persian Gulf oil sheikhdoms there were riots in Bahrein, rumoured trouble in Kuwait and a reported strike and cutting of an oil pipe-line at Qatar.

In Pakistan, Singapore and Indonesia there were anti-British demonstrations. The Pakistan Premier was reported to be seeking concerted action with other Muslim States of the Bagdad Pact—Iraq, Persia, Turkey—to stop Anglo-French action against Egypt.

Dispatches from the capitals of the older Commonwealth countries indicated the anxiety aroused there by the British Government's policy.

Nutting
Suez

Primate Lea
Urging '

By Our Politic

WHILE Sir Anthony Eden wa defending the Government a special Saturday session of th Commons protests against h policy were coming in from over the country.

They were given an added poi during the afternoon when M Anthony Nutting, Minister of Sta for Foreign Affairs, became the fir member of the Government to resi because of the Egyptian adventur ' . . . I do not honestly feel." said in a letter to the Prime Ministe " it is possible for me to defend th Government's position either in Pa liament or in the United Nations."

In fact, Mr. Nutting gave in h resignation on October 31, but d ferred the announcement " in view the imminence of military ope tions."

Mr. Nutting is not a member the Cabinet and has never carri much weight in the party. All t same, his resignation is bound create still more uneasiness amo the rank and file in the country. had been at the Foreign Office sin 1951, and Minister of State fro 1954.

That he should have felt con pelled to leave the Government w also be a deeply wounding blow the Prime Minister. Up to now M Nutting has been one of his favour sons.

Churches' Appeal

The protests against the Gove ment's policy have rolled in fro widely different quarters. First, the have been the churches. The Brit Council of Churches yesterday se a deputation to the Lord Chancell led by the Archbishop of Canterbu the president, urging that " ev

Attempt to Block

U.S. Makes Two

Iraq Sends Troops to